ALMOST FAMOUS

ALMOST FAMOUS

AN AUTOBIOGRAPHY

DR. PAM MUNTER

WESTGATE PRESS
Beaverton, Oregon

Manufactured in the U.S.A.
First Printing: October 1985

Library of Congress Cataloging-in-Publication Data

Munter, Pam, 1943-

  Almost famous.

  1. Munter, Pam, 1943-   . 2. Clinical psychologists—United States—
Biography. 3. Entertainers—United States—Biography. I. Title.
CC339.52.M86A33 1985   157'.9'0924 [B]   85-13621
ISBN 0-9614926-0-0

Cover photograph and author portrait by Barbara Gundle.
Book design by Susan Applegate of Publishers Book Works, Inc.

Westgate Press
225 Westgate Square
3800 Cedar Hills Boulevard
Beaverton, Oregon 97005

FOR AARON
my son, my friend, my companion

CONTENTS

FOREWORD

I'd heard about Pam for several months, if not years—she had a fine reputation as a shrink. I first met her as a peer, at an oral licensing exam of the Board of Psychological Examiners. I was immediately drawn to her chutzpah. I didn't know the woman driving the hot yellow MGB with the top down was Pam—but I noticed the boldness of the driver as she wheeled into a parking space. Then, enter Dr. Pamela Osborne Munter. Hellos were said and introductions made. Then and here's where I got hooked— she asked for some lunch. It sounded like a minimum expecta-tion—you drag me out of my office in the middle of the day, you provide my lunch. I immediately wanted to know who was this person who walked in and not only appeared to be in total control of herself but displayed mastery of the situation, apparently unin-timidated with the environment, the people, or the task. She was hungry, she asked for—and got—something to eat. I was in-trigued, fascinated—it was like announcing to the world that you had to go to the bathroom. In my experience, anyone that direct who expected her demands to be met was a rarity.

Never mind what rock I crawled out from under—that's an-other whole book—from then on I've never been the same, and thus began the best years of my life. Actually, thus began my life: the beginning of discovering what it was like to be a person in control of my own destiny. And content—I can't think how my life could be much better. It all started with the blonde demanding to be fed.

My next contact with her was a phone call during which I said, "I need a good shrink, can I come and see you?" Her response still rings loudly, a simple "Sure." So we started the psychotherapeutic process of me defining myself and making significant life choices. Among which, and here I've obviously telescoped time and events, was saying "yes" to Pam's request to join her in private practice.

I am writing this foreword seven years later, having had the opportunity to watch Pam, hear how she has affected numerous others, and actually observed her clients from week to week execute changes in their appearance, outlook, way of acknowledging me in the waiting room, etc. More than a few have gone from being overtly dysfunctional to being warm, friendly people. As I said, I know how that feels from having been there myself. So I feel both qualified and privileged to be able to say what this book is all about and toss out some of my observations about Pam and what makes her tick.

She is still a powerful role model for me. I often gawk in amazement as her boldness results in a free night's lodging in a hotel, an extra day on the rental car or the increasing number of zeros on the business retirement fund (which she manages). Being in on the process of writing this book has been a deepening experience for me, has caused me to look within and ask myself some of the same questions she answers about herself: who am I, how'd I get that way, what do I want and where am I going from here? She likes to tell her clients that about every five years we would do well to have an identity crisis so that we can go back and re-process all our raw materials and see who we are from our new perspective. In her book Pam does exactly that. I fully expect we'll see a new book from her about every five years!

Pam refers to herself as being very "demanding." For a long time I was puzzled, as I didn't see her that way. Eventually I figured out that I didn't see her like that because we basically share the same value system, believing in honesty, openness, sharing, growth, struggle, process. But to other people, whose priorities are different, she seems very demanding. Some people see her as "overbearing," "too intense," "driven," "uppity," and "stubborn." She is clear about her values and requires of herself consistency, congruence, authenticity, presence, and directness. She seems to be that way naturally but others often have to struggle like crazy to just stay clear. The net result has often been—burning out people, burning out relationships. It all starts off fine but after a while people can't keep up; they seem to stumble and fade away. It's an issue Pam reflects on a lot because of its obvious significance. In a way, her book evolved out of this very type of examination.

She comes across as if she's got *it* all figured out when the rest of us are still struggling to identify *it*. It's difficult to realize that there was a time when Pam wasn't like this. As a kid, she didn't know how smart she was. Her view of her intellectual capacities was far from what teachers saw and from what the tests indicated. Even as an adult, there are still times when it feels to me that Pam does not appreciate how smart and intellectually flexible she is. She has none of the conceit often seen in very bright people, and is unassuming about it. To Pam, it isn't how many marbles one has but what one does with them and the quality of life that results that is important. Her kind of smarts takes form in words and ideas, generativity, substance, depth and breadth of experiencing the world. It is not a hammer-and-nails kind of build-it-with-your-hands-smart. She is very realistic about her abilities in this area (or lack of them as she sees it), and will often say, "I can't do that" or "I don't do well at that," and it sounds incongruous coming from her, again that demeanor. It comes across not as a lack of ability but more like "I don't DO windows."

Pam has another trait that drives those of us close to her wild: she is so internal, inner-directed. It appears as though nothing ever rumples her feathers, as if everything fits into place. She processes very rapidly and can function on several levels at once, though preferring to be present on one level at a time. "Presence" is another of those hallmark qualities that describe Pam. She is "all there" when you speak with her, as if nothing were more important at that moment than what you're saying. It's a highly validating experience, and very powerful.

Some of this may sound inconsistent, but Pam is the most consistent person I've ever known. Usually it's the other guy who does the shifting or changing—Pam appears to wait quietly while people talk things out or struggle with their varying perceptions. Then she'll jump in, make an observation, summarize or suggest. Her style is remarkably clear and is often in the form of the one-liner.

It seems everyone says this, but with Pam it's true—she has a great sense of humor. Hers uses the incongruous juxtaposition of words and often has a remarkably disarming effect on people. I can banter back and forth with her now, as I have become aware of myself on other levels. That took a long time to learn to do—at first I was pretty overwhelmed and couldn't easily hear on so many levels at once (low self-esteem and preoccupation obviously being two of my old issues). Now I feel like an equal and have ever since we stopped the therapeutic relationship. I admire how Pam handled that process as well—she made certain all my issues were resolved before encouraging the relationship to move toward friendship. Now humor plays a significant role in keeping us both relaxed and focused at the office. The traveling involved with keeping up continuing education credits is always a highlight because the more relaxed Pam is, the funnier she gets. My favorite example of her humor came one night watching a program together on TV. A woman was describing her experiences coping with breast cancer. She mentioned that having bilateral mastectomies was like grand theft—equivalent to a felony in law. Pam quipped, "With me it would be petty larceny."

Pam is very direct, in a tactful way. She is clear with herself, knows her priorities, is highly aware of where her bottom lines are and does NOT compromise herself by going against her values. At first it takes some getting used to when she says, "I'm really not interested in hearing any more about that." Gulp, well, okay and off we go, on to other topics that are more relevant to both of us. The beauty of her approach is that at (nearly) all times, one knows exactly where he/she stands with Pam, and where she stands on topics, issues.

Her book is about who she is and how she got that way. Like the rest of her life, it exemplifies the processing style by which she lives. Because Pam is not an "outcome" person, everything is alive, viable, has meaning, value, in "process." There are no rights or wrongs, blacks or whites, just variations on degree of fit. The book describes the evolution of a person, describes a way of being, the process of searching, honing, defining and living a set of values in a way that is richly rewarding.

Pam has an intense impatience with living life passively, and herein she talks about why, how much it costs for her to be proactive, to be true to who she is. She lives life cliché-free. Uniqueness, autonomy, individuality are characteristics evolved from an early sense of being different from others, from being excluded by adults, not appreciated by peers, judged by others. Her life as she tells it is a series of risks, each in its own way bigger than the last, each more revealing of who she is, and all very much worth it as we find by the close of this volume. She is a genuine person living life genuinely. Pam is a true existential woman.

CHERYL CASTLES, PH.D.
June 1985

PREFACE

Why would anyone—especially a "normal" person known to only a few—want to write an autobiography? Answering that question has delayed this work for several years. As a mother, I would like to be known by my son in a way only premeditated and deliberated disclosures can provide. I suppose I would like to be known so that I am vindicated to all my adversaries, and the memory of all my mistakes is erased. That temptation, of course, is the major struggle of this book. If I am to be honest, the reason I am writing is to experience myself more fully. The quest itself is sufficient.

As I write, common themes emerge. Starting with the feelings of powerlessness in childhood, moving to the brooding melancholy of adolescence, few are unique to my own experience. Most of us flail in our twenties, making partnership and career commitments while seeking financial solidarity. The thirties are often a time of reconsideration and recommitment. It seems every decade recycles the basic identity issues, the years adding context and perspective.

It is only in viewing my whole life that the themes stand out in bold relief. The show-business passion was intended to be a single chapter until it kept on flowing. Its prevailing influence is an organizing undercurrent, along with a feminist orientation. Striving for mastery as a woman born too soon has been a continuing source of pain and frustration.

Let's get back to that temptation, the same one faced by famous people who attempt autobiography. Like a person with an international reputation, I would like to appear brilliant, unswerving in some noble quest, deserving of praise and emulation at every turn. Some of the events and feelings in my life are less than flattering, but I have made the decision that the warts are an essential part of the story. After all, this is about a regular person.

Another problem has been deciding which story or part of the story to tell. In relating historical events, do I discuss the facts as I knew them then, the feelings I was having then, the behavior that went on then, my current feelings about my feelings then, the context as I later came to understand it, or all of the above? A show-biz legend might reinterpret the various tracks of her life in ways that subsequently confirmed her view of herself or that proved consistent with her eventual career choice and achievements. Thus, being exhibitionistic in her fourth-grade class would be interpreted as craving the attention she later found on the New York stage. But maybe she was just an obnoxious kid and show biz was eons away. There is a danger of overinterpreting minor events to ensure consistency. As a clinical psychologist, I know it is easy to fall prey to that trap.

Writing an autobiography has reinforced my belief in the efficacy of process. Each time I read the rough draft, I found a new insight or nuance. It made me appreciate that life is a growing organism, never-ending. To stop re-writing produces an artificial closure. Even as you read this, I will have changed in some way.

I think it is important that regular people write about themselves, and I want to acknowledge the difficulty (not to mention the anxiety) in making oneself publicly vulnerable. Since the internal is what matters, explaining the process of conceptualizing a life seems to have just as much value as the actual writing of it. And so I begin.

P.M.
1985

ONE

The Normal Life

Show biz. How do I describe what that phrase means to me? Do the feelings date from my first performance when I was three on a train lumbering from Los Angeles to Cleveland? Or does it refer to the passion I associated with jazz singing experiences as I approached forty? Sammy Davis Jr., Mickey Rooney and others have celebrated their multiple-decade anniversaries in show biz. How does a person like me celebrate anniversaries like that? I've never played Caesars Palace or the International Hilton, yet my experiences are just as intense to me.

Neither of my parents were in show business. Just your average, middle-class folk. My parents' values were similar, which is surprising in light of their disparate backgrounds. My mother's family came from the Deep South, North Carolina. My grandfather's father was mayor of the small town, and there were Dellingers in business everywhere. My grandmother was reared to be a lady and never worked a day in her life. When they married, my grandfather owned a hotel and restaurant and was a successful businessman. They had four children in rapid succession, first three boys and then my mother. It may have been those relatively abrupt changes that provoked my grandfather to begin to gamble. Eventually he lost everything at the track. They moved to Cleveland to start over, and my grandfather worked for a storage and battery company there.

My mother delighted in telling us the big family secret, one that she discovered only when she applied for a passport as an adult. It seems that Grandma was unable to defy her own mother when it came time to name my mother. She told my great-grandmother that she had named my mother Dorothy May, when she had not done so. My mother's birth certificate says BABY GIRL DEL-LINGER. The deception was the most politic way to avoid a confrontation, a style that has been time-honored by the rest of the family as well. So confused was my grandmother as a result of her mother's pressure that she transposed the birthdates of two of her children. Until the information came back from the records office in North Carolina, my mother had celebrated her birthday on August 16 each year, while her brother, Roy, claimed September 16 as his date of birth. In truth, the dates were reversed! Whether this represents a family in disarray or just an hysteric's oversight is hard to determine.

My mother grew up in a middle-class neighborhood, but the family continued to struggle financially. None of the children went to college, but that was more a reflection of the family values than the lack of resources. All of the brothers developed blue collar values, were highly concrete in their thinking and tended to be prejudiced against anyone who wasn't white, Anglo-Saxon and Protestant. My mother remembers the neighborhood fondly, and especially her close friend, Dorothy Keck. Mom's upbringing was conventional, devoid of serious trauma. When she was a teenager, her picture appeared in the local paper as a Jean Harlow look-alike, but her mother wouldn't let her work as an actress on the wicked stage. That was probably the major disappointment of her young life.

My father was the seventh son of a seventh son, which gave him a feeling of anointedness. He was born in England, the son of a draper in an upper-middle-class background. While they lived in England, the family had servants. The only time my father saw his father was just before dinner. Freshly scrubbed and in formal clothes, he would be presented in the drawing room. All nine children were then led to a separate room where they dined together.

One of my father's older brothers made his way to the United States and sent back laudatory letters to his mother. Following some discord between the parents, his mother took the six children still living with her and emigrated to Cleveland, where her son had begun work as a building contractor. It took a lot of courage to make that move, essentially without help or support. But then my grandmother (or Nana, as I called her) had had an interesting life already.

During World War I she had worked in a munitions factory. Though she, like my mother's mother, had been reared a lady, she considered the work to be a patriotic duty. Among her possessions when she died was a decal, which read, "There'll always be an England." She took great pride in her homeland. She enjoyed telling hair-raising stories about her factory work and the close calls she had there. She also rolled bandages for the troops during the war.

A woman of independent means, she had earlier invested in the transatlantic cable company and collected dividends until her death. It is said that she never corresponded with her husband, who remained in England, nor ever mentioned his name. Thus it was up to her to raise the large family in her new country. Several of the boys were old enough to chip in while they continued to live at home. My father, Eric John Osborne, was eleven when the move was made.

He had a childhood full of fear. It was difficult enough being the youngest of nine children, as he was frequently the victim of mischief. Because Nana continued to dress him in the little Lord Fauntleroy clothes that had been indicative of class in England, my father was in countless fights on his way back and forth to school. I suspect it was his reaction to living a guarded and fearful childhood that led to his being emotionally withdrawn in adulthood.

While my mother felt close to her father and tension with her mother, my father felt distance with both his parents. There is little evidence that he developed a unique personality during childhood or adolescence; he was one of the crowd. Augmented by the boys' financial help, Nana's income was sufficient that the family could live in a huge house in the nicer section of Cleveland. Throughout my father's late adolescence, parties were the order of the day. All the Osborne kids were good-looking and social. The family would throw formal dress parties, complete with tuxedos and long dresses, compatible with Nana's regal air. My father had assumed a dashing, Clark-Gable-like demeanor. It is not surprising, then, that my mother found him to be a romantic, glamorous figure.

Mom's friend, Dorothy, was dating Dad's brother, Terry. There may have been some competition involved, as they both married about the same time. My mother was twenty, my father twenty-four. Both families were delighted with the match.

A short time after the wedding, Dad's sister moved to California and like her brother earlier, described it as a promised land. Within a few years, Mom and Dad moved to California, followed shortly by more of the family from both sides. Dad had several jobs, working as a hod carrier and bus driver, before he was hired as a technician by Douglas Aircraft in Santa Monica. He had some technical training, but most of what he knew was the result of hands-on experience. Neither parent was comfortable with formal education, and no one on either side in their generation went to college.

Ultimately, however, all the siblings did well. They were part of that Protestant ethic generation, conditioned for hard work and self-sacrifice. Two of my mother's brothers started as a policeman and fireman, but later founded the first discount department store in California, a membership store for municipal employees. Her other brother became a designer for Ford Motor Company in Cleveland. Several of my father's brothers continued in the construction business in Indiana, taking advantage of the postwar building boom. Another brother ran a successful condiment business in Cleveland. None of them, with the exception of my mother's brother Roy, ever learned how to live well.

After Dad went to work for Douglas, my parents began working toward having a family. Reared conventionally, they wanted two children, one of each. It was bitterly disappointing when Mom lost the first two in pregnancy. They weathered World War II in relative comfort. My father was deferred from the military because he was working in a "vital defense industry." In fact, none of the immediate group went to war. My father worked in civil defense, which for him was a poor substitute for the real thing. I recall him telling me when I was very young that a skin flap on his neck was the result of being shot by the enemy during the war. It wasn't until I was a teen-ager that I found out he hadn't served in the military at all.

When I was born on March 27, 1943, there was great joy. My mother had successfully carried a child to term at last. My first name was selected because it was typically British, with Erica the runner-up. My father's name was Eric, so it is puzzling why this option was not taken. My mother's name, Frances, was not even considered. Though they had been married almost eight years, it was like a new beginning. With Nana now in residence, the family constellation had grown to the four of us.

The excitement was dulled when my father's sister Rene died of a massive stroke while on her way to visit me and my mother in the hospital. Some of the family have taken an almost mystical view of this, attributing this to some perverted act of fate. Hers was the first death of a sibling on either side. She was said to be the most vivacious of the Osborne family, spontaneous and flapper-like. I found the rest of the Osbornes to be rather somber, and wish I could have known Rene.

Pacific Palisades in the early 1940s was a small suburb of Los Angeles. There was a shopping center, where everyone greeted each other with friendliness. For those who missed the word-of-mouth news, there was a weekly paper, the *Palisadian*. Several years later, the Palisades became a two-newspaper town when the *Post* was born. Our neighborhood on Hartzell Street was solid middle class, a charming street lined with fragrant eucalyptus trees. In the back yard towered a jacaranda tree along with a smaller fig tree, which I delighted in climbing. It was a visually pleasing area, clean and benign.

Mom and Dad had an active social life. The siblings gathered together and were often joined by Nancy and Bob Church, who became my godparents. My middle name was after Nancy, since they had been neighbors during the early days in Santa Monica. Bob was a restaurant manager. None of the women worked. My earliest memories are of lots of company and parties. Soon after we moved to the Palisades, my father built a badminton court as a setting for the gatherings.

I shared a bedroom with Nana, which must not have been very pleasant for her. I had colic for several months. Given Rene's death so soon after my birth, the tension in the home could have contributed to the condition, which is known to be sometimes psychosomatic. Nana's presence may have caused some stress, too, since she was clearly my favorite person. It was an irony that she had been such a remote parent, but a doting grandmother. We were inseparable. I was a bright and responsive little kid, easy to love. The colic soon disappeared and I became most comfortable in the company of adults. Being the firstborn in a family of three adults, I was the source of much attention. I was verbal at an early age and learned how to entertain others. That, of course, is a major theme in my life and has its roots in its relationship-building power.

All three adults were performers of a sort. My mother sang to me often, and I learned the words to all her songs. My father played the organ, guitar, accordion, piano and banjo. Even Nana played the piano, and I can still see her playing "The Blue Danube Waltz," swaying in time with the music. Social gatherings were characterized by all taking turns performing. I could sing and dance and was the hit of the party.

Nana didn't seem to care about my function as an entertainer. My memories of her are dominated by our adventures together. The Santa Monica municipal bus ran up Hartzell Street in those days, and for a nickel we could ride all the way into Santa Monica on the big blue bus. We would get off at Palisades Park and walk along the cliffs overlooking the Pacific Ocean. Nana knew I liked to climb on the cannon and walk down the hill to the Santa Monica pier. She was in her mid-seventies by this time and still physically active. We had great times together.

She was quite a baker. She would make delicate pastries from scratch, and I would hang around pleading for samples of raw dough. Each day we had tea together, a remnant of her English heritage. Nana was also a major contributor to my religious education. She had been a staunch member of the Church of England, and had joined the Episcopal Church upon arriving in the United States. Neither Mom nor Dad was religious, attending only at my christening and other special occasions. Nana would take me to church with her when she could manage to get there, and saw to it that I was enrolled in religious education classes in school (this was before they were declared unconstitutional by the Supreme Court). I hated the religious rituals, but I loved being with her. Many of my early memories are of her, rather than my parents. So I had mixed feelings when my brother came along. It meant Nana had to move away, as there was not enough room in our two-bedroom house for all of us.

Another early memory is eagerly awaiting my father coming home from work. He would take his lunch pail into the kitchen and sit down with me and the evening paper. We would read the comics, each of us reading every other word. With this kind of help, I could read by the time I was enrolled in kindergarten. My father was particularly fond of reminding me in my adulthood that he was the first person to put my "little fingers on the piano." Those were golden times, and among the few times I felt close to him. Most everything else after that seemed like a negotiation, especially after my brother was born.

My mother spent lots of time with me, reading to me and teaching me things. When we weren't together, I knew I could find her on the couch, reading a book, or entertaining neighbors and drinking coffee. She was a voracious reader, consuming a book a day with ease, usually murder mysteries and romance novels.

Most of the kids in the neighborhood were boys, so my parents often imported other girls to play with me. They were the kids of their friends and of assorted ages. However, I found the boys more interesting. I became a tomboy. When it was allowed, I dressed in boys' clothing and kept up with the boys' conversation about sports. I would sit on the curb, watching the McClure boys playing baseball or football in the street, hoping in vain they would ask me to join them. I admired my older cousin, Allen, who was an athlete. We would go to his Little League games and I was very envious. When I found out my mother was pregnant, I was hoping for a brother. If I had someone in residence to play with, I would no longer be at the mercy of the boys in the neighborhood. Perhaps a brother would provide me with a passport to that elusive world of sports.

Once again, carrying a child to term was a problem for my mother. She had lost another child before successfully delivering my brother. Mom was undecided on his name. He would be named either for my father, Eric John, or a reversal of that, John Eric. I voted for the latter and vetoed an idiosyncratic spelling of the name. Mom thought it distinctive to call him Jon. At the age of five and a half, I thought it an unnecessary burden on him. My fantasies grew as I watched him grow. Soon I would be able to play catch whenever the mood struck and always have someone to pal around with. It was almost enough to distract me from the loss of Nana, who had gone to live with my father's sister, Mimi, in Pasadena.

Though John and I became close, he never fulfilled my ultimate fantasies. It turned out he was interested in working with his hands. If he deigned to play catch with me, I had to pay him a penny a throw!

For the Freudians among the audience, my earliest memory comes somewhere between the ages of three and four. By this time, my father had enclosed the front porch, producing a dining room. We continued to eat in the kitchen, keeping the dining room for special events. The small pump organ, on which my father played nightly, was housed there. I remember him playing "San Antonio Rose" and "When the White Azaleas Are Blooming" while my mother sang along. The music was so moving that I began to cry.

My father stopped playing and they laughed, probably thinking my reaction was cute. I ran from the room in tears, returning to my bedroom, where I quickly recovered once out of the range of the music. After that, I would have to steel myself when the music was played. It was the first time I became aware of my own intense emotion, and the first time my intensity was punished.

Around this time, the family took a train trip to Cleveland to visit the relatives still living there. My memories here are clearly secondhand, but the story has become legend in the family. Apparently I entertained the passengers in the club car hour after hour with my repertoire of what my mother says was over a hundred songs. I don't remember it, but it fits. As long as I can remember, many of my fantasies have been show-biz or fame-related.

With the large extended family, backyard barbecues were well attended. There was much kidding around among the uncles, always of the put-down variety. Someone would be the butt of the joke, or jokes would be told deprecating some minority group. Once the meal had been served, the women would retreat to the kitchen to clean up. Their conversation centered on the men in the other room. Though the men were clearly in control of the family, the women would discuss them as though they were cute but errant children. I was baffled by the apparent paradox, and wondered how they could ever carry on an intimate conversation when alone. They appeared to be on different sides.

Sex was never openly discussed, but looking back, I realize the horseplay had sexual overtones. At one family gathering, one of my aunts came over to my father, undid his shirt and laughed as she tousled the hair on his chest. Those moments made me exceedingly uncomfortable, though I didn't understand the reasons.

The year my brother was born was the same year we got our first television set, 1948. I spent every evening watching the little TV from the security of the big box in which it had come, cuddled with a blanket and a pillow. My big hero was Hopalong Cassidy, and I was overjoyed when I received a Hoppy outfit for my seventh birthday. I watched the Friday night fights with my father, more out of camaraderie and fascination with the medium than out of true interest. Since TV was a social event, the neighbors would gather in our living room each week to watch *Your Hit Parade*, taking turns at guessing which song would be number one.

Johnny and I shared a room, and I liked having a roommate. I talked to him and about him constantly, crowing about his accomplishments as though I were his parent. When he was old enough to understand, I would read him stories and teach him new skills, as my parents had done with me. Because there were almost six years between us, there was little competition. I was older and had more privileges, including a later bed time. The time I was to go to bed was an emotional issue for me, and negotiations for a change in that time were invariably tearful. I felt as though I were asking for the world. Like most kids, I would stay up as late as I possibly could, until the final commercial was over and the station break appeared on the screen.

On weekends I would be glued to the radio. *The Shadow*, *Nick Carter*, *The Fat Man*, as well as comedy shows like *Our Miss Brooks* and *A Date With Judy* were my favorites. Special times were the evenings when I would lie there in the dark, listening to Mark Scott broadcast the games of the Hollywood Stars, the Pacific Coast League baseball team. He was an obvious partisan and I loved his enthusiasm. He always signed off with "And whether you win or lose, be a good sport."

When my parents would go out for the evening, or would play badminton on our court, I would be allowed to fall asleep in my mother's bed. These were agony-and-ecstasy times for me. I hated it when they would go away or would banish me to my room while they entertained late at night. They would use references around adults I could not understand. Sometimes their friends would talk down to me, very much the way I saw the women talk about the men. I resented it and felt alien. Yet I was able to listen to my beloved baseball games and lose myself on the imagined diamond. I knew all the players' names and positions and could make an educated guess at their batting average. By the time I was eight, I was a real fan. I had learned to escape pain via the media.

At three, I was dancing and doing acrobatics at the Ebsen School of Dance, run by the sisters of MGM star Buddy Ebsen. This was the mid-1940s, at the end of the Shirley Temple era. Everybody's children—at least in the upwardly mobile Palisades—were thrust into dance lessons. I danced with Buddy once or twice, and I caught up with him later in my life to confirm the memory. More painful were the involuntary lessons with cute little girls who were nothing like me. I felt like a steam shovel, with awkward movements, bulky and self-conscious. Worse still were the home performances required at every turn: "Pam, sing a song." "Pam, do your ballet dance." "Pam, do your tap number." I did it, sometimes with pride but often with resentment. We have home movies of a frowning little girl doing a mechanical dance that has obviously been a command performance for the camera.

It might be noted, though, that many of the performances were of my own volition, especially if they involved dressing in boys' clothing and dancing to an up-tempo record for an audience. I loved boogie woogie, and Hadda Brooks' recording of "Near You" would set my three-year-old tootsies moving any time. The music would begin and there I'd go. Those were the first moments of exhibitionism that I remember with fondness, but they were not always performed when I wanted.

Other significant events that I do not personally recall were the post-wartime shows that my father helped stage at Douglas Aircraft. By that time, he had risen from technician to electrician, and took responsibility for setting up the equipment for the shows. The evenings featured such talent as Hedy Lamarr, Marie Wilson and Lana Turner. One of my father's favorite stories about me was when Hedy Lamarr held me on her lap during a rehearsal and talked with me. My recollections center more on the band instruments and the sounds they made. I wandered around, looked at them but didn't dare pick them up. This was a scene I was later to repeat with some regularity. My father made recordings of their performances which he later played at home for the neighbors. I was very impressed that recordings were possible. One of my early alienating memories was that he would not share his outtakes with me. Movie stars had blown their takes and sworn, and he did not want me to hear that. This is important in that my father tended to distance me in many ways, and this is the first time I remember it happening. I could not even imagine what could be so bad that I could not handle it. Another fascinating mystery of adulthood.

The world of adults seemed riddled with such secrets, known only to them. Shared glances, smirks and whispered allusions all made me feel like an intruder. I longed to be included in this elite society where everything was known. As I grew up, those uncomfortable moments grew into an intense need for information. Politically, the idea of censorship became abhorrent to me. And personally, I developed a strong sense of the value of honesty in relationships. Lying, especially the sociopathic art of lying by omission, is intolerable.

One night my father took me to the Bay Theater to see a movie, a rare occurrence. We seldom went anywhere by ourselves, and almost never to a film. That was the province of my mother and my friends. The night was special, an opportunity not only to see a movie I wanted to see, but to share my growing film passion and internal world with my father. He was standing in line to buy the tickets when some of his friends from work came over to say hello. I was standing by the posters advertising the movie. When I walked over to be introduced as I had been taught to do, they were in the middle of the conversation. The woman leaned toward him and began to tell him what was apparently a joke. He asked me to stand aside, far enough away that I couldn't hear it. I was hurt at the exclusion, but also disappointed at this obvious lack of respect for me, a devaluation of our relationship. I tried not to cry, but I was deeply hurt; I had been cut out again. It wasn't the joke I missed, but the intimacy.

In early childhood, I was a mimic and praised for being "on stage." My father had his share of the theatrical spirit, too. Each year, he played Jacob Marley in the community production of *A Christmas Carol*. But somehow I was embarrassed and ill at ease in seeing him do that. It seemed so out of character. Perhaps it was another example of suppressing my intense reactions.

Looking over the home movies and photographs today, it is clear that I was shot more often than my brother. It may be because home movie equipment was fairly new when I was little, and my father liked gadgets. As a person uncomfortable with groups of people, he could have used the camera as a tool to structure interaction. His role was well defined in the family. No one else in the extended family took pictures at anywhere near the clip my father did.

I can remember being dragged outside before leaving for anywhere. I was given instructions to walk down the path, and whatever I would do, smile, smile, smile. And wave. Long before the era of *cinéma vérité*, I had to appear to be having a good time, always coming or going. It may be why even today, when some well-intentioned jerk tells me to smile, I feel like punching his lights out.

The only honest action films came at birthday parties, many of which were held at Beverly Park, an amusement park now defunct. So we see little Pam at three riding around the track in the caboose of a train; then a little bigger Pam at four, five, and six, around the same track. There's little Pam, smiling and waving. It was certainly easier to be photographed there, as it did not interrupt my fun.

It is interesting to note that I was never photographed performing in some passionate activity. None of my Ebsen School of Dance recitals are chronicled, no record pantomimes or street baseball games. My father chose to see me on his own terms, his very own Shirley Temple, endlessly coming and going. It may have been this frequent posturing that led to a childhood self-consciousness. I knew every frame would be shown to the entire family as well as the neighborhood and critiqued by all. It encouraged the show-biz fantasies, but placed a definite emphasis on maintaining a pleasant, if phony, demeanor. I resented the constant posturing and the intrusion in my life. The home movies were another example of the focus on externals over internals in my family. It was the appearance of things that mattered.

My home was filled with the murder mysteries devoured by my mother. My father, on the other hand, read very little. Other than our reading the "funnies" together when I was learning to read, I don't remember seeing him read anything but the newspaper. Mom read to me all the time and was a powerful role model in the joys of reading. I was well prepared for school. Kindergarten sounded like fun, a place where reading was encouraged, and I was looking forward to that first day.

As I walked hand in hand with my mother across the street toward the big white building, the excitement was immediate. She pointed out several other little girls also putting their best foot forward on this important day. It must have been a small entering group, since it was late January and included those inconveniently born in the spring months.

Kindergarten turned out to be not what I had imagined. Instead of books, we were placed in front of easels and encouraged to finger paint and draw with paint brushes. During play time, I would retreat to the sandbox, playing by myself. Indoor play was sex-role stereotyped. The boys played with building blocks in the center of the room, while the girls combed their dolls' hair in the corner. While I wanted to join in the block-building, I felt I belonged to neither group. I guess I hadn't been sufficiently socialized. My parents were not yet discouraging my tomboy attitude, but it didn't fit at school. There was obviously a code, but I didn't know the rules. Somehow in the course of that year, I figured out a strategy to deal with this alien world: I would relate with the teacher instead and achieve academically as best I could.

By the first grade, I knew how to read fluently, which set me apart from my peers. Still a tomboy, I liked climbing on the jungle gym and relished being called by a different boy's name each week. My teacher, the warm and accepting Miss Erickson, tolerated it all, though it must have caused her some discomfort to call me "Larry" or "Phil." I loved recess and playing with a ball, any ball. Games were still not well organized, but it was clear that I was more boy than girl. The girls all seemed sedentary and lacking in curiosity.

The differences were later confirmed when my mother signed me up for Brownies. I didn't like the idea, but Kathy Berry did, and she was my best friend. It seemed all the girls my age were doing it, and that was enough for my mother. If this seemed like the beginning of a double message, it was. I was indeed unique, but I had to fit in. It was quite a conflict for a seven-year-old, and was the centerpiece of later identity crises.

There were ten girls in the troop, with two of the mothers as leaders. In sharp contrast, several of the girls were excessively feminine, passive to the point of crying at any disruption. There were others who were destined to social heights. Almost all of them were compliant kids and a few were quite intelligent. It was safe for little girls to be smart until they hit adolescence. We learned all the "womanly activities," from sewing a carrying bag to learning how to cook in the leader's kitchen. Of course, all these efforts were rewarded with merit badges as soon as we graduated to Girl Scouts. To my bitter disappointment, even the camp-outs were focused on learning to cook outdoors, which spoiled the whole thing for me. But I went on to earn more badges than any other girl, emphasizing my own areas of interest, such as boating and radio/TV.

By the second grade, we were learning basic arithmetic using lima beans kept in a cigar box that smelled wonderful. While I felt more interpersonal alienation, I continued to spend time with Kathy Berry, who lived about four blocks away. She was also a performer, and we took turns singing for each other. We often spent the night together, huddled under the covers with a flashlight reading comic books and telling stories. I cried the next night, though, from the loneliness created by our being apart.

I was thoroughly into baseball and played whenever I had the chance. Unfortunately, in the early 1950s there were few opportunities for girls to play baseball. At nine, I began attending cousin Al's Little League games and asked my uncle why I couldn't play. He told me it was because I was a girl. I remembered reading in school about Americans petitioning their government to redress grievances, so I composed a petition allowing girls to participate in Little League.

Since the Palisades was my playground and many of the merchants were friends of my parents, it was logical that I would wander around town to seek the signatures I needed. I ran out of steam by the time I had thirty names. There were usually snickers or smiles when they signed, but nobody turned me down. Now that I had the finished petition, I asked my parents what to do with it. They didn't know; it seems no one knew. Somehow it disappeared and was forgotten amid the events of childhood.

I was still angry, though. After hearing about some boys' clubs playing each other in team sports, I decided to form a girls' baseball club and named it after a boys' club, the Lancers. I recruited girls to play ball every Saturday morning, thinking all of them were equally angry at the discrimination. Eventually we had a cadre of four or five girls, enough to field a street team. The giant eucalyptus trees on Hartzell Street served as the bases, the street as the infield. The yards across the street were the outfield, and we had to be careful to avoid the picture window in center field. Luckily I was a pull hitter, and the only one capable of hitting the ball that far. One day I came across a baseball catalog in my cousin's room and asked if I could keep it. Afterward I spent many an hour formulating ways to buy real, honest-to-God bases and a real elevated pitcher's rubber.

It was around this time that my parents began contracting with me for the things I wanted. Wisely, they seldom bought me things outright. I would have to earn part of the cost, usually half. At various times, I sold greeting cards, mowed lawns, babysat, cleaned houses and even bought candy at wholesale prices to be resold at a profit in the neighborhood. Most of the income went into the baseball fund, along with the weekly ten-cent dues required of the members. When there was enough in the treasury, I went to the sporting goods store to inhale the sensual smells of leather and buy some baseball paraphernalia.

By the fourth grade, I had learned to keep the club a secret. Latency was in full swing, that time when little boys hate little girls and ridicule everything they do. I'm not sure that attitude is really ever unlearned; probably it's merely rechanneled. Anyway, my efforts to have a girls' club were demeaned, though I continued to be the top athlete in my class, of either sex. The best time I could imagine outside a movie theater was a special trip to see the Hollywood Stars baseball team play. Mike Sandlock, Carlos Bernier, Bobby Bragan, Jack Phillips, and Dale Long were all heroes.

We would make the long drive to Gilmore Field next to the Pan Pacific auditorium. The biggest crowds came for the intercity rivalry between the Los Angeles Angels and the Stars, and those contests were most exciting. I would almost gasp each time I arrived at the top of the stairs and saw the diamond for the first time. The beauty of the contrast between rich green grass and the dark brown infield stirred me. For one of the Angels-Stars games, it was so crowded (more than 2000), we had to camp in left field in a roped-off section. That game is memorable as the one in which I bitterly fought for and successfully recovered a home-run ball hit by Carlos Bernier. Many an hour was spent in fantasy of actually being able to play on that field, or any field for that matter. It took thirty years to play that fantasy out.

A highlight of this period was my relationship with Arden Farms. We had our milk delivered twice a week, courtesy of a kind, smiling man named Bill. He offered to take me for a ride in his milk truck. One thing led to another, and soon I was doing his deliveries with him almost every week. He brought me one of his old work shirts, with "Arden" written on the back. Even more exciting than riding in the doorway were the people I met on his route. Television actor Leo Carrillo and Mario Lanza were Arden customers, and I looked forward to delivering their milk. My favorite was Deborah Kerr. She lived in an older mansion in the Palisades, complete with maid and maid's quarters. Bill and I entered the kitchen each week, to be greeted by the maid and a piece of cake. Sometimes Miss Kerr (or Mrs. Bartlett, as we called her) would offer a greeting. I had seen her in *King Solomon's Mines* and thought she was wonderful.

While I was living in fantasy of a career playing first base or starring in the latest MGM musical, my academic career was humming along. An IQ test led to my being skipped from the last half of the third grade to the last half of the fourth grade, which made me even with the school year. The fourth grade, though, held terror—Mr. Skopp was a reputed tyrant who allegedly broke rulers over heads. I was hoping my teacher's-pet skills and IQ status would protect me from his wrath. Within a few weeks, I had won him over.

It was in this grade that I became more acutely aware of anti-female sentiment and the pressure to conform to "appropriate female behavior." Naturally, I felt in conflict with those expectations. On top of the baseball identification, I had become interested in national politics. Eisenhower was running for president and my parents were going to vote for him. They were not especially vocal in their interest, but I was from the minute I inadvertently wandered into Republican Party headquarters. I liked the buttons and colorful bumper stickers. I walked up and down the middle of Swarthmore Avenue, handing out GOP propaganda. People viewed this with indulgence, but with polite dismissal. One of the neighbors said it was unfeminine, which surprised me. I didn't see what being a girl had to do with sports or political activity. No one was taking me seriously about anything.

I began to challenge the ironclad dress code which demanded that girls wear skirts or dresses to school. Making up excuses that ranged from no clean clothes (which was a lie) to having a cold (also a lie), I wore pants as often as I felt I could get away with it. This would require a note from my mother, who complied on occasion. Falsely pleading nausea or headache, I would stay home from school at times when I saw a Freddie Stewart movie listed in *TV Guide*. I relished those B movies and loved his singing, as well as the apparent camaraderie of the college kids.

More seriously, I began to act out my increasing frustration by hitting other kids. If someone didn't run out a ground ball during recess, I would deck him. If someone made fun of me, I would slug him or her, or pull the chair out from under him. This was always done impulsively, never premeditatively. Inside, I was a real coward and constantly feared retribution. Friends who would play at my house would be subject to my bossiness. They had to play by my rules. If they didn't, I would slap them over the top of the head with my ever-present baseball cap. I had seen this modeled frequently by Muggs McGinnis in the 1930s *Eastside Kids* movies, featuring the tough Brooklyn kids. Most of the time, I managed to get away with these futile attempts to gain respect. Once in a while some kid would rat on me to the teacher and I would be sent to the principal's office.

Miss Allison was our aging leader, stern but fair. I lived in fear of her, for I knew corporal punishment was frequently practiced in her office. By this time, though, I had learned how to con my elders. When sent to her office, I was frightened, but not too scared to line up my defenses. By the time I reached her office, I felt cooler. After a while the scene became a familiar melodrama. She called me into her office and sat down behind her massive desk. She scowled, and told me she knew I knew better and how disappointed she was in me. This was an old line from home and I knew how to deflect it, though at home I wasn't so successful in avoiding the guilt. I apologized, explained away my impulsive behavior and promised never to do it again. As long as my infractions were spaced over time, she bought my act. So far as I know, my parents never found out about these episodes, which is probably for the best. They wouldn't have known what to do, short of punishing me again. Problem children were outside the family experience.

I learned how to escape serious punishment and to live a double life. I became an angry, alienated kid on the inside. On the outside, I was an achieving, studious, athletic kid who was participating in all the expected activities.

The pressure escalated in the fifth and sixth grades. My fifth-grade teacher apparently had some problems of her own and couldn't handle the class. She sent me to the principal with some regularity, much of the time without cause. I complained to my mother, who spoke to other parents, and the teacher was eventually canned. Fifth grade also marked the triumph of the school nurse over my mother. Every year she had sent home a report that declared my need for glasses. Though my mother was also near-sighted, she took no action. By the fifth grade, I was getting up out of my seat to read the blackboard, though I was sitting in the front row. Ultimately the glasses were purchased. The harassment I received over having "four eyes" was superseded only by the teasing about my athletic performance.

Jacquie Weiss and I walked the same way to school in the fifth grade and we became friends. She didn't seem to fit the mold either. She was gawky, and from an immigrant Jewish family. She was friendly and compliant, and shared my movie passion. Though she was far from athletic, she joined the Lancers and indulged me in the weekly baseball games. I teased her about her awkward throw and she never did learn to stand correctly at the plate, in spite of my relentless coaching.

And I had the writing bug. I began a club newspaper, called *The Star*, after my favorite baseball team. It came out monthly, in four pages, with two typed columns each page. I would write an editorial and feature stories on various Hollywood Stars players. There would be humorous articles and jokes. It was a money-making enterprise, producing the vast sum of ten cents per copy. Since the Xerox had yet to be invented, I had to type each page several times, using carbons. It was time-consuming but emo-tionally rewarding, even with its small circulation. The paper was "published" regularly until the eighth grade, when I capitulated to sexist pressures and abandoned my imagined baseball career and the Lancers.

Writing helped me cope with anger. I had learned to substitute words for fists. My sixth grade teacher, Mrs. Ziegler, also had something to do with that. Nicknamed "The Black Widow" for her characteristic choice of clothing, she scared the daylights out of me. I heard she walked into the girls' bathroom at recess and peeked over the stalls, challenging the girls' right to be there without a pass. I wasn't going to mess with her. Her other function in my life was to traumatize me to math. Up to then, I had sailed through timed tests, finishing well in advance of the deadline. Mrs. Ziegler, however, attributed my one or two mistakes to my speed and forced me to slow down, even if it meant giving me extra work to do. When I claimed not to be cut out for the pursuit of arithmetic, she countered, "Then you'd just better cut yourself out, young lady." No nonsense, indeed. Her early discipline, whether it was to quell my temper or to learn to memorize the Gettysburgh Address, helped prepare me for the all important junior high school years.

TWO

Are You Sure
I Can't Be
Doris Day?

Among the high spots of my middle childhood years were trips to
Pasadena to visit Nana and Aunt Mimi. Though I loved my
brother, I enjoyed the prospect of getting away on my own. My
family would make the hour-long drive, stay for dinner, and leave
me with Nana for days at a time. Mimi owned a health food
manufacturing plant called McBride Products. She worked hard
all day, then came home to dinner and her Seagram's Seven, not
necessarily in that order. By about eight o'clock, she was in a
stupor and made her way slowly up the wooden stairs to bed.
During the day, I had a choice of going to work with her or staying
home with Nana. Often I would go with her, relishing the smells
of the soy and malt and being able to tinker with the typewriter in
the front office. She ran the business mostly by herself, and it was a
modest success.

The Pasadena house was a large, white, two-story wooden
structure with colonial pillars supporting the front porch. There
was a large front yard, a vacant lot next door. The railroad tracks
ran across the street from the lot. When I would hear the train
starting to rumble, I would run outside and wave to the engineer.
If he saw me, he would blow his loud whistle, sending adrenaline
rapidly through my body.

The house had been built in the 1920s, and had been fitted for
gas fixtures. There was a sun porch downstairs, a kitchen with a
cooler, and sliding wooden doors that disappeared into the wall.
The stairs were of dark wood and curved upward in a narrow

spiral that produced ominous fantasies. Upstairs were three bedrooms and a bath. Off each of the end bedrooms was a sun deck.
No one ever used it, but I worried about falling off the roof and
considered it a possible means of escape in case of fire.

I should mention that by middle childhood I had developed a
terrible fear of fire. That the Pasadena house was a firetrap was not
lost on me. I spent some sleepless nights worrying about getting
out of the house, and wondering where the fire might break out. It
didn't help that everyone in my family smoked. I worried far more
about the fear involved than about the possibility of dying in the
blaze. I don't think I so much as heard a fire engine in Pasadena,
but I had experienced several nocturnal neighborhood fires. The
flashing red lights and wailing siren would waken me out of a
sound sleep. No one had as yet diagnosed my nearsightedness and
myopia. When I saw the lights reflected on the wall, I couldn't tell
what was going on.

By and large, Pasadena holds mostly positive memories. Nana
would play with me by the hour, usually card games like Fish and
Old Maid, and we would listen to soap operas together on the
radio. I didn't always understand what was going on, but I liked
the warm feelings of being with her, whatever we were doing. She
would sometimes give me a dime to take to the gas station to get a
pop. On hot days, she would offer another dime to buy her a Nehi
Orange. The only harsh words we exchanged were when I wanted
to bring in geraniums to set up a jungle on the living-room floor for
my toy soldiers.

Mimi dated several men, all of whom were nice to me. One in
particular would take me along with them. There was a little
restaurant around the corner, the Old Virginia, with red check-
ered tablecloths on the tables and a fire in the fireplace. It was cozy,
and I loved it when they would take me there. I was in a world of
adults in Pasadena and seemed to be taken seriously.

The big event was New Year's Eve. We set up the card table in
front of the television set to watch Guy Lombardo. Some time
during the evening, we brought down the dinner gong from upstairs and set up the food. Mimi was a chocolate freak and we

always had a nice box of See's candy, as well as other treats. Mimi let me have a cigarette and a watered down glass of bourbon and water on that night. We brought out pots and pans from the kitchen, along with spoons. Nana would retire about eleven, and I would go upstairs once or twice to splash cold water on my face to be able to stay awake. When New York announced it was midnight, Mimi and I would pound on the gong, beat on the pots and pans, then sing "Auld Lang Syne" with Guy. Then we would open the front door and throw the doormat on the front lawn. Mimi said it was like throwing out the old year and starting over. It was always a stirring occasion. I continued to spend New Year's Eve in Pasadena until I was thirteen years old and began babysitting for the neighbors at inflated rates. Now, on that night, when the ball drops in New York, I think of those exciting, memorable evenings. Mimi could really get into it.

By the time I was nine, Mimi received word that her niece in Ohio had been orphaned by the death of her brother and his wife. She offered to adopt her, saving her from an orphanage. Mimi handled me with great sensitivity, taking me aside before cousin Nancy arrived.

"Even though Nancy will be my daughter, you'll always be my queen bee," she said with a smile. It reassured me and set the stage for a less competitive relationship to come. While we fought on occasion, Nancy and I had a lot of fun together. We were only nine months apart in age but had had very different experiences. We walked to the community plunge together in the summer, went to the movies, played with soldiers, went for walks, and even shoplifted together. Nancy didn't have my academic interests, but she was a good sport. There was no issue of competition for Nana, either. I never worried about that, as Nana made it clear I was her favorite. Those Pasadena trips were among the real highlights of the middle childhood years, though my only contact with show biz was the weekly movies at the Rialto Theater. I first saw *Annie Get Your Gun* there, and immediately fell in love with Howard Keel. Nancy and I went to every movie that played there when I was in town. She liked Esther Williams, and we'd act out the dramas after we got home.

From the time I was eight, I had sung with records and acted out scenes from the films I had seen. I had been going to movies on a regular basis since I was five or six. At eleven, I discovered record pantomiming. My fame fantasies took new flight. My friend Jacquie and I imagined ourselves Frank Sinatra and Bing Crosby doing "Well, Did You Evah?" from *High Society*, and Rosemary and Betty Clooney doing "Sisters." We would take our records and tour the neighborhood, stopping housewives in the middle of their work to perform for them. I even conned my brother into doing pantomimes with me as we mimicked "Mutual Admiration Society." I was always getting into someone else's identity via the vicarious learning associated with show biz.

John and I were practically inseparable but we teased one other mercilessly. My mother bought popcorn in huge red cans with metal lids. John and I each had our own cache of lids with our initials carved in the center. When either of us wanted to annoy the other, the silence would be broken by the clatter of a lid being tossed on the metal heating register just outside our bedroom doors. When a lid was thrown from any distance at all, the sound was akin to a rifle shot and sure to get the other's attention.

By the time I was twelve, I had discovered Doris Day and was truly in love. She was everything I wanted to be. She was cute, feminine, perky, and clever, found herself in interesting situations, and sang real well. There was always an orchestra with her wherever she went, fulfilling my most opulent fantasies. And, of course, there was the proverbial happy ending. It was not unusual for me to see one of her films ten or twelve times, spending all day Saturday and much of Sunday studying her every move. If only I could perfect her style, her words, my life would be complete and I would be happy forever.

There was a single glitch in this fantasy: Jacquie. She felt a competition with me for Doris' affections and began to keep a scrapbook on her, as I did. To my chagrin she came up with obscure articles and glossy photographs of Doris that would drive me crazy, and would never reveal her source. I assumed she had some help from her uncle, character actor Herb Vigran, but she wouldn't give me a clue.

As a gift, she presented me with an autographed picture of Doris, which produced mixed feelings. I was excited to receive a personal treasure like that, and the thought that Doris herself had been exposed to my persona was beyond joy. But Jacquie had one-upped me by getting that close herself, and it drove me bonkers. Jacquie and I often went to Doris Day movies together. That area of the competition was all mine. I always did better with the dialogue memorization and in singing the songs along with the soundtrack. The real capper was that I looked a little like her as well. Blonde hair, blue eyes, an open smile and the all-American girl look produced a passing similarity.

Another of Jacquie's coups was sending my photo to *Screen Stories*, a popular movie magazine. It was one of the seemingly endless magazines we read and digested every day at the Rexall drugstore. One day Jacquie was acting more coy than usual as we made our regular daily trip to the magazine rack. She handed me *Screen Stories* and asked me to look through it. When I saw the article in which my picture was juxtaposed with Doris as a look-alike, I stopped breathing. Then I saw Jacquie's letter suggesting the similarity and my feelings became mixed again. Somehow she had horned in again on my Doris Day fantasy and even seemed to get credit for it. But this was just a minor part of my reaction. The appearance of the article renewed my fantasy of "being dis-covered," just as so many big stars had been over the years. I knew that once someone saw I existed, knew of my talent and special qualities, they would seek me out. This is a theme that is replicated at various times in my show-biz life. Not unexpectedly, however, only a few friends saw the article and then only after I dropped heavy hints they should peruse the magazine for interesting articles.

One of my early memories about the fame/destiny theme dates to those drugstore raids. Even before meeting Jacquie, I would go to the Bay Drug Store to "arrange magazines," pretending that it was my "job." Among the magazines then popular was *Confidential*, well known in subsequent years as a target for libel suits. It would print scurrilous information about celebrities that I would not hear anywhere else. It was like getting in on an adult world that I couldn't seem to crash any other way. I kept wondering if Doris Day would ever be in any of those revealing articles, but she never showed up there. Even at the age of eight or nine, I was fascinated by those awful secrets. I figured the only way *Confidential* would know these things was to watch people when they didn't know they were being watched, or to corner friends and entreat them to reveal sensitive material. For a few years I became paranoid about my friends and obsessed with loyalty. More than that, I would fantasize that a reporter from *Confidential* was watching me, even when I was watching television or doing some mundane activity. This served a double function of making me self-conscious, but also of developing an alter ego. This other part of my person would be me watching me, in order to gauge the impact I might be having. It gave me a sense of power and celebrity, if only in my imagination.

The "*Confidential* magazine complex" was an important aspect of my early fantasy life. By employing imagination, I was pretending I was being watched. It gave me the illusion that I was at least as important as the people discussed in the magazine and every bit as interesting. And it helped me develop the skill of monitoring my own behavior. Simultaneously, I was participant and observer. My behavior was directly experienced, while another part of me watched and determined its appropriateness. More than making judgments, it helped develop a sense of demeanor. I began to think about what other persons must feel on the inside, though I might only be privy to their external behavior. It was an intense course in empathy.

All this cross-comparing and internal-external blending seemed to produce a strong sense of self for a young girl. Others commented on it, and adults were often intimidated. There was an intensity and integration unfamiliar in children. It fed into my feeling of uniqueness, but also my sense of alienation. Was there nobody like me out there? And if the answer was no, what did this mean about who I was and my acceptability? It is not surprising that I would identify with other unique people, seemingly alien to the rest of the world, such as movie stars. *Confidential* magazine coalesced much of what was happening within.

In junior high school, the school day changed from a static classroom to a situation where my environment and teacher changed every forty minutes or so. In my first year at Emerson Junior High, I had a young teacher in her first year of teaching. Velma Cottle was responsive to my fantasies and supportive of my specialness. She had a cutting sense of humor, a quality we shared.

Miss Cottle came into my life at a propitious time. Shortly after entering Emerson, I broke my little toe. I had been chasing John around the kitchen table to tickle him when my toe caught on the table leg. Emerson was a half-hour's school bus ride from home. The pain in my taped-up toe was continual, but worsened when someone stepped on it in the rush to the front of the bus line. Miss Cottle was kind enough to keep me in during recess, so I would not have to risk more pain. I kept her company while she prepared for the next class. And while I sat, we talked.

She was witty and benevolent, interested in my thoughts and opinions and I began to trust her. I don't think I ever shared my show-biz fantasies with her, thinking they were too bizarre. So it was a special irony when I returned for the eighth grade and heard that Miss Cottle had become Mrs. Nagel and was teaching drama. Better than that, she had married an actor. It was beginning to feel safe to pursue some of the fantasies.

That summer I had an opportunity to act in a Girl Scout play, but chose to take tickets instead. I was afraid of embarrassing myself, but more fearful of not getting the part I coveted. Immediately regretting my cowardice, I memorized the play and silently mouthed the dialogue as it was being presented. At any rate, when I reached the new junior high, I decided to use my one elective to take Drama I. As usual, Jacquie decided to follow in my footsteps, and made the same decision.

Drama I was uneventful and disappointing. Acting out these little scenes and pantomimes was for amateurs. I felt unrecognized as the pro I knew myself to be, destined for greatness. My classmates humbled me, as I became aware of the number of kids who were more directly linked to show biz. The children of Bob Crosby, Paul Henreid, Victor Mature, Harry Morgan, Robert Riskin, Herbert Yates and others were certainly unimpressed with this pudgy little waif with the sense of destiny. It was deflating to be taking social studies with one of the Mousekateers or Ryan O'Neal. Another classmate was always meeting her father at the studio and showing up with promotional material for the latest films.

It is still a wonder to me that, in the face of the stiff competition, I managed to maintain not only my fantasies, but the acute sense of destiny. I knew lots of these kids had a head start on me, but I believed that talent would win out. There was little doubt in my mind that if I worked hard enough and prepared myself I would ultimately get what I wanted. My cynicism would come later, after disillusionment.

The humility I developed on the outside did nothing to mitigate the inner intensity. Another blow came in Drama II, when we began learning Shakespeare. That's when I began to realize not all show biz is created equal. My fantasy life centered on musical comedy. Shakespeare not only had no bearing on those thoughts, I deemed it anachronistic. Even serious drama bore my scorn. I did a scene from *Tea and Sympathy*, but lacked the sophistication to understand what it was all about. The kid with whom I performed the scene was no more enlightened, but he managed to cut a hit record a few years later with another drama classmate. They called themselves Dick and Deedee and soon faded into oblivion, but not before I was humbled again.

As an adolescent, I burned people out. My friends wanted to talk about how dreamy Elvis Presley was or who was dating whom. I was interested in why Elvis had such appeal, the kinds of people who worshiped him; and I wanted to know what made some people popular and others not so. The feedback was that I was too serious and asked too many questions. One friend told me she was tired of my intensity. Actually, the seriousness was tempered with an imitative, dry humor that was documented in yearbooks throughout school. It sometimes got me into minor trouble in class, but the prevailing impression was one of quietness and seriousness. I suspect the same is true today.

The science fiction writer Ray Bradbury once wrote, "The ability to fantasize is the ability to survive." Fantasy had always come easily for me, a natural bridge between reality and the possible. It allows for anticipatory problem-solving, constructing scenarios and solutions that sometimes preclude the need for actual trial-and-error. Potential mistakes are weeded out internally. More important, maintaining an active fantasy life has kept me in touch with the deepest part, the person I am becoming. It has motivated me to keep seeking, to keep working, even when the odds are against me. Certainly there were times during adolescence when fantasy saved me from complete withdrawal, even from myself. Knowing there was more and the ability to see myself being more produced an ever-enlarging sense of self that experience alone could not provide.

The danger with fantasy is living there exclusively, of settling for the rich internal life and avoiding direct experience. It can remove a person from the immediacy of the now, allowing a total retreat in the face of adversity. I admit to having used fantasy as an outlet to ward off disappointment and to feel powerful in vanquishing my enemies. But in general, it has been a positive force, propelling me beyond what I thought were my limits.

Drama II allowed me to write and participate in "radio." The school, which by then had been christened Paul Revere Junior High, had a morning public address broadcast linked to every classroom. I was recruited by Mrs. Nagel to write some of the messages in a humorous way, and performed several of them in my Louella Parsons impersonation. By the end of the ninth grade,

I had participated in a few school-wide productions, but they fell far short of my fantasies.

The conscious sense of destiny had been developed somewhere between ten and twelve. In most cases, that implies a dependence on fate, a passive state in which one merely waits for her just desserts. Mine was a bowdlerized view of fate, in which I would get those rewards, but only because I exerted maximum effort. True, the fantasy of "being discovered" in a drugstore was omnipresent, but my responsibility was to be there, to be well trained, to be well schooled in show-biz theory and history, and to make contacts. To this end, I read plays and just about everything else I could find in the Hollywood bookstores I raided each week.

This expectation explains why junior high drama was both threatening and disappointing. While it called my bluff, the quality of the material was as embarrassing as the Girl Scout play. The hackneyed plots involved childish humor, moronic misunderstandings and slapstick. I couldn't relate to it at all, which made me more nervous than ever, since mastering the material was essential. Mrs. Nagel made no attempts to bring us into the world of musical comedy. The highlights of those classes for me were the record pantomimes I did in class, which was the closest I got to what I really wanted to do. I always had trouble fitting myself into someone else's mold.

Concurrent with drama came my involvement with band and orchestra. Music goes all the way back. Other than our singing together, my mother decided I should learn to play the violin. I was about six at the time, so the instrument seemed a strangely masochistic choice. After several group lessons, I made a deal. I would practice at home and learn on my own. And if I could learn to play a real tune, she would buy me my most coveted possession at the time, a motor scooter. Surprisingly, she underestimated me and agreed. Within a week, I could play a popular tune, not well but all the way through to the end, but it was at least recognizable. I never got the scooter.

Shortly thereafter, Mom switched gears on me. When I was seven years old, she escalated her efforts to socialize me by importing an obese, frizzy-orange-haired woman to teach me the piano. She would come to the house every week for my half-hour lesson. It wasn't the practicing I minded, though scales weren't exactly inspirational; it was her bulk and body odor. I would hear her car arriving outside and I would immediately find a place to hide. Unfortunately, I would always be found. Eventually, I guess, Mom got tired of the hunt. I moved on to Mrs. Lindsay, whose house was a short walk away. An older, exacting woman, she continued the time-honored tradition of prescribing my music. Neither of the teachers asked what I wanted to learn, so it was scales and cute little numbers. I had hoped to learn to play the songs I was memorizing, the popular tunes of the day. But, no. Once a week, after school, I would walk to Mrs. Lindsay's, hoping she would be sick or the house would have burned down.

One day one of the hoods in my sixth-grade class asked where I was going. I complained about the lesson and he said he would take care of it for me. Not giving it another thought, I went on to my lesson. I had no sooner sat down to reproduce some scales when there was a large thump on the roof. It took a second to realize that it was probably the hood making his move. I stifled a laugh when Mrs. Lindsay looked around puzzled. After a few more salvos, she left to look outside. By the time she had returned, there were only fifteen minutes left of the lesson. I was grateful, but fearful that I would be implicated. Though I was never confronted with the dreadful deed, within a few weeks my lessons were shifted to another teacher.

Mr. Barnaba was a stereotypical old-school music professor. Doddering and rumpled, he had a thick Eastern European accent and smelled musty. We had been working together a few weeks when I noticed the other musical instruments in his small studio. The room was in the back of a music store that had recently opened in the center of the Palisades. By this time, I was so sick of the piano I would have picked up anything. The five years of lessons had not lessened my disdain for the piano; I figured another instrument might be better, since it was clear my mother was continuing to insist I play something.

I should mention that by this time I had developed an affinity for the Navy, after seeing *The Caine Mutiny* fourteen times. As a result, I had sold greeting cards and done chores for the neighbors in order to save up the sixteen dollars for a bugle. I taught myself all the standard bugle calls and regularly woke up the neighborhood with reveille and bade it good night with taps. With some of my allowance and babysitting money, I rented a trumpet for a three-month stretch for five dollars per month. It is sad that my parents didn't pick up on this obvious motivation to switch to the trumpet, which was the instrument I really craved to master.

So when Mr. Barnaba's grouping of instruments appeared in his studio, I thought of finally getting some backing to switch to the trumpet. Mr. Barnaba and my mother had one key attitude in common: neither thought the trumpet was very feminine. I had my choice of a flute or a clarinet. I picked up the clarinet and began home to convince my mother that a change would be desirable. It would make me a better musician to learn more than a single instrument. When she agreed I was so relieved, I cried. It wasn't a trumpet, but it was better than the piano.

When I reached junior high, Mom suggested I join the band with my clarinet. I agreed, though I kept my eye on the trumpet section, and even had fleeting fantasies of learning to play the drums. I worked hard to increase my skill level on the clarinet, and was even inspired for a while after seeing *The Benny Goodman Story*. I bought the soundtrack record, the first LP I owned, but ended up playing my drumsticks and brushes on my practice pad with the songs.

This mini-drama regarding the change of musical instruments illustrates some ingredients in my upbringing. I was allowed to negotiate with my parents, though I was much better at doing it with my mother. She wasn't rigid about too many things, and would change her position if my reasoning were sound. I also learned to subvert when I didn't get my own way. It was true that I continued working on the clarinet and enjoyed it, but I also persevered with the trumpet and bought drumsticks, brushes and a practice pad. It was a way of paying the piper, and knowing when I couldn't buck the rules. But also I learned to do something for myself. Subverting the system occurred only when it came to some kind of show-biz situation. Nothing stood in the way of the passion.

In the Revere band, I found another mentor and role model in Miss Mary Alyce Marshall, in her first year of teaching. She had an effervescence and was generous with her humor. She communicated a respect for her students so important to an adolescent. What was more significant, she offered a no-lose way to excel. Since she gave extra credit for book reports and concert attendance, I began a campaign of reading and writing which dwarfed the second-highest point maker. I would meet her after school, write her notes, and come in during recess. When we would have Christmas programs, it was difficult for me to choose between doing the play for Mrs. Nagel in drama and playing in the band for Miss Marshall. When Miss Marshall moved me from the first to the second section to lend my strong support, I felt betrayed. After that time, drama became the easy choice. In my mind, I became quite the hotshot at Revere, performing at every opportunity.

Halfway through my eighth grade year at Revere, Nana died. My parents had been called to Pasadena several times because of a medical emergency since Nana had been living in a rest home for more than a year. Though I had visited her as often as was allowed, it wasn't the same. She knew who I was, but conversation was stilted and vague. I began to prepare myself for the inevitable ending by reflecting on our good times together. It was on one of those emergency trips, when I had been sent to stay with the Church family, that she died. Mom and Dad walked in the room to pick me up and I knew. Mom handled it with sensitivity and compassion and in the only way she knew. She told me Nana lived a good life and that it was time for her to go. That was too fatalistic for me, though I couldn't deny the wisdom of her words.

A few days later, we drove to Pasadena for the funeral. Her room in the house was filled with her possessions and we all took turns retrieving those with sentimental value. Perhaps it was my preoccupation with my own grief, but it seemed no one was crying. It was businesslike, detached. I wanted those objects which evoked her for me—her ticking clock that kept me awake when I slept in her bed; the quilt she made and kept on her bed that smelled of lavender cologne; the bracelets she wore that produced almost an altered state as I listened to their idiosyncratic rattle. I wanted her appointment book, which contained evidence of her writing, and where she had documented my importance to her as she recorded my date of birth. As I looked across the bed where the objects had been placed, I was struck by a card that read "There'll always be an England." Seeing the well-worn card brought tears of recognition and insight, reflecting the British flavor that infused her personal style.

At the funeral, everyone was quite reserved. Later, I realized that epitomized the Osborne way. There should never be an overt show of emotion. At age twelve, though, it alienated me and made me feel as though I were overreacting because I was crying. Even my father seemed without feeling, but by then that was consistent with my sense of him.

Returning to school the next day, I must have been subdued. Over the next few months, my manner changed. Gone were the jokes and impressions. Friends were sufficiently concerned about the length of time it took me to recover that they threw a surprise party for me. My concern for their concern brought me back physically, but the pain continued for many years. It was probably fifteen years before I could hear "The Blue Danube" without welling up with tears; that was the one song I could remember Nana playing on the piano. After the surprise party, my grief went underground and I returned to the performance arena, in more ways than one.

THREE

Stars I Have Known

All that performing in junior high only reinforced what I had been doing for years at home. Family and neighborhood gatherings were frequently held at our home, where entertainment was commonplace. My father played the piano while others sang. When given the least amount of encouragement, he also played his guitar, his banjo or—God forbid—the accordion. We teased him mercilessly about the quality of his playing, but it provided a forum for all of us to show off. Sparky, our venerable Springer spaniel, once lifted his leg on the accordian. After that, Dad could never play it without the rest of us paying laughing tribute to Sparky's critique.

My parents never discouraged my show-biz fantasies, but then they did not know the extent of them. One summer we vacationed at the private ranch of Donald Douglas, president of Douglas Aircraft, where my father worked. It was a remote ranch, its perimeter defined by a six-foot fence. One night we heard a voice call out for help but no one was visible when we looked out the window. My father, always dependable in a macho sort of way, went out with a shotgun in one hand and a flashlight in the other. The intruder was a Mexican farm worker lost in the valley. Dad came back in the house and called the sheriff; the whole episode over in less than an hour. I wrote my first radio drama about it and titled it *The Spurious Assassin*. By then I had discovered Roget's *Thesaurus*. The play was dramatic, emphasizing the individual reactions of the people inside the darkened house. Notations were included for sound effects and commercials. The rather lengthy play wasn't bad for a twelve-year-old. Real life was only a foil for my show-biz aspirations. I think it was around this time I discovered that I could buy movie star maps with addresses. I began to write fan letters and began a collection of photographs. I wrote several fan letters a week, mostly innocuous notes asking for photographs of the people I most admired. Much of the time, the photos would be eight by ten glossy prints, autographed personally to me by the star. After I had accumulated about a dozen of these, I decided to frame them and put them on my bedroom walls. Within a year, all four walls were filled with movie stars' pictures and bookshelves, representing the passions and a schism. There was the part that was creative and fluid, that fantasized about grandiose happenings. Then there was the other, that read and studied and sought to master via the intellect.

It was because of one of those letters I received a telephone call from Jerry Lewis. This was around the time he was breaking up his partnership with Dean Martin and I had written sympathetically to Lewis. As I was getting ready to go to a dreaded cotillion one evening, I was called to the phone. I didn't believe it was Jerry at first, but then he referred to my letter. He said he appreciated my support and thoughtfulness. When I told people at the dance that evening, few believed me. Later, Jerry Lewis became the first Honorary Mayor of Pacific Palisades and I would see him driving around in his convertible. I would smile and wave, hoping he would know it was the same girl he had called that special night. Each time I think of him making that call, I am warmed by his generosity.

Lewis wasn't my only real contact. By the time I was twelve, I had met and talked with James Whitmore. My brother had joined Indian Guides, a kind of prelude to Boy Scouting. Whitmore's son was also in the group. When I knew he was coming to our house for a meeting, I planned my questions. I knew his work after seeing the science fiction film *Them* six times. After we met, I rushed over to the library and looked up his biography so I could casually refer to his career statistics when we talked. After Indian Guides ended,

I saw him occasionally around town, usually at the Brentwood Country Mart, and he was always cordial. He remembered my ardor many years later, at my brother's graduation from high school. His son eventually became a pretty good actor, too.

It must be evident by this time that for a starry-eyed fan, Pacific Palisades was the place to grow up. I was virtually surrounded by show biz. There were not only show-biz-connected kids at school, but stars in the markets. Seeing these people produced a reaction in me of awe and intimidation. It didn't occur to me that becoming one of them would induce these feelings in others. While the lifestyle was appealing, my focus continued to be on actually making a film or a television show. The idea of being a journeyman actress didn't sound good, for that meant I would have to appear in anything. More and more I was aware I was seeking to approximate a fantasy. I wanted to use all of me and be valued for doing so. The intensity of show biz would be an ideal match for the intensity I felt inside.

Somewhere during these years, I also developed an identification with Joan Davis. Though Doris Day was an alter ego, Joan Davis was funny and I learned to win people over by being witty. *I Married Joan* was at the top of the ratings, and I never missed the show. One day as I was wandering through the telephone directory for movie stars' names, I saw a "Joan Davis" listed, living in Bel Air. I called Jacquie on the phone and we planned our next move. The very next trip to Rexall Drugs, I coaxed Jacquie to make the call to check out this Joan Davis. As soon as the phone was answered, Jacquie recognized the voice of Joan Davis. In a state of panic, I quickly whispered to Jacquie to give our stage names, which we had long before decided would be the Stewart Sisters; she was Joan (after Joan Davis) and I was Pat. We had several follow-up conversations with Joan Davis, discussing various aspects of her career and seeking advice on how to replicate it. She was most gracious about the intrusions into her life, which were episodic for a year. On her birthday, I cajoled my father to drive us to her home on Bellagio Road in Bel Air to deliver some glasses we had pooled our money to buy. Unfortunately, Joan wasn't home. I don't think I could have taken the excitement if she had been. Within a year or so after our last contact with her, a fire wiped out her home and she moved to Palm Springs, where she later died of a heart attack. I felt as though part of my childhood had died with her and wanted to go to the funeral. The mourning was personal as well as symbolic.

Jerry Lewis and James Whitmore were typical of the celebrities seen around the Palisades. Though the area was in its infancy as a celebrity retreat, many celebrities maintained residences there. It was common to see James Arness in the drug store or Vivian Vance in the market. Silent screen star Francis X. Bushman lived two blocks down the street. As a student of Hollywood, I also came to recognize the character actors such as Gladys Cooper and Jerry Paris. All of this contributed to the fantasy of being discovered. It seemed Hollywood was all around me.

The Fifties were the last decade in which movie stars were mysterious and elusive. They were larger than life, simply because the media were not covering their private lives with all the warts and imperfections. We didn't know who was an alcoholic, how many suicide attempts someone had made, or who was beating their children. It wasn't until they died that we read all the dirt about Joan Crawford, Errol Flynn and Judy Garland. So it was in this ballyhoo context that I studied them. Movie magazines might chronicle Doris Day's move to her home on Crescent Drive in Beverly Hills, but it would not discuss her marital hassles. These days, we know when Elizabeth Taylor enters a treatment facility. It makes her more of a real person, multi-dimensional. But in the Fifties, the only way to obtain information about a movie star was firsthand expeditions. Thus, I would take the bus to Beverly Hills and walk by Doris Day's house, getting more of a "feel" for who she might be.

Studios were vast empires where access was controlled by uniformed guards. There was no such thing as tours. Tickets to shows were coveted. These days, *Daily Variety* prints ads that offer famous producers in seminars, actors in workshops and even open casting calls. The system was more closed before, which made it that much more intriguing. Today, there are many more points of exposure. In the past, damaging information was slipped to Hedda Hopper or Louella Parsons, who would use it at their discretion. Any information was grist for my fantasy mill.

From the time I was eight or nine, I was spending as much time at the movies as my parents and allowance would permit. Almost every Friday night, my mother would take me to whatever was playing at the neighborhood theater. The most exciting events I can remember were when the theater hosted major studio previews. In place of one of the pictures on the advertised double bill would be a surprise, a new film unseen by anyone outside the industry. The suspense was high and the theater was crowded on those nights. Often there were searchlights and photographers. When the opening credits flashed on the screen, there would be an audible sigh or groan from the audience. We really felt we were in on something special. At the end of the film, everyone would go out in the lobby and fill out preview cards, rating the actors and the movie. More times than not, one of the stars was in attendance, sitting in the back in the dark, gauging the effect of the performance.

I recall especially one preview happened shortly after Elizabeth Taylor and Eddie Fisher created a furor when Fisher left Debbie Reynolds. After the film, when the preview cards were being filled out, there was a murmur in the crowd. Everyone turned to see Liz and Eddie coming out of the theater. People moved back, like the Red Sea parting, and there was hardly a word spoken to them. This was quite unusual, and demonstrated what much of the public felt about their flouting convention at that time. I felt as though I were taking a risk just being this close to "immorality."

I often spent weekends at the movies, and it was typical for me to spend five or six hours on Saturdays and/or Sundays, watching the movies twice through. If it was a Doris Day picture or a musical, I was sure to stay. The impact of these films is hard to describe. One of Rod Serling's teleplays on *The Twilight Zone* probably comes close. In it, Ida Lupino played a silent screen actress who spent all her time watching herself in forty-year-old films. Her whole life was wrapped up in the past. At the end of the program, her maid comes in to find Lupino has left this world and rejoined herself on the screen. There is some philosophizing about how much happier she will be now. In spirit and emotion, my life was on that screen, too. The more sentimental the film, the better.

It is a real challenge to describe what I experienced as a kid in the theater. I was totally consumed. Not only would I identify with a particular actor in the drama or musical, but I would enter into a whole fantasy life about the setting. In *The Caine Mutiny*, I identified with Willy Keith, played by Robert Francis. While watching the film, I practiced my empathic skills, reading in much of what I thought he might be experiencing as well as what was portrayed on the screen. When I would leave the theater, I thought about being in the Navy, experiencing the conflicts and frustrations as Keith must have. I wondered what the rest of his life might have been like. I would imagine him in other scenes and would place myself in his situation to work through that fantasy. At the same time, I became obsessed with reading about the actor Robert Francis in the movie magazines. It was an incredibly complicated process, and it took a lot of information and fantasy to feed my drive for information.

Other films were closer to my experience. The Doris Day movies of the early and middle Fifties portrayed a young tomboy growing up (*On Moonlight Bay* and *By the Light of the Silvery Moon*), and of a person being discovered or growing into womanhood (*My Dream is Yours* and *Calamity Jane*). *Young at Heart* and *Pajama Game* were special favorites, explaining to me how women meet and deal with early love. I could play those parts, I would tell myself; I have had those feelings. When she was tough on the surface, her feminine side lying dormant in *Calamity Jane*, I took note. I just needed someone to come along and open me up. The theme continued in *Pajama Game*, where I learned I could be a career person so long as I married the boss.

Movies were life's textbooks for me and I believed just about everything I saw. The screen biographies were powerful vehicles for me, as they almost always involved someone overcoming obstacles toward conspicuous public success. Eddie Cantor, Gus Kahn, the DeSylva-Brown-Henderson songwriting team, Jane Froman, Benny Goodman and Glenn Miller were all documented in film during the 1950s and I was converted to the inevitable cause-and-effect of success.

By thirteen, I became aware of the disparity between the person I worshiped on the screen and the real Pam Osborne. Doris and the others didn't have identity conflicts, concerns about popularity or loneliness, at least on the screen. I watched Audrey Hepburn in *Funny Face*, in which she fell in love with Fred Astaire. Audrey could be unconventional, which was reassuring, and even experience loneliness, but she could be bought by a trip to Paris. My disenchantment coincided with the decline of the musical in American film. For by 1958, even Doris had moved away from the musical and was into light comedy.

Sometimes when I thought of our differences, I was scared. If Doris was significantly disparate, where would I go to find out about how to live and to be? The intense sense of uniqueness I felt was never approximated on the screen. And loneliness, at least in females, was usually resolved by falling in love. While I had doubts this would happen to me, it had little relevance to my life as a young teenager. At the same time, it forced me to focus more clearly on who I was. If I was not the light and lively Doris Day type, then what was the alternative? At early adolescence, there were elements of Doris, but also of Katharine Hepburn, Bette Davis and others. The later teen rebels were too high-risk-taking for me, with alcohol and fast cars. So I began to discern who I was via contrast.

Around this time, the Duchows moved in across the street, a young couple with a daughter about my brother's age. I campaigned to be their babysitter and developed an infatuation for the man. He was working as a pool cleaner, but looking for another job. To my delight, he was offered a position as an artists and repertoire man for Capitol Records. When the Duchow family came to our musicales, I would be sure to sing especially to Pete

Duchow, hoping he would be the one to discover me. What he did instead was to offer to sell me his secondhand records, the ones his company was giving him free. I was disappointed, but this was the age of the record album and my collection would be improved by his offer.

The best thing Pete did for me was to expose me to his friends. One was Bob Bailey, who enjoyed a long and successful career on the radio. When I met him, he was the star of *Yours Truly, Johnny Dollar*. Bob was a droll and unassuming guy, flattered by my syncophancy. I would ask him hundreds of questions about acting and what it was like for him. He would entertain me with his show-biz stories and keep me in old CBS radio scripts. I began to go to the studio with him on Sundays when he would record his show. I would sit in the control booth and watch every move. The work of the sound and music men caught my eye. I could hardly wait to try out that little booth they used to make it sound as though someone were on the telephone. The *Johnny Dollar* group consisted of many of the same people doing different characters, almost like a repertory company. Those versatile actors had successful TV careers as well, such as Virginia Gregg, Barney Phillips and Parley Baer. Of course, I kept hoping that Bob would ask me to play a part on the show, but I was afraid to mention it to him. Instead, I would recite the dialogue from the current script in the car on the way down there with him. He was amused by this young girl trying to sound like a macho insurance investigator and probably enjoyed the hero worship. I also liked the potent smell of his characteristic Old Spice; to this day, I still think of him when I smell it.

One summer Pete and his wife were asked to house-sit for Edmund O'Brien, the talented actor and Academy Award winner. Somewhere into that summer, the Duchows invited us to the O'Brien home for a swim. I could hardly wait. I had been in Bob Bailey's house and James Whitmore's house, but they were still not stars. Edmund O'Brien was an established institution who had won an Oscar! I might even get a look at the statuette. My family was looking forward to the pool, but I wanted to see the house.

When they went down the long steps leading to the garden-surrounded pool, I stayed in the house under the pretext that I wanted a drink of water. (I would again use thirst as an excuse to invade a star's home, as we will later see.) What I really wanted was to drink in the atmosphere. I found the den, stepped inside, and there it was. The gleaming little man. I felt as though I were at a shrine. There was also a resolve that some day I would also have one of those little guys. My reverie was interrupted by the realization that I had been in there too long. As I turned to go, my eye caught an address book sitting on the otherwise barren desk. When I opened it, my eyes nearly fell out of my head. Almost every major star was listed there along with an address and phone number. Given my mania for finding this kind of information, you can imagine my excitement. I found a piece of paper and a pencil and started copying down numbers. I knew I would never use them, but just having this knowledge made me feel important. When I got home, I copied all the names and numbers in my own book, just as if I knew those very famous people.

This might be a good time to explore my worshipful attitude toward the Oscar, and in later years the Grammy. It wasn't just the achievement, though I had long known the sense of safety that can come from that. I wanted to experience the top of the heap for its own fulfillment. The emphasis was on the process, on the moment, rather than the outcome of the award. I could imagine the tremendous sense of one-ness that could come from putting together the record or the film; feeling satisfied with the work, knowing it was the best I could do, that all of me was in that. And then having it acknowledged would be like having me acknowledged. I knew it would be a validation from my peers, which I'd seldom had, rather than a popularity contest, which I knew I could never win. I was too much out of step with the norm, it turned out, for either of these to occur.

Within a few months of the O'Brien escapade, I was spending a quiet Friday evening at home, watching one of my favorite programs, *Mr. Adams and Eve*. The show starred Ida Lupino and Howard Duff as a prototypical Hollywood couple, and I liked the insider's feel it had. It was a particularly good show that night, involving their discovering a young girl and offering her a part on their show, which of course left me drooling. I don't know what possessed me to do it, but I decided to call Ida Lupino (one of the numbers in O'Brien's little book) and tell her how much I liked the show. My parents had gone out for the evening and I have always felt more courageous when alone. I dialed the number and waited for an answer. The voice said the usual "Hello," and I asked if Ida was there. I assumed it was a maid and my familiarity would be sure to get me through to her. When the voice said "This is Ida," I felt a worse panic than when Jacquie and I had contacted Joan Davis on the phone. Vamping like mad, I told her we had a mutual friend from whom I got her number, and that I was calling to tell her how much I enjoyed her show every week. Taking courage from the fact she had not hung up on me, I casually mentioned I was an aspiring comedienne myself. Her comeback was "Well, perhaps we can use you on the show." Was this how *it* happened? I couldn't believe my ears. She asked if I had an agent. When I said no, she suggested I get one, then get in touch with her casting director, whose name she gave me. I thanked her and hung up. I couldn't believe what I had done, and what might lie ahead of me as a result. I had learned the value of chutzpah.

Finding an agent isn't like locating an exterminator. They have to want you in order for them to risk their time and energy. How would I go about finding one? The chutzpah had worked with Ida; maybe it would work with an agent as well. I called several, including one that specialized in children and adolescents. They all replied that they would have to see photographs first. I must have gotten the courage to tell my mother what I had done, for she supported me in seeking out the help of my drama teacher, Mrs. Nagel, and her actor-husband, Don. They came over one evening to take pictures. As I look back on this today, it's hard to comprehend the amateurishness of this. Why didn't my parents spring for professional photos, with so much on the line? Was it a lack of information or a lack of support? At any rate, the pictures turned out to be so unflattering I was embarrassed. It was another in the series of unpleasant realizations of who I really was, compared to who I wanted to be. When I saw the photographs, I saw an overweight, intense-looking person who was not nearly attractive enough to be on *Mr. Adams and Eve*, much less taken on by an agent. I went through a long period of mourning the death of my idealized image.

Not only had I failed to attract the attention of my idol, Doris Day, but a record industry pro had failed to see my talent, regardless of the repeated exposure. Hanging around radio, TV and movie stars didn't seem to change things either. And I had even blown an opportunity that was handed to me in person by Ida Lupino. Where would I go now? How could I crack this seemingly impervious world of show biz?

I decided to make more direct incursions into the show-biz community. The years between eleven and fifteen were the beginnings of bus trips to faraway places like Beverly Hills and Hollywood. I discovered the so-called rapid transit district and the Santa Monica municipal bus lines and the adventures they could bring. As I edged into my teens I relished the freedom that came with getting on a bus for an hour and exploring adult worlds. It took over an hour and a half and two bus transfers to get to Hollywood and Vine, right across from Music City, where the stars bought their sheet music. A few blocks down Sunset was CBS, where Bob Bailey had taken me to watch him record *Johnny Dollar*. One of my favorite things to do was to enter office buildings and look at the directory to see if I recognized any names. In those days, writers and producers had offices outside the studios, so there was lots of fantasy-fodder for me. No matter how often I would go to Hollywood, I always enjoyed walking in the forecourt of the big theaters, which were laden with history. Grauman's Chinese was fun, but a tourist trap, and not nearly as nostalgic for me as the Egyptian or the Pantages. Rudolph Valentino and Pola Negri seemed to be haunting every corridor.

For sheer excitement and risk, though, there was no place like the Brown Derby. The original restaurant was outside the Hollywood area, on Wilshire Boulevard, in Los Angeles. (There was another one in Beverly Hills, which I didn't discover until my late teens.) Because much of Hollywood production was still in Hollywood in the 1950s, many stars and executives lunched at the Derby on Vine Street. As often as I could, I would save my allowance so Jacquie and I could trek to the Derby. The place was just plain magical for me, from the male waiters to the cartoon renderings of movie stars on the wall; from the phone jacks at every table to the woman who would page famous names every few minutes. I felt like I was in a movie just being there. But the menu items were expensive, requiring that I spend a little less on the books at the Pickwick Bookstore and spend a little more time babysitting or cleaning houses that week.

About the only thing I could afford was the Cobb Salad, which had been named after one of the early owners. It was filling and took long enough to prepare that we could scope out the restaurant to see who was there. If the waiter looked friendly, I would ask him if there was anyone famous there that day. Sometimes I would intrude on their lunch and ask for an autograph, but that was unusual. Mostly, I would just gawk and wait to be discovered. We worked very hard at looking grown up, and the staff treated us with great benevolence, considering how obvious it was that we were just kids. One humiliating day, Jacquie dropped her Cobb Salad in her lap and called the waiter over to our table to retrieve the greens. I didn't speak to her for hours.

The Derby was known for having phone jacks in every booth, all the better to service the busy entertainment executive who might be lunching there. On one occasion, I entreated Jacquie to go outside and call the Derby while we were eating there, and ask for me. They would page me discreetly over the P.A., and rush a phone to our table. I wanted to know how it would feel, forgetting how it might look for this kind of service to be rendered a pre-teen. She was kind enough to indulge me and I was paged. "Pam Osborne. Phone call for Pam Osborne." I guess someone noticed that I was no one, as no phone was forthcoming. I walked over to the maitre d' and took the call quickly near the operator. A few moments later, we resumed our lunch. It was still exciting. All those execs and stars had actually heard my name!

I confess I still like lunching at the Derby, and still ogle the celebrities. The only difference these days is I go to the one in Beverly Hills, I can afford something other than the Cobb Salad and I never ask for autographs. No longer do I expect to be discovered, but the memories of earlier trips are nonpareil.

I was an avid reader from the time I could read. Much of my money went toward books, mostly about show biz. There were many bookstores in Hollywood and Beverly Hills that specialized in that kind and I was a frequent patron. I began devouring biographies and autobiographies of show people, a practice I still carry on today. In the early days, I was reading about film history, soaking up the vibes of the industry any way I could.

Among the books that were important to me then were auto-biographies of Mack Sennett, Eddie Cantor, Jesse Lasky and Fred Astaire. My reading ranged from pictorial histories of the silent screen and the American theater to plays and film annuals to books on radio production—anything that would offer a histor-ical perspective. As the years went on, the list expanded.

Jacquie and I would send off for free tickets to television shows, such as *Do You Trust Your Wife? It Could Be You*, *Meet Millie* and *Fandango*. When the new NBC studios opened in Burbank, we would ride the extra hour or so to see the *Dinah Shore Chevy Show* and its summer replacement with John Raitt and Janet Blair. For much of this, we were just twelve, the minimum age for admis-sion. But with the expert use of demeanor I had learned at the Brown Derby, we were never challenged. We would hang around the studio after the show, Jacquie to seek autographs and I to absorb the atmosphere. It felt so good to be there, so right.

We waited for up to an hour after a television show was over, outside the entrance. I had had a big crush on John Raitt since *The Pajama Game*, so when he hosted the *Dinah Show*, I tried to be there as often as we could get tickets. Though Jacquie and I were manifestly fans, it was important to maintain a cool demeanor. We never carried a camera on our various trips, though now I wish we had. It was important to avoid the stigma of being a tourist, that dirty word. It wasn't easy to reconcile the image of coolness with the long wait outside a studio gate in the rain to watch someone drive by and wave.

Our trips to Beverly Hills would always incorporate a leisurely walk past Doris Day's house on Crescent Drive. I had read that the Beverly Hills police were tough on intruders and vagrants, so we kept moving. We would stroll past the houses of Burns and Allen, Jack Benny, Hedda Hopper and others. We kept hoping that Doris would emerge from her house, immediately recognize her biggest fans and invite us in. The closest we came was when a delivery man arrived during one of our marches. We couldn't even see who answered the door. It was very frustrating.

By this time I was using some of my babysitting money to subscribe to *Daily Variety*, which I read religiously. It told me who was in town, when Doris would be making a new film and who was seen at the Brown Derby the day before. Nobody I knew subscribed, which made me feel like an insider. After that, movie magazines seemed just hype. *Variety* was the truth, the facts read by those in the know. It seemed an auspicious way to enhance my preparation.

Though I was performing frequently in junior high plays and concerts, it wasn't enough. I began recruiting friends to do improvisations with me. I would describe a situation and assign the roles, so we could ad lib a scene. There were times when these were rewarding and creative; other times they would deteriorate into soap opera. Some themes replicated movie or television plots, but most of them were original. When the scenes involved men, I was able to try out behaviors I never would have had the nerve to do with the boys I knew. It was during those plays that I became increasingly aware of the discomfort I was having in these male/ female plots. The women were too flighty and passive, not to mention manipulative. The men, on the other hand, were too controlling and macho. These were the sexually stereotyped 1950s and it was hard to find a comfort level with either gender.

I wasn't really feminine, and I wasn't really masculine. I was both of those, which in the Fifties meant I was neither. To be truly female was to eschew anything that was male. There were my qualities of assertiveness, risk-taking and independence, but also empathy, sensitivity and supportiveness. Another example of simply being out of step. On a more positive plane, though, it gave me a sense of empathy with both genders. Some twenty years later, I was drawn to the emerging concept of androgyny. By definition, it refers to having the healthy characteristics of both sexes; and it was finally seen as a new standard for mental health. Too bad that orientation was not prevalent as I was struggling with my identity in those days.

This ability to assume either sex role may have made my teacher impersonations so devastatingly accurate. My classmates would be in stitches, as I captured the essence of many teachers and administrators. In time, I turned my satiric talents to the students themselves. These carbon copies, my Louella Parsons broadcasts, and my penchant for humorous record pantomime all gave me a reputation for being a comedienne. Many of the remarks written in my ninth-grade yearbook refer affectionately to that role. They, too, expected that I would fall into a career entertaining other people.

Mrs. Nagel wrote, "See you in *Variety*." A friend wrote, "To the funniest comedienne I've ever known." Another penned, "To the funniest gal I've ever met; you will go far as a comedienne or whatever you choose." Even an acquaintance noted, "Lots of luck in all the skills you try. Here's hoping you and 'Oscar' are good friends." It was a kind of validation by my peers, and a reflection of the surroundings at Revere. At fourteen, I felt I was well on my way.

Graduation from Revere Junior High was bittersweet. I desperately wanted to grow up and move on, but these two years had been intense and rewarding. Though I suspected there were many teachers who looked askance at my antics and androgyny, I had received opportunities to gain acceptance through the show-biz activities. And the support from Mrs. Nagel and Miss Marshall would be missed.

Two events of that graduation week still stick in my mind. Like all upscale junior high kids, we had a prom with a live dance band. I had been going out with a gangly but cuddly boy named Jim Lowry for two years and he invited me to the prom. While the other kids were dancing and enjoying each other, I was fascinated by the band instruments and the impact of the music they were making. I felt as though I were the only person in the room who was feeling the power of the music. During a break, I waited until the musicians had left, then quietly went up to the bandstand and sat behind the drums. A popular song at the time was Elmer Bernstein's "Man With the Golden Arm." As I sat there, I could imagine myself playing with the group, providing the driving beat to that tune. I had practiced on a pad at home with my drum sticks and I was ready to try it out for real. The drummer, however, wisely denied my fantasy.

As I look back on that night, I am struck by the level of risk, but more by the sense of isolation. Only Jim knew of my intent. It is another experience that tends to characterize that era, sometimes positive, often negative and discouraging. The fantasies were very resilient and durable.

The other strong memory is of graduation itself. I played in the band, in the coveted first chair clarinet position. Miss Marshall staged weekly challenges, in which a lower chair would challenge a higher one. Another clarinet player and I were in constant battle for first chair, and it shifted regularly. But for the all-important graduation, first chair was mine. Jacquie gave me a copy of Eddie Cantor's autobiography for graduation, which seemed appropriately show-bizzy, and my parents gave me a watch. An era had ended.

FOUR

Negotiating
with the Fantasy

University High School was one of the bigger secondary schools in the Los Angeles Public School District. There were over a thousand in the entering class at Uni, so homerooms were assigned alphabetically. I felt completely anonymous. Starting all over was not at all appealing. I announced I was not going to college and declared myself to be a music major, signing up for both band and orchestra. At Uni, a heavily academic school, music majors were outsiders. Most of us did not take physics, chemistry or advanced math. Many of my musical peers were people for whom music was their whole life, and I felt like an interloper. Chair challenges were prevalent here, as with Miss Marshall's band class, and I kept up the effort. But I was no competition for these semipros. While they were home practicing every weekend or playing gigs for money, I was off exploring Hollywood or Beverly Hills. They were studying the lives of famous composers while I was reading about King Vidor or Louis B. Mayer. We managed to meet over musical comedy and George Gershwin. Clearly, the differences were accelerating and the stakes increased.

Uni represented an even higher level of show-biz competition. First trumpet was Warren Luening, who was playing every week on Lawrence Welk's television show. Performers in school musicals also worked in professional theater in their spare time. In addition to the usual spate of celebrities' kids, we had Sandra Dee and Nancy Sinatra. I felt the gap widening between what I had and what I wanted. The spector of this high level of competition focused my attention that first year on the band. In order to push out boundaries, I started to write lyrics. One of the musical geniuses in the band had written a blues tune for which I supplied lyrics. It was an accurate reflection of my feelings when I named it "The Unihi Blues." One of the verses went,

When I awake and come to school each morn,
I get that same old feeling, why was I born?
School starts too early now and I am forlorn.
I've got those Unihi blues.

Feeling socially alienated, I also joined a Tri-Y club, the Harlequins, which was like a junior sorority, a seeming social necessity. My only significant function there was to stage the club's musical entry in a citywide songfest. The Harlequins consisted of an unlikely group of compatriots, and I had difficulty feeling as though I belonged. I didn't seem to fit, and managed to gain acceptance though the lyrics I supplied to the tune "Has Anybody Seen My Gal?"

Harlequins, Harlequins, we're the jolly Harlequins,
Everybody give a cheer
Let's all clap, let's all scream
Harlequins, we're on the beam,
The greatest club at Unihi

Toward the end of my first year at Uni, *Teacher's Pet* was released, starring Doris Day and Clark Gable. A week before my fifteenth birthday, my parents called me into the living room and ceremoniously gave me two tickets to the world premiere! Movie premieres were glamor incarnate, and places where celebrities tended to cluster. Here I had a ticket, and maybe even a chance to see Doris in person. But who would accompany me? I was between boyfriends and was beginning to feel anxious over the possibility I would have to go with my mother. It is hard to maintain that slick Hollywood demeanor when one is with one's mother. Finally, at the last minute, my godmother's son, who was a few years older than I, offered to go with me, and I was grateful. It would have been nice to arrive in a limo, waving to the screaming fans in the bleachers erected to the occasion. However, Robin had an old clunker. Beggars could hardly be choosers. I waved and smiled at the fans anyway, hoping to convince at least some of the more naive ones that I might be somebody.

As we walked in, I noticed a large crowd of reporters around Clark Gable, who looked dapper, but old. He wasn't my type. Besides, I was looking for Doris, who was nowhere to be seen. Poor Robin wasn't into this scene at all, and was just humoring my rubbernecking. He strongly suggested we enter the theater and find our assigned seats. My head on a swivel the whole time, we went in and sat down. A woman in a fluffy white fur sat next to me. She was looking at me with disdain, as I kept turning around trying to find Doris. When I took a better look, I realized it was Rhonda Fleming. While I was more careful, I was still preoccupied with finding Doris. The lights dimmed and the film began. I was captivated. This film was different in that Doris played an achieving female who was in control, at least most of the time. While she got the guy in the last reel as usual, she didn't have to abandon her identity to marry him. It started me thinking.

In *Teacher's Pet*, Doris played a journalism instructor, Clark Gable a newspaper editor. There was an abundance of newsroom scenes. I knew Uni had a school newspaper. Ever since junior high, teachers had been trying to get me into accelerated writing classes or journalism, and I had demurred. There were too many other things I wanted to do. But now that Doris was indirectly sanctioning it, perhaps I should explore this world. Journalism One was taught by a portly martinet, but this did not deter me. I loved every minute of it. One of the first assignments was to write a movie review. While I had written several television reviews for Mrs. Nagel, I had never done a film review. The teacher was impressed and accused me of copying the review from a newspaper. The work was truly mine, as plagiarism hadn't occurred to me. Once he was convinced of its originality, I became a real teacher's pet, as the journalism teacher offered me the position of feature editor on the school paper, the *Warrior*. This was a major decision point for me, as the paper staff met during the same period as band.

Feeling that I had exhausted all possibilities as a competitive musician, I found it an attractive option to join the *Warrior* staff. I was assigned a desk and told to fill one of the paper's four pages each week. One of the articles could be my movie review. My by-line would be Pam "Doris" Osborne, a tribute to the person who was continuing to exercise such a profound influence on my life.

At first I would be reviewing the very same films that other students were seeing in the theaters. To gain an edge, I began collecting reviews of not-yet-released films from *Daily Variety* and the *Hollywood Reporter* and would rewrite them as though I had seen the movies myself. Within a few weeks, though, I was relieved to find that my letters to the studios were being noticed and I was extended invitations to trade screenings, along with the rest of the Hollywood press. Several nights a week I was in a theater or a studio screening room, taking notes in the dark. The admission to a studio lot was an escalation in the passion. Driving up to the guard and showing him my pass gave me entrée to 20th Century-Fox, Warner Bros. and Columbia. It was like dying and going to heaven. I didn't give a damn about reviewing the movie; just let me loose on the back lots. I felt transported to another world as I walked down the New York street or the Western street or through the prop department, all in secret and totally alone. There was a feeling of belonging. If the only way I could gain entrance into show biz was to write about it, so be it. This was the closest yet.

My reviews were well received. By the end of the year, the teacher asked me to be managing editor for the coming year. It seemed to be a fitting reward. Of course, I continued my film reviews, which were among the running articles appearing in the *Warrior*. Late in the year, I used my title as managing editor to contact Doris Day's husband/manager, Marty Melcher, in his office on Cañon Drive in Beverly Hills. I wanted an interview with

Doris in connection with the release of *Pillow Talk*. I would have the safety of the press, and the reassuring structure of an interview to ask the probing questions I had been sitting on for years. Marty said he'd get back to me, but never did. I was disappointed but not surprised. I had read that he insisted on approving every word written about her. While he need fear nothing from me, he didn't know that. And he didn't know Doris and I had already met.

For years, I had been plotting ways to meet Doris. Friends had told me places they had run into her and I had frequented them. Pete Duchow, who now, coincidentally, worked for Marty Melcher, was still no help. Here, directly across the street, was probably the one person who could have fulfilled a longtime dream. Whenever they met with the Melchers on a social basis, Pete's wife would enchant me with every detail of the conversation. Either Pete didn't know his power, or he didn't want to jeopardize his position with his boss. I was becoming more and more impatient and frustrated. After the Edmund O'Brien raid and the Ida Lupino phone call, I knew I would have to do something more to get what I wanted. It was simply naive to expect other people to cater to my fantasies. The good news was that Pete's persistent lack of action rid me of my crush on him.

It was right around April 3, which was both Doris' birthday and her anniversary. Knowing from all my reading that Doris liked Tootsie Rolls, I bought a giant box with all my allowance, grabbed my current boyfriend for support, and set out for her house in Beverly Hills. I dared not fully consider the consequences, as I was already trembling enough as it was. After the hour-long bus ride to Crescent Drive, we walked up the driveway that had become so familiar. I asked Nick to ring the bell. A few seemingly endless moments passed during which I hoped I would not faint. Her son, Terry, answered the door. I told him I was bringing his mother a gift for the double occasion and asked to speak with her. He told us she was having a fitting. God knows where I got the chutzpah, but I pressed him, saying it would not take long. He paused and closed the door for another interminable period. Then the door opened and there she was. I must have turned stark white, but the practiced demeanor held sway. I handed her the gift-wrapped box of Tootsie Rolls and wished her a happy birthday and anniversary. She was friendly without being open. The conversation died when she did not pursue it. I thanked her for her time, smiled and left. The whole thing probably took less than three minutes. I managed to get to the edge of the driveway before I let out a muffled scream of glee that I had finally managed to meet my heroine. She existed! That the event didn't match my fantasies was of little consequence.

We had planned to celebrate Doris' occasions by making still another trip to the Paramount Theater in Hollywood, where *Teacher's Pet* was playing. I had the dialogue down, as well as all her non-verbal reactions. Nick would watch me, not Doris, and got a sense of the whole film. But by the time the bus let us off in front of the theater, I was feeling weak from the overwhelming emotion. I spent almost half the film in the ladies' lounge, trying to keep from throwing up and warding off my dizziness. It was the first time I recall having physical symptoms that were so obviously caused by my emotions. It was worth it.

That intense moment, though, was the beginning of almost ten years of headaches, nausea, diarrhea and occasional dizziness that inevitably followed stress. I really didn't conquer it until graduate school in Nebraska, when I developed a more complete repertoire of stress reduction techniques.

While I was writing for the *Warrior*, I met Joe Bugental, a prominent psychologist's son, who seemed the All-American boy. He had acting aspirations as well, and had been feature editor the year before me. The summer between my junior and senior years at Uni we decided to write our own show and produce it. It was to be a review, called *Like Wow!*—one of the popular expletives of the day. Joe would direct and act in it; I would write the book, coordinate the music and lyrics, sing and dance. We met almost every day that summer to write it and cast it from all the people we knew. My association with musicians from the Unihi band was handy in putting together the pit band. By early September, we had it written and began rehearsing. The two shows were well attended, even though they were in the basement of the church Joe attended. I ended up writing very little original music, but focused instead on the comedy skits and on writing the blackouts. As I look back, I'm proud of having put it together, and of singing "My Heart Belongs to Daddy." When I turned to go off stage, I had a big red rose pinned to my rear end. It was a Joan Davis touch. We even made money on the production and split it fifty-fifty.

In an emotional moment, Joe and I agreed to meet again ten years to the day after *Like Wow!* was produced. On Sept. 9, 1969 I checked the Los Angeles telephone directory to locate him, but the name was nowhere to be found. And by that time, I was about to leave for graduate school in Lincoln, Nebraska. It might have been a moving and triumphant reunion.

Just as Mrs. Nagel held a link to Hollywood with her marriage to an actor, one of my high school teachers was wed to a powerful 20th Century-Fox publicity executive. I was watching *What's the Name of That Song?* on TV one night when Jeanne Prince appeared as a contestant. She knew all the lyrics to a popular song and even sang it well. I was envious, knowing all those lyrics myself, and wondered how she got on the show. Mrs. Prince became one of my staunchest allies in high school, but I never confided my show-biz fantasies in detail. She encouraged me to continue with my education, gave me good feedback emotionally and worked to maintain our camaraderie when I was feeling down. It was only much later that I learned of her marital relationship. Again, so close and yet so far.

High school marked the decline of my affinity with Doris. She had shifted gears in her career with the making of *Pillow Talk*, a sexy comedy in its time. I was mildly embarrassed by it and couldn't relate to it. In my world sex was not an issue yet, and I was disappointed that she would allow herself to appear in a film in which sex was such a central theme. I had the feeling she had sold out. I stopped writing about her in my column and no longer made trips by her home. I had been driving through her back alley regularly to see if I could get a look at her swimming in her pool. The frustration of the unrequited hunt began to get to me and I started to see that we really weren't much alike at all. This may have been pushed along by my harmony teacher, who took me aside one day and told me she was concerned about my admiration for Doris. It wasn't natural, she said, and I should have outgrown it by now. I was offended at her intrusion but had to admit she was right. It was clear I was outgrowing my need for Doris as a role model.

The Doris Day identification was separate from the show-biz interests. My success as a show-biz writer in a show-bizzy school encouraged the continued fantasies, rechanneled though they were. When it came time to announce life ambitions in the senior yearbook in 1960, mine was listed as "motion picture administration." If I wasn't attractive or talented enough to be a star, I would be in control of the product. I imagined myself as a mogul. That would at least get me on talk shows from time to time, and might grant me more power than I would have as a star. Certainly it was more secure. It seemed like a good compromise with myself.

The year after I graduated, I picked up a copy of the *Warrior* to discover another student was writing film reviews under the by-line "Pam Doris." I was flattered, but felt violated.

My yearbook at graduation was filled with references to Doris Day and our similarities, as well as to my promise as a writer. There were lots of comments such as "See you in the movies." One buddy wrote, "You're great! Anyone with your talents for song-writing and your natural charm and magnetism is going to be fantastically famous! I want two front row tickets to your first big *My Fair Lady* type musical—knowing you has been a privilege." Such remarks were encouraging.

I was particularly fortunate to have experienced few actual failures during school. Most of the disappointments were private ones: experiencing my limits on musical instruments, inability to capitalize on seeming opportunities for overt success (Pete Duchow and Ida Lupino, for instance), and generally maintaining my show-biz anonymity. I had hoped to be working my way up the ladder by now, hoping to have found a mentor in the business. Because of these disappointments, I learned how to internalize and switch gears. By the time I graduated from high school, my fantasies had progressed from comedy to musical comedy to recording to acting to writing to being an executive in motion pictures. Each of these changes involved an internalized dialogue, a coming to terms with limitations, both mine and those of the sexist realities. Like a flowing river with one branch blocked, I rechanneled.

As with most adolescents, I found disillusionment painful. I had my ideals, and it was hard to see they might not be compatible with the real world. While they were shaped by trial and error, I refused to abandon them and conform to external expectations. In the late 1950s and early 1960s, a young woman's choices were few. She could marry, which was seen to be the most desirable, or she could have a career. But even the nature of that work was severely limited, especially in show biz. The number of female producers, directors and screenwriters could be counted on the fingers of one hand. There were few female film or television executives. So while I might maintain the alternate fantasy of working behind the scenes, in reality the opportunities were limited to being a reader or a script girl, or working in the makeup or costuming department. Though I didn't realize it at the time, thinking I would become a film executive was an even more radical plan than being a film or television performer.

Leaving University High School was no sad experience. The size and diversity of the student body was overwhelming, and it was impossible to relax and get in a groove. By the last year, I had a calendar on the wall in the newsroom. With great ceremoniousness, I tore off one day at a time, each page a day nearer to leaving high school. Though I had achieved some fame as managing editor and film critic, I still felt the same isolation and anonymity that I had felt upon entering three years earlier. Graduation was a relief. After all, I was about to begin my takeover of the motion picture establishment.

I had not planned to go to college. Few film pioneers were college graduates, and I didn't see what function college would serve in my life. I had not counted on Clara McClure to change all that. Clara and Don were a middle-aged couple who lived across the street. I used to watch their boys playing football, sitting on the curb hoping for an invitation. The younger, Doug McClure, grew up to be an actor, making his mark in the *Checkmate* television series. Clara was a feature writer and columnist for the Santa Monica *Evening Outlook*. She asked about my plans and I mentioned I was not going to college. In the next edition of the *Evening Outlook*, she commented in her column on my decision. She saw it as a tragedy and a waste. My mortification and chagrin were somewhat tempered by feeling flattered and surprised. I decided if someone whom I respected believed that strongly, perhaps I should reconsider. I enrolled in Santa Monica City College, declaring myself a theater arts major.

SMCC had been a haven for the unemployed as well as the ambitious actor, as Bobby Darin, Ty Hardin and Beth Adlam had all been students there. The department was a professional one, since two of the full-time professors were working actors. Joe Brown became Victor Millan as he played a series of smaller roles on television; Bert Holland was a stock character on some of Jack Webb's shows. It was a chance to break into show biz by apprenticing with working actors and "being seen." This was an escalation in competition from University High, as the department was supercharged, the denizens totally devoted to the profession. In spite of my obsession with show biz, I was also interested in other things, like politics and sports. My theater arts colleagues seemed concerned only with show biz and themselves. My bluff had been called.

For years I had dreamed of being consumed, of having the time to be totally immersed in show biz. Other things could be put aside; I would worry only about my characterization, or memorizing a new song. At SMCC I could do just that, even taking a full load. The quality of instruction was good, the facilities modern. Once again, though, I felt I was in the wrong place at the wrong time. Their version of show biz was Chekhov, Tennessee Williams and—God forbid—Shakespeare. No contemporary light comedy, no musicals, no radio, no television. This was conservative, traditional theatrical training.

One of the major themes in my life has been the struggle between isolation and power. Only at rare times has that conflict been in resolution. Feeling unique left me shy and subassertive within my peer group. I was not like the others; my interests were divergent and my value system often at variance. Yet I hungered for security, to come to a unification with my fantasies, which involved others. I longed for congruence, when I would feel powerful and secure. There would be no need for artifice, or for meeting other people's expectations. That fiction gave me a lot of trouble in entering show biz, which seemed filled with phoniness and pressure to conform.

At Santa Monica City College, the demand was for exclusivity. The theater arts majors hung around together and seemed to talk of nothing but the theater. Their common passion and willingness to restrict their interests bound them together. For a lot of reasons I was uncomfortable in their midst, the biggest one being my tendency to be alive only from within. At the age of seventeen, there was no way I could translate passion outside of myself, and it even seemed trivialized to share it. It became a classic double bind: damned if I did, damned if I didn't. Success in the social whirl remained an uncertainty. The likelihood was minimal, since my own area of show biz was less Tennessee Williams and more David Merrick. That was perceived by academics as schmaltz, fluff. Sharing would have been a big risk, though I might have found a peer. Several of the SMCC crowd became influential industry figures, among them Gary Essert, founder of Filmex. On the other hand, if I withdrew my fantasies could be sustained, but I would remain frustrated and unfulfilled. In the spirit of compromise, I edged into SMCC show-biz society slowly and with caution. Out of that experiment, I learned the centrality of my preference for relating one-on-one. There is no doubt that my ineffectiveness with small talk and parties contributed to my limited success in show biz. Ironically, it was equally instrumental in my being a good psychologist ten years later.

I spent two years at SMCC taking the courses, trying to shove the square peg of my musical comedy into their round hole of academic theater. In acting classes I chose scenes from *Gypsy*, *Pajama Game* and *Picnic*. When cornered, I did a scene from *Streetcar Named Desire*, but it felt uncomfortable and stilted. By the time Joe Brown staged his Shakespeare festival, I was looking for a way out. I volunteered to write the narration that could tie together the play segments, and worked behind the scenes building sets and setting the lights on scaffolding high above the stage. Anything to avoid doing Shakespeare. It was to be my last brush with academic theater.

My intellectual curiosity at SMCC yielded an unexpected benefit: I developed another coping device. In response to reading Emily Dickinson for my American literature class, I began to write poetry. Over the years, poetry was the distilled reflection of my life situation. It is not astounding, then, that the first poem written in 1961 focused on the intensity of friendship:

Nothing is there sadder than to lose a treasured friend.
To ne'er replace the vacuum an angel could not mend.
Through death but more through anger, a friend is soon
    removed.
A word, a phrase, or just a glance sufficiently unsoothes.
Together joyous cheer is shared, the hours everlasting,
Two lives begun blend as one; they know not time is passing.
Then the blackened day arrives, unkindly words are tossed;
Two—separate, lonely, weeping—at last discern their loss.
But, ah, departed is the time when laughing friends adored.
Experience advances men to seek self, higher soar.

In spite of the frustration, or maybe because of it, the SMCC years turned out to be informative and productive. I discovered a community theater group in Pacific Palisades at the Jewish Community Center. They were putting on a 1920s musical, *Good News*. It had been an MGM hit in the 1940s, with June Allyson and Peter Lawford, and featured a catchy DeSylva-Brown-

Henderson score. I tried out with much anxiety, and won the secondary lead, the femme fatale. The cast was a motley group, from an engineer at Douglas to semi-professional actors. The leads were taken by the latter group, and I felt right at home. Brad Trumbull, a professional actor, directed the show. Again, here I was in the lap of professional and semiprofessional actors—so close, and yet so far.

As "Pat," I did a number of the songs and dances, and had a solo about the girls in the sorority. While I would have preferred more of a comic role, I was flattered at being considered attractive enough to be competition with the gorgeous blonde who played the female lead. The show played for two weekends to full houses.

A fringe benefit was meeting the Lyfields. Harry was our piano player and could transpose like a whiz. His wife, Hank, was an enthusiastic ball of fire. They held frequent musical evenings for the cast at their house, where Harry would tirelessly accompany each of us as we took turns performing. I got the chance to try out new material that I would never have a chance to perform in public, always to Hank's wild applause. She made me feel I belonged in their company. We started having lunch together that summer, usually on Saturdays because I was working for Douglas Aircraft during the week. Dad had helped me get a clerical job there for the summer. Hank was nearing sixty, but I think she considered me an equal. We were a mutual admiration society.

During one of our lengthy conversations, Hank mentioned that she wrote music. Instantly we decided to collaborate on a musical comedy. Though I looked forward to working with her, I was afraid my inexperience would get in the way. I had done only the limited writing for *Like Wow!* while Hank had forty years' experience on me. Nonetheless, she began writing the tunes, while I fleshed out a plot.

The show was called *Jamaica Ginger*. The plot involved a family being transferred for business reasons from a penthouse in New York to Jamaica. Action would center around the individual family members' adjustment. The show would open with a big production number (naturally), featuring husky moving men singing about working, while the family sang in counterpoint of their anxieties about the move. I spent all my free time at work designing the sets after finishing each scene. It was a labor of love, and saved me from the boredom of clerical work at Douglas. Hank and I were on the phone at various times throughout the day, she singing me her tunes while I recited the latest dialogue. We would make occasional suggestions to each other, and it was a dream collaboration. I just knew we would have a big hit. Even so, the process itself created a bond.

By the time we were well into the second act, the summer was over and I returned to school. I had decided to work on my brain and followed my instincts toward political science. A poli sci course at SMCC had aroused my curiosity, setting up fantasies of becoming a lawyer. I was admitted to the University of California at Los Angeles as a transfer student, a junior in political science. My workload was huge, and I needed to find a job. In an effort to maximize my college opportunities, I started writing for the *Daily Bruin*, the campus newspaper, and had auditioned to work as a disc jockey on the new campus radio station. Feeling confident of my writing ability, I supplemented my political science classes with courses in journalism. When one of my professors told me there was a position available with an advertising and public relations firm in Beverly Hills, I ran for an interview. To my surprise, I was hired. My schedule was unbelievable, and *Jamaica Ginger* became a casualty. Hank and I discussed it, deciding to shelve the project until the following summer.

I thought about her often during that school year, but like many busy people, I didn't take the time to call. At the beginning of the next summer, I had committed myself to working full time at the advertising agency, but I wanted to pursue *Jamaica Ginger*. Most of all, I wanted to share more of that warmth with Hank. Reflecting on my thoughtlessness, I was reluctant to call, afraid of a chilly reception. Instead, I wrote a cheery note, telling her of my wish to continue and hoping she was in good health. A few days later, the phone rang. It was Hank's adult son, Bill.

"I'm sorry to tell you Hank died a little over a month ago. She knew she had cancer, but she didn't want anyone else to know."

A mumbled, "I'm sorry" seemed inadequate.

"I want you to know she felt close to you. She didn't want anyone to make a fuss about her illness."

It was a moment that transcended tears. We had been close only a short time, and I had blown it. I had thrown away the opportunity to continue a relationship, to be supportive in what must have been a lonely time. Harry had died over a year earlier, and I was unfamiliar with other support systems she might have had. I felt a personal loss, but I also lamented the death of *Jamaica Ginger*. Our friendship had been so tied up in that show; now it would never be finished. Hank's death reinforced my own growing sense of mortality. The imminence of the now began to assume greater importance.

My enrollment at UCLA didn't ease the lack of confidence about my intelligence. While my grades had been mostly As in junior high, I wasn't devoting as much time to study as my friends did. By the time I got to high school, it was more of an effort. Getting a C became more than a rare occurrence. My overall scores on national achievement tests were all within a few points on either side of the ninetieth percentile, but I was aware that several friends were closer to the ninety-ninth percentile, and got better grades as well. In contrast to the uniqueness I typically experienced when it came to show biz, I felt intellectually ordinary. At the time of graduation, the administration announced our standing in the class. I was in the top ten percent in our class of over a thousand, but I wrote it off, attributing it to my music and journalism courses.

By the time I got to SMCC, I was painfully cognizant of the gaps in my knowledge. I seldom read fiction, had no interest in science, and knew next to nothing about world affairs. Looking around, I felt insecure and decided to fill the holes as best I could. I took several literature courses in one semester and barely made a B in each. I struggled through a botany course, earning a B only through my creative saga of the life and death of a petunia named Howard. Then I took a political science course, and got turned on. As with my earlier drive for information on an interpersonal level, I was fascinated with gaining access to the secrets of national and international politics. I began to include books on the American political system on my reading list, emphasizing biography and autobiography. Since I had had little interest in social studies in school, I was behind in the accumulation of hard knowledge. This was a major reason for my feelings of inferiority, and it convinced me I was hardly a towering intellectual.

Somewhere in college, I began to experience the schism between the pure intellect of political science and the creativity of show biz. The split grew with my increasing need for substance to feed the emotional intensity. Yet I continued to be pulled by the exuberance of the musical comedy fantasies. Singing was still my activity of choice, if only in the privacy of my own room.

In political science I was unable to integrate the intellectual with the creative part of myself. In fact, my primary interests there were constitutional law and international relations, which seemed even closer to the intellectual extreme. The inquiring minds I found in the political science department only dramatized the contrast to what I perceived to be the insularity of my friends in the theater arts department. At SMCC I had been awarded an academic scholarship to pursue criminal law, as a vote of confidence in my potential as a political science student. The schism continued.

There were two major universities in Los Angeles that offered credible entertainment majors, UCLA and the University of Southern California. In the area, USC was considered to be a "rich person's school." UCLA, because it is a state school, lacked the budget of its privately subsidized rival. In the early 1960s, UCLA was known for its theater department, though it had also developed limited course work in television / radio and motion pictures. Many working actors took courses there. The campus was also the setting for many of the then-popular television programs, such as *Medical Center* and *Route 66*. It was not unusual to see a crew shooting somewhere on campus as we trekked from class to class.

UCLA was an academic factory, the biggest school I had ever seen. My switch to political science was as much an appeal to my academic side as it was a rejection of academic theater. UCLA was "the big time" in educational theater, and I feared more of the SMCC pretentiousness. I was still surrounded by show biz. Everywhere I looked there was a familiar setting, one often captured on TV and film. To get to my classes, I had to pass by the Kenneth McGowan Theater, which produced at least five minutes of active show-biz fantasy to start my day.

Being a disc jockey on the campus radio station was a holding action. It kept me performing, this time on radio. My "boss" was Harry Shearer, who became famous as a writer and comedian. Bob Bailey would have been proud of me. I had four hours every Sunday to fill with my "Music for Happy Listening." Shades of Doris Day. My choice of a title was undoubtedly conditioned by my mother's stated attitude about life. "Happy" was definitely above "fulfilled." My intent was to play music that wasn't on the top 40. Included were foreign tunes, some old big band songs, and earlier works by singers currently in vogue. I loved sharing my wealth of trivia, especially when it came to old show tunes. Often I would select a show of a prominent composer that had been an atypical failure, such as Irving Berlin's "Mr. President" or Rodgers and Hammerstein's "No Strings." At the same time, I was becoming disenchanted with Los Angeles and was considering moving to Berkeley for my senior year. There I could find the intellectual stimulation I sought, without being "contaminated" by the trappings of show biz that were all around me in L.A. I was continually fighting the seduction.

My radio show was originally piped only to the dorms, but then it spread to the general Westwood area. The anonymity of it was driving me mad. It seemed so insular to arrive at the underground parking lot, walk to a closet-like studio, chat with the engineer, do the show, get in the car and go home. No feedback. A little publicity couldn't hurt.

I went to my trusty typewriter and wrote a story about being the first female disc jockey in Los Angeles and sent it to the *Palisadian Post*. I figured they'd like the story of a local kid doing something interesting, particularly if it sounded pioneering. The following Thursday, my picture was all over page one, second section. I clipped it out and sent it to the printer, where I had 250 copies printed. For the next few years, I used it as publicity in my efforts to secure other show-biz employment.

As I look back on these first eighteen or nineteen years of my life, there seems to be a wealth of amateur show-biz experiences. Writing, acting, composing, playing in a band and orchestra— these all seem like considerable and valuable experience to me now. But there is a pace about Los Angeles that made us all competitive. Someone else was always better, faster, richer. There were times when that stopped me from going on; other times that tempo was invigorating. There is simply no way to master it, to feel on top. Had I known a broader context, my fantasies might have been more quickly modified. As it was, my contiguity with the Hollywood scene was like a continual influx of adrenaline. It was always a factor. That insidious pressure was responsible for my taking alternative roads, namely the writing, when it was not really the activity of choice. Switching gears had caused me to say at the time of my high school graduation that I wanted to go into motion picture administration, when I really wanted to be a performer. That bargaining and flirting with the truth of my real ambition is a major theme of the first two decades of my life.

One of my more successful detours was my work with Bernie Kamins. He ran a one-man public relations and advertising agency on Cañon Drive in the heart of Beverly Hills. Bernie was a kind but remote man who was trying to get out of representing actors, which he had done for many years. His current thrust was into financial public relations. I signed on as a typist-shlep. When he found out I could write and was interested in helping him with his Hollywood clients, he was delighted. For $1.50 an hour and ten cents a mile, I would transcribe his dictation, write articles, and ferry them to various newspapers in town. In time, he trusted me with delivering records and gifts to his most prized Hollywood clients.

Bernie had a Wheeldex almost as good as Edmond O'Brien's address book. He even had the number of the phone in Louella Parsons' bedroom! One of his clients was Dora Hall, whose husband owned the Dixie Cup Company, and who was apparently subsidizing her singing. She cut a record and Bernie was hired to sell it around town. I was excited about helping with the promotion, for it meant going through that glamorous Wheeldex and meeting some of those legends in person.

My experience with Dora Hall gave new dimension to my fantasies. I had been committed to the ideal of hard work, high energy and adequate preparation in order to make it big. It hadn't occurred to me to buy fame. I still thought one had to be discovered in order to make a record. Money had never been very important to me, but the thought of money opening doors was an intriguing one. How much would it take? $20,000? $100,000? Could one buy an appearance on a television show? Could one buy a television show? And if so, why weren't more exhibitionistic rich people on television? I had thoughts of buying commercial time on TV along the lines of the back of the comic book with the little dog in the teacup. Won't you give this girl a break? And how could I possibly save or earn a sufficient amount to make a dent? Up to this time, all I could afford was a tiny one-inch ad in *Daily Variety* announcing my role in *Good News*. It cost all of fifteen dollars, but my satisfaction was worth it, though it failed to bring out the Darryl Zanucks and L.B. Mayers. Knowing Dora Hall's experience of having a husband who bankrolled her career added to my growing cynicism about the need for talent in gaining fame.

FIVE

Journeys
from Beverly Hills
to Paris

I was twenty years old when I went to work for Bernie. I had entrée to the city rooms of all the L.A. daily newspapers and to both Hollywood trade papers. I was sure to impress someone with my talent and sincerity. While the treasured thought of the Lana Turner/Schwab's find was still there, it would have been acceptable for some city editor to proffer a job writing about movies and television. I could always slip into performing later.

From seeing *Teacher's Pet* so many times, the newsroom of the *Herald-Examiner* looked very familiar. Bernie sent me there to deliver copy to the editors of the various pages, often copy I had written. I was fascinated with the city editor, Agness Underwood, the only female city editor of repute. She was a legend in her time, hard boiled and professional. I never got close, but watched her behavior and her interactions. While her persona felt closer to mine than did Doris Day's version of a journalist, I was too afraid of the consequences of having that kind of power.

This was still the era of strong sex-role conformity. Women who broke the mold were suspected of being gay, or at least bisexual. I wasn't sure what sexual category described me yet, but I lacked the courage to associate with anyone who might call attention to my nonconformity and uncertain femininity.

The need to belong is underscored by my persuading Bernie to sponsor me for membership in the Greater Los Angeles Press Club. It was one of the original "key" clubs in L.A., providing a pleasant and impressive setting for taking clients to lunch. Local television newsmen would be on hand to hoist a few. I was self-conscious in such company. My face was not recognizable. None-theless, the anonymity did not stop me from bringing friends there to lunch among the celebrities. It was like my own personal Brown Derby.

Bernie assigned me two main clients in addition to Dora Hall: Marvin Miller, who had become famous as Michael Anthony on *The Millionaire*, and my old dancing partner, Buddy Ebsen. Be-fore I delivered a to-be-published story on Miller to his home, Bernie advised me not to stay too long if he answered the door in his bathrobe. I laughed, thinking he was being overprotective. I had read enough about Hollywood casting couches that I was not about to put myself in that position, quite literally. His warning confirmed my major concern about competing and working in Hollywood. I never could comprehend how one could be up-wardly mobile while in a supine position; the power of sex eluded me. As it was, Marvin Miller did answer the door in his bathrobe. I stayed a few uncomfortable minutes and left. He was always a gentleman when we would meet, but I constantly expected the worst.

Buddy Ebsen was different. There was nothing sexually threat-ening about him, since he was associated with my childhood and my naivete. In an unusual move for an actor, he paid Bernie to keep his name out of the paper. I wrote only a few stories about him, mostly of his involvement in the community activities in Balboa, where he maintained a residence. The first time I saw Buddy in my new role was at a state fair. In his *Beverly Hillbillies* character, Buddy was appearing with the other members of the cast, performing skits based on the show. While I was not a fan of the program, I was excited about the possibility of seeing him again. When the show was over, I explained to the backstage manager who I was ("I represent Mr. Ebsen for Bernie Kamins") and moved behind the curtain. It was steaming hot, and smelled of greasepaint. There was mass confusion with well-wishers and friends pushing to see their favorites. After I was ushered in to see Buddy, I introduced myself, delivered my package, then popped my question. Did he by any chance remember dancing with a little blonde girl at his studio about fifteen years earlier? He said he did, and referred to the scene specifically enough for me be convinced he really did remember. It made me feel wonderful. A famous TV star knew who I was. Unfortunately, it was also the last time I saw him. My work for him involved preventive publicity and I spent most of my time talking with newspaper columnists, rather than Buddy himself.

Another opportunity occurred when he was making *Mail Order Bride* at MGM. I had visited that studio when I was writing film reviews, but it was the one studio I was unable to wander through freely. There were guards everywhere, even in the parking lot. Bernie asked that I deliver some papers to Buddy on the set. What an opportunity! The closest I had come to a set was being in the audience for all those television shows with Jacquie, and when attending a Desilu stockholders' meeting. One of the members of the board of directors of Desilu was George Murphy, who took interested stockholders on a tour of the studio. Now, though, I had fantasies of sitting in a director's chair next to the kleig lights, while the real director yelled "Action." And, needless to say, if someone came over to offer me a part or a screen test, well, who could refuse?

The pervasiveness of this fantasy must be evident by now. It was a daily temptation and a regular possibility. Here I was, working in the heart of the West Coast show-biz world. If it wasn't on my terms, certainly I was closer than I had ever been. It was not difficult to maintain the dream.

I double-timed it to the studio in my MG, which I was hoping would beguile the studio guard. Then I saw the Mercedes-Benzes and Rolls Royces lined up and I figured I would be lucky to get in at all. I told him who I was and why I was there. He sent me to the office of the producer, Richard Lyons. Lyons, one of the last salaried staff producers on the lot, would have to approve my being on the set. He had an office in the Irving Thalberg Building, only a few hundred feet away. The Irving Thalberg Building. The very name echoed in my mind, as I recalled all I had assimilated about the halcyon days of MGM and the great genius, Thalberg. My sense of history grew heavier with each step toward the building. I checked the directory for Lyons's name, and gasped when I saw Gene Kelly had an office there. I had seen almost all of his films, and fantasized him as an ideal partner for me. We would restore the great musical comedy era to MGM. I made a mental note of Lyons's office number, then went searching for Gene Kelly's office. What would I do if I saw him? Who knows? His office was locked, which was probably for the best. My best intrusions were at least minimally thought out, and this was a serendipitous escapade.

Returning to Lyons's office, I found that it was also empty. I went in and sat down. I was hoping he would come in, find me irresistibly spellbinding and ask if I'd like to watch the shooting. There must be a way to get on that set. Fifteen minutes went by, and discouragement set in. Within a few more minutes, a young man came in and asked where Dick Lyons was. He looked vaguely familiar, but I couldn't place him. We made polite conversation, and he left. I decided to leave the papers on Lyons' desk, since no one was around. As I walked down the corridor, I suddenly realized my small-talk partner had been Keir Dullea, who had gained fame in *David and Lisa*. I kicked myself for not being more alert, but shrugged, knowing he was one of many I was bound to run into now that I was hanging around the studios.

Delivering those Dora Hall records provided opportunities to visit famous people. Some I never saw. Hedda Hopper had her maid take the record. I gained entrance to the showplace that was conductor-composer Johnny Green's home. He and his wife were enjoying a late breakfast. One of my deliveries was to Johnny Mercer, the morning after he had won an Oscar for writing "Moon River." He, too, answered the door in his bathrobe, but it was because I had awakened him after a night of revelry. I wanted to break into song for him, but reality overcame fantasy and I resisted.

Another delivery was to Steve Allen. An honest-to-God Renaissance man, it seemed there was little he had not done or could not do. We shared the same politics, and I had attended rallies for his group advocating a Sane Nuclear Policy. He seemed natural and unaffected by his genius, and I was looking forward to engaging in a lively conversation with him. He was clearly a person of substance. The day I was to make the delivery, I took pains to dress especially well. Even the car had been washed and waxed. His rambling home was just over the hill in Sherman Oaks. I pulled into the driveway and, almost as an afterthought, remembered the Dora Hall record. I knew he'd hate it, but expected he would be polite. Endless conversational gambits sailed through my mind as I waited for the door to be opened. It never occurred to me that anyone but Steve would answer. A dour-looking maid, complete with uniform, asked what she could do for me.

Once again, I went through the validation rap. Hey, I'm okay. I'm working for a top Beverly Hills agency. The maid reached for the record and said she would "give it to Mr. Allen." Wait a minute, here. You mean he isn't home? No, he was rehearsing in Hollywood. She started to close the door. Quick, think of something. "Uh, could I have a drink of water?" The old Edmund O'Brien gambit! I mumbled something about it having been a hot day and a long drive. I awaited her decision. The least she could do was let me see the living quarters of this fantastic person. Begrudgingly, she led me to the kitchen. On the way, we had to pass through the living room, which was dominated by a huge grand piano. It was an entertainer's dream house. I asked if this was where he composed. There was some pride in her voice as she stopped in her tracks and pointed down the hall. She told me he often played the piano in the middle of the night, composing without any thought of sleep. The old *Confidential* magazine came to mind. Was this how those reporters got their dirt? By asking pushy questions of servants?

We stood in the kitchen while I slowly sipped the water, asking questions about what it was like to work for Steve Allen. She was complimentary and obviously liked her boss. That was pleasing. All those good things I had read about him were true. He was the first "legend" who seemed like a real person. Though I saw him in other contexts over the years, I never came this close again.

Bernie subscribed to all the trade papers, and I spent my lunch hour reading about the industry. It was an effort to continue my self-directed study. One that was new to me was the *Screen Producers Guild Journal*, full of erudite articles which impressed me with their thoughtful content. Bernie explained that the editor, Lou Greenspan, had been instrumental in coordinating the film industry's efforts during World War II, inserting subtle propaganda into movies. He was eager to divulge all this, since propaganda was one of Bernie's longtime interests, starting with his days as a student at Harvard. I asked to meet Greenspan. He had access to a whole new area of information, more insider stuff. And, as Bernie told me Greenspan's history, he was an integral part of an important but seldom documented era in Hollywood's history. He was also a producer, which was the highest source of power I had reached so far.

Greenspan was a kindly-looking man for whom the Screen Producers Guild had been a mission. He was one of the founders and enjoyed talking about its form and function. In some ways, he seemed the consummate Hollywood mogul. Though he had never controlled a major studio, he knew everybody and was powerful. I decided to confide my performance fantasies. He was encouraging and asked what I had done about them. Mentioning my amateur appearances was embarrassing. What I wanted was screen credits, but I didn't know how to go about getting them. I knew about the Catch-22. I couldn't get a part in a film without a card in the Screen Actors Guild and I couldn't join the Guild without having a part in a film. What to do? There was a pause, then Greenspan pointed to the smallish couch in his office and smiled. I thought he was putting me on. He seemed so benign, so benevolent. Looking him square in the eye, I declared my antipathy for such dues payment. He shrugged his shoulders, which said I was obviously making a choice.

"All the major stars have spent time on the couch. Even your Doris Day."

I sensed he was trying to shock me into compliance. I was momentarily disarmed by his nonchalance. Silence, then he spoke again.

"How much do you want to be famous?" One of his eyebrows cocked upward.

"It's hard for me to believe what you say," I stammered as I studied the floor. Then, I stood up, walked to his desk and shook his hand. I thanked him for his advice and asked to receive the *Journal*. My heart was beating fast, my face red, my dreams flying out the window. When Bernie asked me how it had gone, I was too embarrassed to tell him the truth. Somehow it was my fault this famous producer had tried to seduce me. In the climate of the Fifties, the woman was usually blamed for this kind of scene. But if this was how it was done, then maybe I was fantasizing about the wrong business.

I didn't know if it was okay to feel good about feeling bad. I was angry but felt guilty about that, too. Was it acceptable to be offended at being considered a piece of meat? I felt naive for putting myself in that situation, and for not recognizing its inevitability. Could I have avoided it? What did I do wrong? I felt that somehow all that was within my control. At the same time, I was aware of my personal bottom lines, and that was one of them. I would not sell out. I sensed that Greenspan thought it was merely an exchange of services. Somehow, I had learned to trust myself in those areas. But it remained a conflict. Was he right? Had I made a decision that precluded the realization of my fantasies?

When I left for my senior year at the University of California at Berkeley, Bernie kept me on the payroll. I would cover Northern California for him, which meant taking care of his Hamm's beer account. But as graduation time neared, I realized I would no longer be content working for $1.50 an hour plus mileage. As much as I enjoyed the varied experiences, I resigned. I had applied for graduate school in the journalism department at UCLA, though my heart really wasn't in it. At that point, I wanted to go to law school, but lacked the self-confidence and probably the grade point average to apply.

I worked for Bernie for two and a half years. It was a rewarding job, in that I could be creative in my writing. The work was timely, almost always published, and I would learn about many other subjects in addition to show biz. He was a fatherly man who patiently taught me a lot about journalistic public relations. It was to serve me well later.

The transfer to the Berkeley campus represented an emphasis on the intellectual. I had become disenchanted with show biz, having tried every conceivable way to become an integral part of the industry. Between UCLA and Cal, though, I did my usual summer thing. I worked in a local music studio as a receptionist/telephone solicitor, and reveled in the fact my boss had been a stand-in for Gene Krupa in *The Gene Krupa Story*. The studio was in a suite upstairs from the Gregg Toland photography studio. Toland had been the photographic architect of *Citizen Kane*, among others. As much as I fantasized being "shot" by him, there was no way I could afford it. In my spare time, I sang to records, which long before had become a staple of my stress reduction techniques. And, with my brother, I drove into Hollywood and Beverly Hills on regular forays. By now I had added Bel Air, since that's the home of so many celebrities. I would point out the sights as we would drive. I still couldn't shake the habit of driving through Beverly Hills via Crescent Drive.

Considerable anxiety followed my decision to go to school in Berkeley. Sally and I had met at University High but did not become friends until we both worked at Douglas Aircraft in the summers. She was sharp and perceptive; it wasn't long before we were spending considerable time together. Sally was a student at Berkeley already. My bravado in going away to school was largely based on our bond. I felt safe with her. Though Sally and I had been close, part of me was afraid to test the relationship. I had written several poems about her, one of which characterizes my emerging awareness of its transience:

People are like negatives with faces, lives transparent;

Pretending, nodding, living lies, their smiles are snarls
   apparent.
A precious few are solid, to whom love is not new;
Real and warm and beautiful, innocent and true.
But all too soon they're grabbed away, the friendship turns to
   haze.
And then the secret is revealed: they've come to live, not
   graze.

Though I considered her a friendly foe, because of her supportive badgering, I was also growing into the knowledge of the importance of disclosure:

To be happy is to love,
To love is to reveal,
To reveal is to remove
The dented inner shield.

I wasn't sure what was awaiting me at Cal, but I sensed a major shakeout within.

I slowly fall apart as life withdraws its meaning;
Too advanced to regain my start, the floor becomes the ceiling.

The ostensible reason for transferring to Berkeley was that it offered an undergraduate journalism major, which was not available at UCLA. My second week on campus, I made an appointment with the editor-in-chief of the *Daily Californian* and presented my string book. My collection of by-lines was formidable and included not only those articles from high school and the UCLA paper but the countless articles I had had published while working for Bernie. When the editor said she was impressed I quickly added that I would like a weekly column in which I would comment on television and film, with an occasional review. Of course, it would be by-lined. And, oh yes. It would not be cut in any way. What did I have to lose? She could only say no. To my surprise, she agreed and asked when the first piece could be submitted.

Thus I became probably the first television critic writing for a daily paper who did not own a television set. I had to gain access to a TV set quickly or lose the job. Fortunately, one of my classmates saw my first article in the *Daily Californian* and complimented me. We became friends almost immediately, having little to do with the fact she owned a TV set.

So here I was, having initially chosen Cal to get away from Glitter Gulch. Within two weeks of wading into intellectual waters, I had lunged for the raft of safety. Seduced again!

The change to writing about television was definitely an accommodation. Movies were my interest; TV was for peasants. All us literati knew that. But, since TV was easily accessible and there were then no movie studios within four hundred miles of Berkeley, I would write the most literate column possible. In my weekly articles, I commented on the banality of commercials, the wasteland that was the current season and the decline of the star system in Hollywood, and praised the quality of the old *Dick Van Dyke Show*. They were well received, though I took a lot of flack from my five roommates. Often kidding me about my public relations background, they surprised me one night when I arrived home after a date. On the ceiling was a seven-foot-long set of smiling teeth, done with white shelf paper. It was a testimony to the perennial smile necessitated by the phoniness of public relations. In spite of their position, I suspect several of my roomies engaged in finessing people, in doing what you had to do to get what you want. Certainly I got an argument when I described the Lou Greenspan episode. Few could comprehend my feeling of violation. Once again, I felt alone in my feminism.

Many of my roommates' values were foreign to me. I had not been exposed to sanctioned sex outside marriage, drunkenness for sport, abortions or even the total dedication to study. And I was unprepared for a shocking discovery: Sally had neglected to tell me she was sexually involved with her boyfriend. I felt betrayed as I had falsely assumed a mutually youthful idealism. She claimed she tried to tell me, but I had failed to pick up the innuendoes. I felt manipulated by her, especially when she spent most of her time with her male friend. I struggled with the traditional values I had been taught, trying to integrate them into the new world around me. The pain is evident in my poetry at the time:

I lie here suffering as though my world has come to an end.
Life and love are full of woe; branches refuse to bend.
Viewing in perspective helps not the one who cries.
Reason, logic, intellect cannot reveal the prize.
There's good in all, or so I'm told; perhaps it is believed.
But down below it's damp and cold and I feel bereaved.
Like something's gone—the past, of course. The inner self emerges;
I shudder, cringe, refuse, deny the truth that crowds and surges.
Onward! Glance between the bars and cast out doubt and fear.
The world is liberation! You're shedding freedom's tear.

The newspaper column immediately lowered my anxiety about competing with the super-intellectuals on campus. It set me apart, giving me a claim to fame on my own turf. I liked the writing, and the respect I received for producing the column. In deference to my new reference group and growing maturity, I shortened my by-line by eliminating the "Doris." I was not in the mainstream of show biz, not even close to the center of journalism in terms of show biz. Yet I was having fantasies of writing for *Daily Variety*. To my knowledge, there were still few women writing about the industry other than gossip columnists.

I qualified for the honors program in journalism and chose to write my senior honors thesis on film criticism. I wrote to John Waugh, who was the Hollywood editor of the *Christian Science Monitor*. He invited me to meet with him in Los Angeles the next time I was in town. The very next weekend, I called him from the Palisades, and we set up a lunch meeting at Frascati's, a popular show-biz restaurant in Beverly Hills. As we sat talking about being a film critic, Jack Albertson stopped by the table to pay his respects. Waugh was friendly with many celebrities as a result of his work. As the salad course was drawing to a close, I looked up to see Jack Lemmon approaching our table. I had long been a fan of his and was star-struck. We had had one previous encounter, which he undoubtedly had forgotten. In the late 1950s, he was making an appearance in a local discount store to plug his record album. I made the drive there to see him. He signed the album jacket but I wanted more time to talk. All I had with me was a jar of pickles purchased for my mother. I asked him to sign that as we talked. I wonder how many pickle jars Jack Lemmon has signed in his lifetime.

At any rate, Waugh was cooperative, and I began to wonder if I might work as a film critic somewhere. If Jack Waugh had Hollywood wrapped up, perhaps I could cover the East Coast.

Close to the end of my senior year, I decided to apply to the *Christian Science Monitor* for a job as a copygirl, which I had seen advertised in the *Monitor*. I also applied to the master's degree program at UCLA's School of Journalism. I had fully intended to sublimate my performing instincts into writing about others doing what I had wanted to do. Still, the *Monitor* was in Boston, close enough to the New York theater.

Though my life had taken an intellectual bent, hardly a night went by that I did not listen to my musical comedy albums while I studied. When my roommates would leave me alone long enough, I rushed to my "Judy at Carnegie Hall" album and sang with it for all four sides. Weekends, many of us would head into San Francisco and the Red Garter, where singalongs were the attraction. Unlike my pals, I knew the lyrics to all the songs and would be out front, leading the singing. The more beer I drank, the more fervently I sang. My friends were surprised at my repertoire, and I was surprised at their surprise. I didn't know that everyone didn't know those tunes. It was just second nature to me.

Cal was a lesson in the diversity of normality. Growing up in Southern California, I thought being surrounded by the glamor of show biz and being fascinated by it was normal. I thought everyone developed their identity through media role models. It wasn't until my early twenties that I realized normals aren't all alike. It took a while to appreciate the fact that different is not inferior or superior, just different. That realization was a potent lesson, one that significantly reduced my adolescent judgmentalness. As with other emotional data collected in this era, that lesson was useful later in working as a clinical psychologist.

By the time I graduated from Berkeley, I felt I had grown up and accepted the reality that I was not Doris Day and that I would not be discovered. Becoming a star was a serendipitous event, outside my control. It was not to be, and I had finally accepted that.

The summer I graduated, my parents gave me a trip to Europe, which is to say I was invited to join them. It was a difficult trip because, unknowingly, I had mononucleosis the whole time and was drained of energy. The plans had been made early in my senior year, and I had asked Sally to come along. By the time of the trip, there was little friendship left between us. The tension of that, coupled with the personality conflict between Sally and my mother, made the trip nearly unbearable. The verbal contests and discord became daily events, with me in the middle. When we returned home in September, I was ready to ship off to Boston to be a copykid with the *Christian Science Monitor*.

It was in Europe that I had decided to go for the *Monitor* job. I was burned out academically from the year at Cal, so much that I didn't know if I could maintain my 3.8 grade point average in journalism. As in the time after high school graduation, I was tired of reading about what I wanted to do; I wanted to do it. I applied to the *Monitor*, thinking I could write about show biz for a national newspaper. Los Angeles was a haunted place for me, mocking in its missed opportunities. Boston was a perfect place to test my wings, get away from the past. It would give me a chance to begin life as an adult.

SIX

Tilting at Windmills:
Ethical Struggles

Boston was the first time away from home as a permanent move. Friends and neighbors had a going-away party for me, with much well-wishing and emotional intensity. Though I was leaving good friends behind, I was moving to the east coast to seek fame and fortune with one of the top newspapers in the country. I set a goal of five years as an apprentice period. By then, I would have my first professional by-line and would be writing in my chosen field. In the meantime, I would work hard and learn what I could.

Boston was an unfamiliar culture. Buildings were crowded together and the city seemed to be constantly buzzing with stimulation. The numbers of people in the streets were vaguely threatening, especially as I walked to work in the dark. I felt alone and frightened but exhilarated by the challenges of the city and the job.

Being a copykid demanded high energy. We were to be at work by 6 a.m., and required to deliver newspapers off the press to everyone in the building four times a day. Copykids were the gofers of the publishing society, constantly on the move. At any time of the day, a buzzer ringing near our table signaled that some editor was calling us to run an errand or deliver a message. My colleagues on the copykid desk were immersed in their jobs, most of them having fulfilled their highest ambition. I was reluctant to share my methodical plans with them.

Delivering the mail was my favorite job, as it put me in direct contact with all the editors, "producers" of the world of journalism. As I walked around the newsroom, I fantasized writing for the book editor, the theater editor, the sports editor, the international relations editor and even the business editor. After extensive exposure under Bernie, I was ready to tackle any subject. To my surprise and pleasure, there were two editors who were open to conversation. One was the drama editor, Fred Guidry. Fred wrote all the film, television and stage reviews, and it was his job I coveted. There was no problem confiding this, and within a few days we were chatting for five or ten minutes each time the mail was delivered. After my experience with Lou Greenspan, I was wary of possible sexual involvement. Naively, though, I felt safe since I knew he was married. And, after all, he was a devout Christian Scientist.

Within a week or two, Fred offered to take me touring. I found out his wife was on vacation for several months and he had time on his hands. For three weekends in a row, we trekked all over, from the Kennedy Compound at Hyannis to the colorful mountains of central Massachusetts. Once Fred asked if I were threatened sexually by him. I lied and said no. Perhaps if I feigned innocence, he would be less likely to take advantage. I don't know if it was my *belle indifférence* act, or his gallantry, but sex never got in the way.

My other ally was the Latin American editor, James Nelson Goodsell. Jim was a latecomer to Christian Science, and previously had labored in the newsroom of the St. Louis *Post-Dispatch*. His visage suggested he had lived a harder life than one might expect of a pious Christian Scientist; his cynical comments made me feel right at home. The *Monitor* was still under the editorship of Dewitt John, who had recently succeeded the legendary Erwin Canham. Newsroom rules were strict to the point that coffee was discouraged on the job. Needless to say, there was also absolutely no cigarette smoking or profanity. I delighted in treating the rules with a rebellious spirit, and Jim was amused by my irreverence.

Our connection included a mutual interest in international relations. Though I had no direct experience, I had majored in political science at Berkeley and UCLA. My focus in the international area had been the Middle East, but Jim was an excellent teacher. I could learn on the job, which came as a bonus. We did not see each other outside the newsroom, and he was often on assignment in Latin America. But I relished reading his articles from the field, never feeling I had the courage to be all alone in a foreign country as he was.

Even though there was no real connection, I maintained cordial relations with the other writers. When we would discuss their current assignment, I enjoyed the stimulation of the interaction. Of course, there was the hope they would suggest an assignment, even doing some research for them. A lifelong baseball fan, I suggested to the sports editor that it would be truly revolutionary to have a woman writing of the excitement of the current pennant races, and wondered if they had ever considered that. Remember, this was 1964. A woman's place on a newspaper was on the woman's page. The sports editors patiently heard my suggestion, snickered, and thanked me for the mail delivery. Their sexist comments rang in my ears as I returned to my desk.

One of the most intimidating editors was Melvin Maddocks, who ran the book review desk. He scarcely acknowledged me, never even meeting my smile with recognition. Nonetheless, he was included in my campaign, as there was nothing to lose.

Not surprisingly, my first assignment came from Fred: a review of the annual production of *Ireland on Parade*. I knew if done well, it would mean a by-line. It was overwhelming to have my by-line fantasy come true after only two weeks, instead of the five years I had envisioned. I asked another copykid to go with me, to be sure I could find Boston Garden. There was a lack of shared excitement, though I longed for camaraderie. A long time would pass before I could accept the correlation of peak experience with the intensity of aloneness.

In the early 1960s, Boston seemed to be a city carved up between the Christian Scientists and the Catholics. *Ireland on Parade* was more of interest to the latter; I felt a little like a spy. The Irish had their own culture, to which I had never been exposed. I decided to treat the performance as just that, and wrote the review as though it were a play or film. There was an internal pressure to be fair. At the same time, I knew the review would be widely read, considering the vast Irish population in the area. I didn't want to alienate anyone with my first writing assignment.

I took notes during the performance and wrote like crazy back in my little apartment. Writing has always come easily to me, and the review came out fluidly the first time. The next morning, I submitted what was essentially a final copy of my rough draft and waited with trepidation. It wasn't until the next day that Fred said it would go exactly as written. In the parlance of the Sixties, it blew my mind.

Was it really going to be this easy? All those years I had banged my head against the wall of show biz. Two weeks on a newspaper and all those skills transfer directly without sweat? Unbelievable! Two days later, on a Friday, the New England edition was to contain the review. I could hardly wait, and eagerly looked forward to savoring the irony of delivering copies of that very newspaper to all the editors. It was a vindication, and I expected positive feedback.

I knew, from what newspaper experience I had, how unusual it was to have something printed exactly as it was written. There was an entire profession—editing—devoted to tearing apart a writer's copy and rewriting it. Just a few feet from the copykid table was an editor's desk where four men sat, performing that function. It was one thing to get away with unedited writing at the *Daily Californian*, but the *Christian Science Monitor*? Was I that good, or were they that lax?

When Friday arrived, I went to the uncomfortably noisy press-room, to watch them run off my review. I took one of the first copies and riffled through to the entertainment page. There it was! "By Pam Osborne." As I read it over, though, it didn't make sense to me. I read it several times, thinking it was my excitement that precluded clear thinking. Then I saw the problem. The proofreaders had missed a major mistake in the setting of the copy. The lead contained reversed clauses and misplaced words, making it difficult to comprehend. Once the reader moved beyond the lead, it was fine. I felt embarrassed, as though I had done something wrong. It was demoralizing to have the big moment diminished by someone else's oversight. Because of this, many of the comments referred to the confusing opening. Fred apologized and he was, in fact, responsible. I was disappointed that my debut was marred by an event beyond my control.

Within a few days, I was asked by the city editor to cover a local story on a seawall that was deteriorating. Another editor asked me to cover a speech given by Supreme Court Justice William O. Douglas. He was speaking in a coastal town on water conservation. As an avid student of constitutional law, I was eager to meet with him and talk about anything at all. He had just remarried and was looking spritely. I sat in the front row and leaned on every word. The next day, my brief article was printed, again without editing. I began to consider the possibility that I had journalistic ability. That old bluff to the editor of the *Daily Californian* about not touching a word apparently had merit. Within a week, there were several other articles. None of them, though, included my by-line. They read "By the Staff of the *Christian Science Monitor*." On one day, the paper contained three of my articles, and I began to think of myself as staff. But I was still a copykid, earning $64 a week before taxes. There were no overtures to hire me on as a reporter.

But then, why should they? I was working all day as a copykid running errands, and doing my writing at night and on weekends. They were getting two for the price of one slave. The feeling of being used began to gnaw on me. In addition, the writing was almost too easy. It had lost its challenge. I was working long hours without just compensation. Though only two months had gone by since I had moved to Boston and went to work for the paper, active dissonance was fermenting inside. It wouldn't take much for me to explode.

In contrast with the newsrooms of the Los Angeles *Herald-Examiner* and the Los Angeles *Times*, the *Monitor* newsroom was like a morgue. It was almost silent, the ominous nothingness punctuated only by the bell that called the copykids to various parts of the building. A laugh stood out like the Washington

Monument; everything was cool, matter-of-fact. Very professional. I would go home for lunch, though it was a twenty-minute walk, just to get away from the oppressive atmosphere. I had expected stimulation and just a little lightness. But the only zap came from going out on stories and writing them at home.

I had expected to find a mentor, someone who might tutor me in the art of writing. Perhaps because it had come so easily, few had offered suggestions. The *Monitor* was populated mostly by senior writers. They had established their areas of influence and did not see the need to help younger writers. I was not approached by anyone taking interest. Fred and Jim were friends who gave me personal support, but no real feedback. There was little banter in the newsroom, which helps explain the lack of colleague informality that might have led to more learning. In the course of my day, the only contacts were at my instigation, as I delivered the mail or the newspapers. This was hardly conducive to a mentor relationship. It was no one's fault; it was just a matter of tradition and circumstance.

Christian Science had been a byproduct of my addiction to Doris Day. In 1951 she married Martin Melcher, who was a Christian Scientist, and she converted soon afterward. I arrived at a Christian Science church via my adolescent identity crisis at the age of fifteen, an appropriate developmental era for religious affiliation. This was one of the few areas of Doris Day's life that was a good fit. Its intellectual approach, its structured problem-solving orientation and its lack of pomp appealed to my teen-age asceticism. When I reached college age, its behavioral demands were "too establishment" for me and I began to move away, slowly but linearly. At first I took a leadership role, as a soloist in the Sunday school and a Reader at Santa Monica City College's organization. But by the time I arrived at Berkeley, there was little left but the formal affiliation.

No one had mentioned that one had to be a member of the Mother Church, The First Church of Christ, Scientist, to work for the *Monitor*. When I found out in Boston, my sense of equality and social justice was assaulted. I had expected a kind of Super-

Scientist there. Instead I found hypocrisy and human fallibility, as well as a disappointing lack of role models. Being firmly entrenched in my youthful idealism, I decided it would be hypocritical for me to continue to me a formal member of the church. I was not judging its value for others. It seemed likely that I might return to it at a later time in my life, as it had served me well during my adolescence.

The decision to resign was not an easy one. I knew I was casting myself out in an existential sense. All my friends in Boston were church members, and I would continue to be surrounded by its beliefs. But being a loner was not new; in fact, being the outsider was an effective way of helping resolve the identity crisis that was created by leaving home. At any rate, it was something I was convinced I had to do.

As with Greenspan's sexual quid pro quo, the subtle pressures of religion just didn't feel right. There was some central core that was being violated, though I didn't know what or where it was. In talking with staff members, I had to censor my speech, avoiding any hint of my normal mild profanity or any slightly off-color references. I had trouble understanding the proscription against tea and coffee and the almost cult-like reverence for Mary Baker Eddy. In addition, Christian Science discourages the use of physicians, believing it is God's perfect science that can heal the sick and injured. The control inherent in this belief appealed to the ascetic in me; in practice, it was stultifying and downright humorless.

Following the written resignation from the church, I was called into Dewitt John's office. He reminded me of the employment requirement, and asked me to reconsider. He said no one had ever resigned membership after what he called "conspicuous success." He cautioned he could not predict what action might be taken as a result of the inevitable church deliberations. I thanked him for his concern, but left still convinced of the propriety of my decision. It was completely untenable for me to pretend an allegiance I did not feel simply to maintain my job.

Within a few days, I received my summons from the clerk's office in the Mother Church. The Mother Church is a cavernous building, echoing footsteps and whispers with equal clarity. As I made my way to his office to explain myself, I could hear my heart pounding in the hallways. I had fantasies of meeting God or at the very least, Orson Welles. Instead, it was more like Don Knotts. He was kindly and reaffirmed Dewitt John's perplexity. He applied no pressure on me to reverse myself, for which I was grateful. The board of directors was convening the following month in Boston and would consider my "case." Within the span of a few days, I moved from introspection to anxiety to righteous indignation. It was hard to believe they would actually fire me for my beliefs. I thought that was prohibited by the First Amendment of the Constitution. There was no one with whom I could discuss this, since everyone I knew had a vested interest in the outcome. It was another time that I was undergoing an intense emotional experience alone, requiring that I use myself as my best resource. I thought about the situation constantly. Two weeks went by as I continued to work at the copykid desk.

It began to dawn on me that the issue was not whether they wanted to keep me on. The choice was really mine. Did I want to make a career with people whose beliefs would allow them to consider trampling on mine? Though I relished the idea of being an exception to their silly rules, it felt like I was playing on unethical turf. A life of censorship, real or potential was not for me. I wrote a letter of resignation to DeWitt John and delivered it myself, with the afternoon mail.

While under the intense pressure only an encounter with the self can provide, I did a curious thing. I made an appointment to see the rabbi at the Hillel Center at Boston University.

A little background, please.

Most of my friends over the course of my life had been Jewish. There was Jacquie with her strong family ties. I suspected her parents didn't like me because I wasn't Jewish, but they could have had other reasons. In high school, I went to temple with a friend from the band. Then came Sally, with whom I shared a friendship all through college. Her family was close, warm and stimulating. My experience with Judaism was through relationships, including those with men. I became attracted to the Jewish value system focusing on family, verbal interaction, warmth and intellect. While Judaism was seldom discussed, it was manifest in the way life was lived. Hank, for instance, had her giving manner and an intense way of relating; Bert, whom I had dated at Cal, respected my knowledge and was distinctly un-gamey with me. His brother was a rabbi. Then there were all the show-biz folk I had met, including Bernie Kamins, basically comfortable to be around. Until Boston, I had never thought of converting or seriously studying Judaism.

Feeling religiously abandoned, I wanted to talk with someone with a detached perspective, one who could be respected and trusted. When I made the appointment with Rabbi Sam Perlman, I imagined a therapeutic session. I wanted to check out my value system, gain some support for my decision to abandon not only my formal religious affiliation but my career as well.

Rabbi Perlman agreed to see me. I took the long subway ride to Boston University and found the Hillel building. Feeling peculiarly at home, I was direct with him about what I wanted. I was not at all interested in another formal religious affiliation, as I had had my fill of hypocrisy. I sought value clarification and some direction for my thinking. In his wisdom, the rabbi gave me no advice. Instead, he loaded me down with a half-dozen books on values and ethics and asked me to come back the following week.

The weekly sessions came to be an oasis. The rabbi was accepting, never challenging my avoidance of commitment. Each week we met for about an hour while I pelted him with questions. He was low-key, offering the best therapy I could have found at that time. He started me on the path toward learning about Judaism. I didn't realize it at the time, but the existential themes were like putting lyrics to my own tunes. Our relationship and the reading helped get me through those last weeks at the *Monitor*.

Now what? I wanted to stay in the East, and thought about sending a résumé to other Boston papers. After my experiences with the *Monitor*, though, I was soured on newspaper work. I considered returning to public relations and and advertising, and sent résumés to companies in Boston and in New York. The lack of response augmented the feelings of depression and fatigue, due to my battle with the Mother Church and my own conscience.

Fred Guidry set up an interview for me with Osborn Elliott, an editor for *Newsweek*, who later became its editor-in-chief. I was planning one last trip to New York, anyway. Perhaps it would be just as easy to make a name at a news magazine as it was at the *Monitor*. I bundled up my clippings, withdrew money from my savings account, and grabbed a Greyhound to the Big Apple.

"All alone in this big city" was just a line in a song to me until I hit New York. Being raised in Los Angeles with frequent excursions to San Francisco, I felt like the ultimate city kid, street-wise and sophisticated. Until I got off the bus in New York. I took a cab to my hotel, the Sheraton on Park Avenue, and began planning my itinerary. I would spend ten days there, which happened to include Thanksgiving, my first major holiday away from home. That would be an important day to plan in advance or it could be an emotional disaster. And there was the interview. The rest of the trip would be centered on the theater. My timing couldn't have been better.

The year 1964 featured some of the best musicals in years. Barbra Streisand had just opened in *Funny Girl*, Carol Channing had begun her long run in *Hello, Dolly* a few months earlier; *Fiddler on the Roof* was across the street; Sammy Davis Jr. was playing in *Golden Boy* and Steve Lawrence was enjoying his title role in *What Makes Sammy Run?* Hume Cronyn and Jessica Tandy were playing in a drama, *The Physicists*, and I didn't want to miss an opportunity to see them. A second cast was recreating one of my favorites, *How to Succeed in Business Without Really Trying*. I got tickets for all of them, and spent the week immersed in fantasy as part of my healing process.

Hello, Dolly was already a big hit, and I considered myself lucky to get a ticket at all. I bought the last seat in the last balcony in the vast St. James Theater, but I felt Carol was singing to me. It was the consummate musical, perfect in every way. Instead of writing an imaginary review, what came to mind was my belief that I could do Dolly. The performance fantasies returned with a vengeance.

Before seeing *Funny Girl*, my only exposure to Streisand had been on record, which turned me off. But during the show I could see what the critics must have seen, a sensitive and captivating vocal instrument. To experience this theatrical event would cement a peak experience. After the performance, I rushed from my box to the stage door and waited with thirty or so others. Within a few minutes, a person I vaguely recognized as Streisand emerged with a couple of people and walked to her car. The others didn't seem to notice her. It was a lesson in demeanor.

I remember reading a story about Marilyn Monroe walking with a companion in a public park. No one recognized her, though she was at the peak of her career. Her companion was disbelieving, but Marilyn explained it as not giving her Marilyn persona any energy. When he doubted this, she threw back her head, and assumed a posture, becoming "Marilyn," and was soon besieged by fans. That's what I saw that night with Barbra Streisand. There was little doubt that she could become "Barbra" at will. Demeanor was everything.

Since there was a dearth of taxis, I walked back to the hotel after the performance that evening, pondering what I had learned. A light rain was falling and the air was starting to crisp with fall. I saw the famous Stage Door Deli and decided to have a cup of coffee and soak up the atmosphere. By the time I left, the rain was coming down harder and people were rushing for cabs. I continued my walk, passing a jazz club and feeling completely whole. I was where I was supposed to be, back to the show-biz roots, here in New York where it was happening. I knew this was an isolated moment in time, but the elements all conspired to make it a peak experience. Returning to the hotel, it was difficult to get to sleep that night, and I had an interview at *Newsweek* the next morning.

Like most men in power, Osborn Elliot was a polished, personable gentleman. He looked at my writings, made some flattering comments and offered me a job on the spot. I would be a research associate, writing articles for *Newsweek* on a wide variety of subjects. There were a few little glitches. One, there would be no chance of a by-line—ever. *Newsweek* didn't reverse that policy for many years. And, two, all articles were written by committee. I would be one of seven or more who would write and rewrite each other. It was hard to imagine that working out for me. While I appreciated Elliot's generosity, and it was tempting to have such an easy alternative, it seemed like another case of selling out. It was not consistent with what I wanted. I decided to pass, even if it meant going home to L.A.

The up feelings from New York far outweighed the disappointment of not finding my ideal job. Thanksgiving dinner at Jack Dempsey's restaurant made the day special, even though I got up too late for Macy's parade. Eating alone, I looked up to see Jack himself standing there. He asked why I was by myself, and asked if he could join me for a few minutes. It made what might have been a lonely holiday a pleasant celebration.

Other highlights of that memorable trip were attending a daily service at Temple Emanu-El on Fifth Avenue, and walking from the Sheraton on 54th to Washington Square at First Street. The whole walk was just like the movies, and equally as unreal. No matter. I would be returning to reality soon enough. I went back to Boston just long enough to pack my possessions to be shipped, and boarded the plane back to Fantasyland.

It was an interesting coincidence that while I was flailing around in Boston, trying to deal with my latest identity crisis, my friend Sally had just returned from her own abortive attempt to continue her education in Wisconsin. We commiserated and worked at convincing each other that neither of us had failed. No one but Sally understood my reasons for quitting a successful job that was apparently everything anyone could want. Our mutual crises opened another era in our relationship. Though she veered dangerously toward the judgmental, Sally was usually an effective sounding board for my musings.

A poem written the day after Christmas, 1964, underscores the feeling:

This is a tale of friendship endured beyond belief;
Through letters, college, travels, misfortune, fear and grief.
In all this time and turbulence, rare moments pronounce its
    worth;
Understanding, trust and empathy provoke its glad rebirth.
Allusive wit and humor, a knowing grin or smile,
Inclusion in a closed cartel—the things that give it style.
A feeling, warm and deep accompanies the time;
Two friends, who laugh and share a relationship sublime.

In spite of all that had happened, I felt okay about myself; it was
other people I doubted. When I was very young, my father would
put me in a precarious physical position, then let me fall. He
would laugh and say, "Never trust anybody, not even your father." It would anger and hurt me because I would trust him every
time, then get hurt. My mother's messages were more subtle and
positive. She led me to believe that I was special, then would keep
me in line with her unstated expectations of conformity by com-
paring me to her friends' children. While "special" was not a word
I associated with myself, "different" was fitting. Coming from a
long history of feeling alien, I found little relief in Boston. Yet I had
never rejected success before, never been quite so definite in throwing achievement away. While there was little doubt in my mind
that my actions were appropriate, I was unsure where this trend to
live by my own rules would lead. It was a complicated sentiment to
explain to the outside world, especially my parents and their
generation who revered traditional success. They could not understand what I meant when I spoke of the hidden costs.

Having felt different, my personality took on an adversarial
nature for self-protection. This resulted in an oversimplification in
perceiving others. Authority figures were especially trying for me
because I had felt so little acceptance from them.

I took a few months out in L.A. It was necessary to have my four
impacted wisdom teeth removed, the Christmas holidays were
upon us, and I needed time to settle in. Sally was concerned that I
had been home three months and still had made little effort to find

a job. The truth was that I was mildly depressed and confused about what I wanted to do. This was a crossroads. My father offered what he could, a secretarial job at Douglas Aircraft. I suppose I could have returned to work for Bernie.

Instead, I decided to conduct a broad-based search, from a job as a deputy probation officer for the city of Los Angeles to applying as an administrative assistant at Bendix. In my heart of hearts, though, what I wanted was to be back in show biz. I applied at advertising agencies I knew to be large enough to be involved in actual television production. And I checked out the major movie studios, like MGM, Warner Bros., Columbia and 20th Century-Fox. I received a job offer from a syndicated Hollywood writer, but I couldn't see spending my time collecting dirt for someone else's column. While my application list included *Daily Variety* and the *Hollywood Reporter*, I expected them to look at my writing talent. After Boston, I didn't want to be a gofer.

Among the jobs was a position as a clerk in the sales promotion department at the local CBS affiliate, KNXT (now KCBS). Coincidentally, the station was in the same complex as Columbia Records, for whom Doris Day had spent her career recording. Also in the building was CBS Radio, where Bob Bailey had done *Yours Truly, Johnny Dollar*. I pleaded with the employment chief to give me a break. She told me she thought I was overqualified for the job, but I persuaded her. I went to work the following Monday, as a clerk for two young men in a small department. The surroundings provided the payoff.

The fantasies were developed along a double set of lines. The KNXT newsroom was just around the corner from my office, and if I could get a chance to show them I could write, and if things really went well, I might get a chance at an on-camera job. The local CBS affiliate produced no fictional programs, but I thought there was a chance I might be able to work behind the scenes. As I re-read this paragraph, I am struck by how often the word "chance" appears. Had I been as savvy as the personnel director, I might have known chance was an insufficient motivator in the long run.

I am a person with an internal locus of control, not a believer in fate. Most of the things that have happened to me have been as a result of my own efforts. Being in the right place at the right time is a matter of making good choices, choosing productive behaviors that are consistent with my long-term goals. Some feel the "good life" is composed of vacationing, being passive, resting. For me, it is fully experiencing myself, when all the parts of me come together in a single moment. With an internal focus, I feel in control of that happening. If it occurs, I can feel especially good about it since I know I am responsible. If it doesn't happen, I scan my thoughts, feelings and behavior for a clue as to what I might have done differently and how I might proceed. It is basically a philosophy of proactivity and an intolerance for passivity. While it has brought me what I wanted much of the time, the proactivity has also short-circuited me when patience might have been a wiser strategy. Both these elements were present at KNXT.

The job was strictly secretarial, with an occasional research function. Neither of my bosses seemed very ambitious; nor could they find enough work to keep themselves busy, much less their single employee. That was fine with me. I would finish my day's work by late morning, just in time to catch the taping of one of the many shows that week. Within the first week, I had befriended most of the directors at the station, who didn't seem to mind that I sat in the control booth and studied their actions. I watched the decision-making, the camera composition, and realized I was learning more than I had hoped. On other days I talked with the reporters in the newsroom. I volunteered to spend additional hours at work, typing for the newsroom director, hoping to get my writing noticed. But, as with the *Monitor*, the lack of impact soon began to elevate my resentment, so I stopped the long hours. In a conversation with anchorman Jerry Dunphy, he gave his permission for me to observe the major effort of the news team, the *Six O'Clock News*. I sat just to his left out of camera range, a good location to watch the action on the set. I already knew what happened in the control booth. It felt like an internship, where I was interacting with all my instructors on a one-to-one basis. As far as I knew, there was no one else at the station who was taking advantage of these opportunites.

I sought a way to get in on the recording sessions happening in the next building. While Doris wasn't recording anymore, I hoped one of Columbia's many stars would agree to my being there. One of my secretarial colleagues greeted me one morning with the news that Andy Williams would be recording that week. I could hardly wait. Andy was one of my all-time favorites and I had memorized all his albums. Unfortunately, he didn't sing in my key. He was the male equivalent of Eydie Gorme for me, because of the clarity of his voice and his articulation. I sensed another opportunity to learn.

He was to begin that afternoon. I finished my work early and made an excuse to leave. The producer was Bob Mersey, who I knew had worked with some top singers. I had never before been in a recording studio, but I remembered the earlier lessons on demeanor. Off-handedly, I asked Mersey if I could sit and observe. He said he had no objection but that Andy would need to give his consent. Andy arrived a few minutes later, with no entourage and no objections. He had a cold, but would try to sing anyway. I sat back and waited.

I had heard good stereo before, but I was unprepared for the intensity of good studio sound. It cut right through me. As Mersey isolated each set of instruments, I could feel its unique sound, the way it fit precisely into the whole. Little shivers went through my body. When Andy added his voice, it was transcendent. This had nothing to do with hero worship. I liked Andy, and even offered him one of my throat lozenges when he took a break. No, it was the emotion of the pure sound, of those historical fantasies coming together at the same time. It was like a replay of New York, the night I saw *Funny Girl*. I wondered if I would ever have the opportunity to sing in this context, to record. I longed to hear the sound of my own voice through this perfect sound system. Time and time again I returned to the studio, to hear whoever was there. I was in on the early Byrds sessions and a few by Robert Goulet.

The Byrds sessions were interesting to me because their producer was Terry Melcher, Doris Day's son. As I stood there asking for permission to observe, I wondered if he remembered opening the door eight years ago to that chubby little teenybopper, delivering Tootsie Rolls to his mother on her birthday. If he did, he didn't say. He knew what he was doing in the studio, though, and it was a pleasure to watch him work. I listened to how he and the other producers chose the best track, how they selected the ideal balance and level of each instrument. I watched how he interacted with his stars, encouraging them to give their best without adding to their stress. I learned the techniques of positive reinforcement, applied to temperamental people.

One of the fringe benefits at KNXT was status in the entertainment community. I sought out and was granted membership in the National Academy of Television Arts and Sciences and was able to nominate and vote for the Emmy Awards. As a member, I was invited to go to the awards ceremony, but didn't have the nerve. People were to be seated at tables of ten or more, and the mere thought of that kind of social pressure stopped me from going. Besides, none of my friends could have afforded a ticket.

While I was working at KNXT, my parents celebrated their thirtieth wedding anniversary. My present to them was to take them to a Dodgers baseball game, since both of them were baseball fans. Just before the seventh inning, I directed their attention to the giant electronic message board in left center field. I had arranged to have them congratulated by the Dodger organization. It might not have been possible if I had not been able to reach their public relations person and offer to send him tickets to a CBS show in exchange for the prominently displayed message. The sense of power was exciting and seductive.

Within four months, I was spending most of my workday outside the confines of the sales promotion office. My bosses were hardly there themselves. I was getting good feedback from both of them, but getting nowhere fast. I met with the news director, who flatly told me it would be years before women would be accepted as news personalities. Women were just coming in as associate producers (read underpaid assistants). That was my best hope, he told me. My fantasies of edging into backstage production were similarly hampered by my having the wrong genitals. Like the sports editor at the *Monitor*, these men tolerated my passively observing and admiring their work. But that's as far as they would let me go. I began to be aware of the sexism about the time I became angry about the limited future.

I decided to give it another chance. After all, it had been only six months. Achievement wouldn't always come easily. Just as I was settling in for the long haul, a job opened up in the promotions department, as a community relations writer. It was a perfect fit. With my experience, my degree and training in journalism, political science and theater, and my understanding of the workings of the station, how could they choose someone else? I made up a résumé with some of the increasing extra time I had, and submitted it to the reclusive director of promotions. Without so much as the courtesy of a conversation with me, he hired one of his wife's (male) relatives. When I learned that the relative lacked even a degree, I was furious. I prepared a document accusing him of violating Title VII of the 1964 Civil Rights Act, the section that focuses on sex discrimination. In a side-by-side comparison, I listed my qualifications and those of his relative. Copies went all the way up to Robert D. Wood, the station manager.

That got action. Within the hour, the promotions director called me into his office and told me he would give me the opportunity to resign. Again, he refused to consider any of the issues. In an instant, I made my choice. Yes, I would resign, and asked for a month's severance pay. During the time I had been preparing the document, I had confided in my friends around the station, who were supportive of my complaints, especially the women. In the aftermath of my leaving, several of them quit in protest with me. It was a glorious if brief fight, and one that mobilized the forces of the whole station.

It was too reminiscent of the *Monitor*, though, and happened too soon after that enervating battle. I began to wonder what I was doing here. Where would I have to compromise, just to live an internally peaceful life? Was there any place where a woman, and an assertive woman at that, could be comfortable and valued? I was getting tired of playing Don Quixote. While I was obviously threatening major institutions, all I was doing was protecting my personal integrity the way I knew how. I had nothing external to show for my efforts. I was again out of a job.

A pattern was emerging about which I felt ambivalent. I had terminated opportunities in order to preserve my own sense of myself. Lou Greenspan's amorous advances, conflict at the *Monitor*, and now KNXT. Was I being impulsive or decisive? In my self-development, it occurred to me that I might be too protective of this new identity, too threatened by anonymity. After all, lots of people never get what they want, never even have their name appear in a newspaper other than for marker events—birth, marriage, death. Did I really need to preserve my sexual integrity to be me? Why couldn't I conform to religious and social expectations without losing my personhood? There was a feeling of congruence about those decisions, though there was not a strong theoretical base for them as yet. I was well aware that others might choose a different path. While that knowledge weighed heavily on me, it seemed confirming as well.

It is typical of an adolescent to reject conventional values in the search of an individual identity. If it gets out of hand it can be nihilistic. I was afraid that was what I was doing, rejecting others' beliefs to establish my own. Later I saw that my belief came first. Making strong statements could be proactive as well as reactive.

There is an interesting addendum to the KNXT episode. Just before I handed in my letter of complaint, I was offered a job within the station as an associate producer of *Scholarquiz*, the local version of the long-running *GE College Bowl*. I was tempted, but the producer told me there would be no screen credit and no raise. I would still be making $90 a week. Another shlepper deal. No thanks. The producer was Arnold Shapiro, who later produced award-winning documentaries and went on to form his own production company. Sometimes I wonder what would have happened, had I deferred my identity crisis and taken that job. Patience was not its own reward for me in my early twenties.

SEVEN

Politics And Romance

A combination of events bolstered my confidence in my ability to think. My relationship with Sally helped. She found it hard to understand or accept my attachment to show biz when she thought I had an ability to conceptualize and master cognitive material. Her support helped maintain a commitment to my education. And it was our talks which led to my signing up, during my stay at KNXT, for a night course at UCLA in Western European governments. I was beginning to face the possibility that I might be a perpetual student, an inveterate learner.

When things started falling apart for me on the job, I considered going to graduate school. When in Boston, I had taken the Graduate Records Exam in the hopes of going to graduate school in political science. My background was not stellar, though I had completed the double political science/journalism major at Berkeley. Once before, I had applied and been accepted into the journalism graduate program at UCLA, but had chosen Boston instead. The three themes were whirling around in my brain: journalism, show biz or political science. Here it was, a year after I graduated with those three majors, and I still had not made a lasting commitment to any of them. Boston killed journalism for me, KNXT showed me the realities of women in media administration, but I had not yet tested the waters of political science. I took a calculated risk and applied to the master's degree program in political science at San Fernando Valley State College. I was all set to begin another massive job hunt when the letter of acceptance arrived in the mail.

From September 1965 to July 1966, my life was highly structured. My parents agreed to lend me the money so, for the first time since I was fifteen, I would not have to work. With my 2.9 undergraduate grade point average, I had not been the most accomplished student at Berkeley. Thus, I thought that to achieve in graduate school, I would have to give it every available moment. I signed up for the maximum number of hours and settled in for the self-imposed exile. SFVSC did not require a master's thesis, which was disappointing; if there was anything I could count on, it was my ability to write. Instead, I took courses in every branch of political science: political theory, American politics, international relations, comparative government and constitutional law. It was exhilarating, a time when I found I could also rely on my brain.

While at Valley State, I found another female role model, the first since high school. Caroline Dinegar specialized in international relations. She was lucid and inspiring, always using opportunities to relate to her students. I watched her for a time before approaching her. When I did, it was under the safe cover of having achieved the highest grades in her class. Toward the end of my studies, I needed to prepare for the comprehensive exams, three hours each, in three areas of my own choosing. One of them would obviously be international relations. Dr. Dinegar offered to tutor me in a weekly independent study session and gave me a long list of books. I spent about seven hours each day, reading and taking extensive notes. Later, when I taught political science at that same college, those notes were invaluable in lecture preparation. At our weekly meetings, she would challenge me, asking me to work through the issues. A partisan of the United Nations, she nonetheless engaged me in debating the value of the U.N. Should Red China be admitted? Should there be a majority rule in the Security Council instead of one nation having the power to veto any resolution? We probed the issues in Hans Morgenthau's *Politics of Nations* and posed alternatives to Herman Kahn's thesis in *On Thermonuclear War*. I began to feel almost intellectual.

My second area of expertise was constitutional law, which was a complete head trip. Based on the opinions of nine old men, and sometimes legal precedent, con law was fascinating. I was especially interested in what my con law prof called the "gastrointestinal influence"—decisions affected by whether a justice was getting along with his spouse or whether his prostate was bothering him. In reading the cases, I was filled with their inherent theatricality. I began to read biographies of the great jurists, imagining lengthy screenplays.

American political institutions was the third area and offered the opportunity to do the writing I longed to do. Paul Hoffman was the chairman of the department, a portly, giving man who had made my coming to Valley State possible. His seminar in the American political process required a term paper. It was an opening to combine politics and show biz. I knew from my personal experience that I might maintain a commitment to political science if I could somehow integrate my passion.

The previous year had witnessed a senatorial election in California, pitting Pierre Salinger, who had been John F. Kennedy's press secretary, against ex-movie star George Murphy. An analysis of how Murphy got elected took up almost 80 pages. While I was unable to arrange a meeting with Murphy himself, I spoke with several of his workers. Most intriguing was a meeting with Robert Finch, Murphy's campaign chief. Finch had been associated with Richard M. Nixon, and was later his secretary of Health, Education and Welfare. Finch agreed to meet with me for a thirty-minute interview in an old downtown L.A. office building. When I was ushered into his office, I was unprepared for the seediness of the surroundings, the musty smell and the soiled drapes. Finch was quite formal, volunteering only short answers to my prepared questions. Though the environment was disenchanting, I was in the presence of big-time politics.

The title of my lengthy paper was "The Role of Personality, Occupation and Media Exposure in the Election of George Murphy to the United States Senate." I scoured two years of *T.V. Guide* listings to cull out the Murphy movies that were playing on television before, during and after his election. To prove that his "good guy" image may have played a part in his being elected, I also considered the content of the films. It was a joyful combination of show biz and politics. Of course, I sent a copy to Senator Murphy (probably still hoping to be discovered, this time as a political scientist), but he never acknowledged it.

The six years between the completion of my political science master's degree and the finishing of my doctorate in clinical psychology represented a time of intellectual achievement and personal growth. Show biz remained in the background. I continued to sing with my records and play the trumpet to jazz records. These were my primary means of stress reduction. When I was teaching, I often integrated show-biz examples into both the political and psychological discussions. It was an area familiar to many of my students, and equally as fascinating for them.

Finishing the master's degree, I needed to make another decision: go on to a Ph.D. in political science (which is what my major professors were encouraging me to do), go to law school, or go into the Peace Corps. Though I had been too young to vote in the presidential election of 1960, I had been captivated by the spirit of Kennedy's "ask not" speech. I was ready to do something for my country. I sent away for materials on the Peace Corps and decided to apply for a program in Latin America. I would have a leg up on the language, with my four years of college Spanish. The thought of training in a distant state was appealing, too.

When the acceptance letter came, I was excited and scared. Then I saw where we would be training: UCLA, twenty minutes from home. So much for adventure. The training itself was also disappointing, and I felt uncomfortable with the unrelenting pressures of togetherness. There was not a time day or night when I was alone. Halfway through the training, we were to be shipped off to a more rustic setting for more training. It turned out to be the Presbyterian Conference Grounds in Pacific Palisades! Next, it seemed, they would be camping in my living room.

I looked forward to the end of training, when I was scheduled to teach political science in Spanish at the University of Panama. One afternoon we were asked to make lists of whom we would or wouldn't want to share a residence. It was an example of the peer ratings advocated by the Peace Corps. They hoped trainees would select themselves out, rather than be rejected by the Corps. To my chagrin, I appeared on no one's list. In the tight crowd of seventy-five trainees, I was invisible. In my attempt to gain alone time, I had retreated from the group quite effectively.

I had learned to disappear into myself under stress. There was a positive aspect to this. I became aware of the value of the internal as a source of stability, an ongoing and predictable base. A few months into the training, "La Culpa" fell onto a page:

> One cannot blame the universe or mankind or a god
> For what seems to be
> The reality is what we see
>
> One cannot blame the tides, the weather, the stars
> For misfortune, failure, disenchantment
> The sorrow is in the heart
>
> One cannot blame a wandering, legendary spirit
> For desolation, isolation, violation
> The vacuum is created by self

A few days later, Panama had a minor revolution and the Peace Corps was temporarily evicted from the country. I was offered a transfer to a new training program for Africa. It was an opportune face-saving way to get out and figure out what had happened to me.

After the abortive fling with the Peace Corps, I went into therapy for nine months, beginning in January 1967. The Field Assessment Officer who ran all the psychological testing was a psychologist in private practice in West Los Angeles. I liked her directness and her sense of humor; I sought her out as a shrink. Among the other issues, show biz was there, too. Though the therapy was helpful in clarifying my fears and anxieties, it had little or no impact on the fantasies.

Psychotherapy was a strange and frightening process. Ricky, the therapist, reminded me of Sally, who had exercised her judgmentalness at unexpected moments to keep me off balance. I had no sense of the process as a whole and felt out of control. As a consequence, I knew every restroom in every gas station from my house to Ricky's office. In time I learned what to expect and began to fantasize about Ricky, who had readily supplied information about herself. I wondered what kind of music she liked, what her friends were like, what kind of house she lived in, who she was. Anxiety would flood as I imagined running into her outside the therapy room. For a time, my problems took second place as I became preoccupied with Ricky:

Everywhere I look you are there
In the room
In the street
In the car

And I am what you want me to be
Self-assured
Sensitive
Loving

If you were in my view, I would be
Self-conscious
Anxious
Disabled

In this process of transference I feel
Confused
Deprived
Imprisoned

I suspect Ricky misinterpreted my lack of problem-riddled conversation. I was pleased to see her each time and wanted her approval; thus, I would discuss all the good events and feelings. One of the major issues for me was being a wife versus being a career person. How could I do both? Ricky convinced me it was possible, and I did feel better about it. Then, toward the end of one session, Ricky told me she thought I was close to being through with therapy. I had mixed feelings. Still caught up in my fantasies about her, I wasn't ready to let this important person leave my life. Then came the crunching blow. She was getting married and leaving her profession. I was overcome with feelings, but our time was up. We would have one more session, to wrap things up.

By now I had done some reading in psychology, and was relieved to find there was a word to describe my feelings: transference. It was a common phenomenon and to be expected in intense psychotherapy. I felt betrayed by her decision, confused by the apparent double message, abandoned by my friend, disappointed by her ineptness at dealing with my transference, and angry at the whole situation. Still in transference, though, I was unable to share any of my negative reactions. At that last session, I wished her well, summarized my progress as a dutiful client, and left. It would be a year before I could resolve the confusing feelings on my own.

Since I was unable to teach political science in the Peace Corps, perhaps teaching would be possible some other way. I wrote to Paul Hoffman at Valley State and requested an audience. He had been complimentary about my paper on George Murphy and encouraged me to get a Ph.D. At our meeting, he offered me a job, teaching a course in American political institutions one night a week. By the fall of 1967 I was teaching full time, four courses a semester. I toyed with the idea of a Ph.D. in political science (maybe in constitutional law), or perhaps going to law school after all. But the readings I had done in psychology as a way to understand my therapeutic experience pulled me in a different direction.

As a direct result of psychotherapy, I considered becoming a clinical psychologist. I hadn't even known such an option existed until I was in the middle of the process. It would allow me to combine my intellect, creativity and intensity, while working with others.

I began to take courses in psychology at UCLA on the days I wasn't teaching political science at Valley State. It was a peculiar split, demanding and challenging. It was also a commuter lifestyle, in which I touched people's lives only tangentially.

Personally, I was developing a value system that I was eager to share. The Los Angeles of the late 1960s seemed filled with shallowness, unaware of the demands of intimacy. My search for a soul mate was frustrating, as documented in "Betrayal":

The feeling between two people when right cannot be wrong.
But when that bond's betrayed, my youth does not belong.

Betrayal can be imagined, it need not be for real;
The hurt goes just as deep, the breach will never heal.

The knowledge comes but slowly, irrevocable and clear
And childlike trust is doomed again, once love grows into fear.

Life as a teacher at Valley State enabled me to function as a counselor during the early Vietnam protest years. Many of the students were politically disaffected, and demonstrations were rampant.

As a political science professor supportive of the antiwar position, I was in the thick of things. One day when I came to school, I was walking toward the eight-story building that contained my office when I noticed much of the top floor had been burned out by demonstrators. Robert Kennedy was due to make an appearance later that week, so security was beefed up after the fire. The power of the political experience in the late 1960s and my gradual immersion in psychology allowed me to temporarily submerge the show-biz passion. I felt safe in the ivory tower and stimulated by the ideological battles going on around me. I must confess I enjoyed talking with some of the Hollywood celebrities who graced Valley State at the time, many of whom were in my classes. It was also during this time that I met Leo Munter, a student in my introductory political science course.

My classes were popular and there was always a waiting list to get in. Leo sauntered in the first day and asked to be put on the waiting list (along with thirty or so others). He wore scraggly clothes and carried incense but he had the most sincere eyes I had ever seen. When he began his sob story, I told him not to bother, that I had heard all the possible repertoire of reasons to be admitted. In a split second, he fell to his knees in front of the class and began pleading his case. I was disarmed by this histrionic approach, and said if he wanted in that badly, I would let him in. By this time, all of us were laughing at this uninhibited hippie. Immediately, all thirty students also on the waiting list fell to their knees. Of course, I had to let them all in, and continued to step over their bodies every day before lecturing.

The years of teaching were a good surrogate for show biz. I had followers and fans, just as though I were an entertainer. I could use snappy remarks, comments and even impressions to make a point. When lecturing about actors as politicians, I would do a takeoff of Shirley Temple doing "On the Good Ship Lollipop." I loved every minute of it. This was still the era of formality on campus, where professors were called by their last name. I delighted in being the exception.

In the meantime, I was being rushed by Leo. He would visit me during my office hours and leave notes under my door. Returning from spring vacation, I found flowers and a poem on my doorstep. Though he was a student and I his teacher, there was only a three-year difference in age. There seemed to be a generation between us. While I was riding the fringes of the establishment as a mini-skirted radical, Leo was a hippie freak, knee-deep in the rock-and-roll drug culture beginning to emerge in 1968. He surrounded himself with loud acid rock, and was conversant with the latest jargon. Friends were fellow pot-smokers in the days when associates were chosen by whether or not they used drugs. I was fascinated by this alien being, so chameleon-like. He prided himself on fitting in anywhere. When we would talk, he would become androgynous, tender and thoughtful. Poems and flowers became *de rigueur*.

Within two months we were discussing living together. This was in the early years of its moral acceptability and was certainly risky professionally, since he was still in my class. Our relationship was a logical extension of our mutual growth. He was terminally adolescent and began to take more responsibility. I was still sexually naive and needed to broaden my perspectives.

I wrote him poetry, emphasizing the values of openness, honesty and mutual trust. We seemed to share those values, though I came to question that later. Because he came out of a divorced home, he was determined to work on our relationship. Though we were trying to build a bond, the relationship was punctuated by violent battles. The topic was almost always drugs or rock music. He promised to refrain from smoking dope, then I would discover he was lying. He had no problem with ripping off other people and I was finding some major gaps in his empathy with me. I would confront him and he would calmly defend his behavior. He never became directly angry but would continue on a passive-aggressive level. It enraged me. In the year and a half we lived together, I threw a wine glass, a shoe and a vase full of flowers—all at the wall—to underscore my anger. My own potential for this kind of acting-out astonished me. I had never before experienced this level of anger. Eventually he would again promise compliance with the ground rules, write poetry, or put together a tape of romantic songs. I would capitulate, hoping for change.

We were living together in my one-bedroom apartment in Sepulveda when the California primary took place in June 1968. As a political science professor, I was living the stuff I was teaching and active in my support of Robert Kennedy's candidacy for president. Leo and I were lying in bed around midnight, watching the returns, when Kennedy was shot in the kitchen of the Ambassador Hotel. The violence was hard to comprehend, much more so than JFK's assassination. While I had supported JFK, the tie was more personal with Bobby. I cancelled my classes the next day, walking around in a daze. I went through the same process of grieving as if he had been a friend: denial, depression, anger and

Nana and her boys with Dad standing behind her. The two daughters are conspicuously absent.

Mom and Dad in 1935, the year they were married. Dad and car are at their dashing best.

Pam and Mom in front of the house in the Palisades, all smiles!

Intense concentration, trying to master the organ that once made me cry.

Pam, John and Nana. Quick! Take the picture!

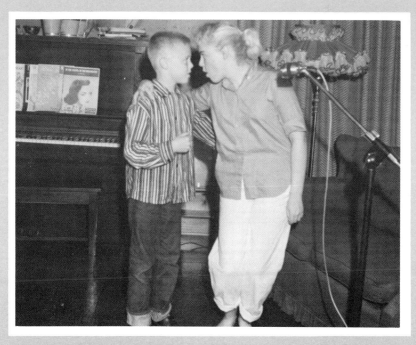

John and Pam in record pantomime to "Mutual Admiration Society."
Performing at every opportunity.

Pam in high school, worshipping at the "Doris Day Memorial Wall."

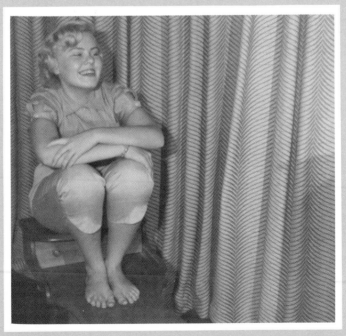

Embarrassing promo shot done at Ida Lupino's suggestion. Another blown opportunity!

Pam in 1959 original production of "Like Wow!" "My Heart Belongs to Daddy" had a Joan Davis ending.

Show biz and political books illustrate schism: feminism vs. the coquettish Doris Day lookalike.

Pam and Leo in 1974 on a nostalgia-themed Caribbean cruise where Pam first heard "Nobody Does It Like Me."

Leo trying to tease Aaron out of his skepticism. Aaron was around nine months old.

The official "happy family portrait," including Leonard, who was like our first-born son.

Pam playing it cool at the Johnny Mercer Studio in Hollywood.

Promotional photo for benefit at Jazz Quarry in 1980.
Eye problems necessitated glasses for two years.

Aaron has his father's expressive eyes and
my show-biz instincts—a special person.

eventually, acceptance. Others could transfer their loyalties to Gene McCarthy; my zest for politics was gone.

Eleven months later, my father died. Leo and I were talking in the bedroom when the phone rang. My heart jumped as he went to answer. There was a premonition that his father had died suddenly of a heart attack. When Leo came back to tell me it was my father who had died, I was stunned, more by the premonition than by the death. Dad had been out driving with a female friend in Topanga Canyon. Apparently he died immediately. Questions about the nature of the relationship with the woman remained unanswered.

So much went through my mind as we made the half-hour drive to the Palisades. I recalled the early years of fun and collaboration. Pictures came back of Dad reading me the comics, exciting trips to Gilmore Field and MacArthur Park to ride the boats, Dad playing catch with me in the back yard, vacations in the sun at the Douglas Ranch. His conversations with me were almost a litany, even in my adulthood. Did I brush my teeth? Did I have a bowel movement today? He would pay me a dollar a pound to lose weight, at the same time my mother was rewarding me with my favorite kind of cookies and ice cream. Had I finished my chores? I remembered angry scenes with him, frequently at the dinner table. So unpleasant were they that when I was twelve, I stopped eating dinner with him. I put my food on a TV tray and took it into my own room, thereby establishing a precedent for the whole family. The only time we ate together was when we ate out.

Dad liked to think of himself as a cross between the casualness of a Bing Crosby and the self-conscious masculinity of Clark Gable. He worked well with his hands, but he had the soul of an Archie Bunker. I tried many times to talk with him, especially as I moved toward my adult years. I wanted to get to know him, but he wouldn't let me in. He simply would not disclose himself. As I drove to the Palisades that afternoon, my sense was that the machine just stopped. He had gone through the motions of parenthood, but we never got to know each other. I felt a wistfulness for what might have been, had he been different or had I been more skilled at getting in.

By the time I got home, the house was filled with grieving, well-meaning friends. My brother had been called in Fresno (where he was going to college) and was told Dad was dying—a typical Osborne euphemism. My job was to pick him up at the airport and inform him our father was dead. I dreaded telling him because I sensed he had shared a close relationship with Dad. When I told him, there was little response. There was no display of emotion at all. The torch had been passed.

In middle-class America, a man's worth is ultimately determined by the numbers who show up for his funeral. If this be the case, Dad was a champ. At home, he was aloof, judgmental and angry, but at work he was a *bon vivant*. Everyone liked him, joked with him. Many told me how he had bragged about me, though he seldom doled out positive words to me. In one of our last conversations, in fact, he scoffed at the fact I was counseling others in marital therapy. Just before I left to go away to Berkeley, Mom had confided in me about his extramarital affairs. I knew they had problems in their marriage, but his criticalness hurt all the same. My reaction to his death was tempered by these moments and my resignation about our relationship.

In the fall of 1968, I began having intense headaches, which I attributed to my Superwoman Syndrome. I was teaching political science at Valley State while beginning the graduate program in psychology at Cal State and maintaining the intensity with Leo. In this context, psychogenic symptoms were not surprising. When I started feeling dizzy and faint, both Leo and a woman friend persuaded me to check into Santa Monica Hospital for tests.

The neurologists suspected a brain tumor, so the diagnostic tests were especially thorough. I took the news without astonishment and began to plan my remaining time. I continued to tape lectures, which Leo took to classes and played. There was a calm acceptance, almost a relief.

The physicians scheduled a pneumoencephalogram, in which air would be injected into my brain via my spinal column. It sounds primitive now, but it was state-of-the-art then. For the next six days, any change from a flat position resulted in a crashing headache. The diagnosis: a low-grade encephalitis, a brain virus. I was given a prescription for Dilantin and sent home. Within a few weeks, I felt fine again and discontinued the medication. I had been given a reprieve.

The relationship with Leo continued in all its volatility. I was impatient with myself for demanding a relationship of emotional substance. Certainly I had never seen any models approximating what I wanted. I blamed myself, as I did at Cal, for my ideological rigidity. During one breach, I wrote

My memory is sharp and clear
Alone but strong I was.
Since you came here, almost one year,
The old me gives me pause.

Now you've gone, how can I be glad
When it was the old me
Who could not take and bend with fad
I never changed, how could we?

But as I became more flexible, I lost sight of any foundation. It seemed Leo's view was "If it feels good, do it," which was too unstructured for my comfort. Confusion is evident in a poem written early in 1969:

Shoot me down
Shoot me down
Stand on shore and watch me drown

Do not aim
Do not aim
Shoot your gun and play the game

If you miss
If you miss
Try once more and blow a kiss

Me offguard
Me offguard
Close your eyes and thrust the sword

Watch me cry
Watch me cry
Then turn away don't watch me die

I realized the reciprocal failures and vainly tried to contain and explain.

You frighten me
I threaten you
So many things we cannot share
Due to mutual fears
Thus love is not enough
If we cannot get close enough to share it

Then, with much sadness, we agreed to live apart. I went into mourning, becoming tearful at the slightest provocation. I was preoccupied with the hope we could make it work. For me, he was everywhere.

Extinguishing old habits
That is the hardest to do
Whenever there's a creak in the night
I know it must be you

A car outside squeals its tires
Like yours used to do
I jump to my feet, my blood flows fast
I know it must be you

Meanwhile, Leo was reactivating his social life. With the resumption of his old behaviors, I slowly abandoned hope. We had discussed having a child, to be named after his father, and strangely, that became the focus of my loss:

The Decision
6/20/69

There will never be a Willie
There will be no married life
He'll never be a father
I'll never be his wife

He'll never find his mate ideal
He'll go through life alone
He'll freak and hope it's all unreal
A lifetime he'll atone

EIGHT

The Andy Hardy Years

As I worked toward my educational goals in psychology, I realized I would have to leave the Los Angeles area to finish. To achieve full independence in private practice, I would have to earn a doctorate. Because I lacked a complete undergraduate major in psychology, I needed to finish a master's degree in clinical psychology first. This was possible at California State University at Los Angeles, commuting 130 miles a day. Given this educational pastiche, there were only certain schools that might accept a student with such motley credentials. Eventually the University of Nebraska accepted me and I, it. It was a convenient time to end my relationship with Leo and return to a stable lifestyle.

My fear was that I was making the traditional mutually-exclusive choice of a career over a marriage. My poetry took on a cynical note:

And when he takes his leave
Just who will fill the void?
Where'll you go for comfort?
To Rogers or to Freud?

As I packed for the Nebraska move, the cynicism was tempered by the hope that he was changing. Knowing of his interest in replacing me immediately, however, I knew I had to leave soon:

I know he'll find another, but much to his surprise

A time will soon uncover, another compromise
He'll think her pure and gleaming, he's finally found his niche
But there's no scheming, dreaming, she's just another bitch.

Then he'll know there's none as good, and he'll cry with soul
That I was misunderstood; could I fill his goal?
Would I be the one to bring him love and will
Would I make him want to sing, say, "I love you still"

On my own those last few weeks, I wrote extensively, since
there was no one with whom I could share the intense pain. A
portent of the Peter Pan Syndrome is seen in "His World":

He is Dylan, the Doors and Fugs
His friends are all on drugs
These objects of his veneration
Bespeak of his degeneration

If he could have his choice
Mick Jagger would be his voice
He'd blow pot with the Stones
Join Hendrix when he drones

He'd freak out with the best
Forsaking all the rest
To spout rock is his goal
And match the Beatles soul for soul

The friends he meets today
Collect along the way
They want to know not him
What's real is Janis Joplin

With frantic effort he'll try
To keep today alive
Increasing time he'll take
In losing self he'll break

And when his youth is spent

Who will pay the rent
Old and lost and grey
Victim of his own heyday

But he wanted so much now
It didn't matter how
There was no time to save
Alone he'll meet the grave

It was over. So if I couldn't make it work, I needed to focus on the next era: life on the plains of mid-America.

After the small-town culture shock wore off, I found I loved Nebraska, feeling a similar kinship I had felt to New England. I spent weekends driving all over, shooting photographs that would capture the rural openness. I had the sense I was living on an MGM sound stage and an Andy Hardy movie was in production. People were clean-cut and straight, uncomplicated and honest. Nobody ever asked me for my driver's license when I cashed a check at the Hinky Dinky market. Though it was a totally new environment to me, I felt strangely at peace. The psychology department was something else.

Though I was a good student, my assertive, driving personality was at odds with the sexist, traditional mold. I pushed to be able to teach my first year, and that was unprecedented. I thought my two and a half years of experience teaching at Valley State would be of value and would ease my transition into the subservient role assigned to graduate students. My request resulted in major personality clashes with one of the professors. And it didn't help when I was voted the most popular teacher in the department by the students when the end-of-semester ratings came in. I was invited to be guest of honor at a sorority house, as their favorite teacher.

Leaving Leo behind in California didn't stop the grieving. If anything, it was exacerbated by the isolation and loneliness that was engulfing me daily. Nights were a microcosm of my own darkness:

It's getting late

Yet I cannot bear
To enter the cold world
Of darkness

In the light
It's less of a strain
To deceive the desolation
Of darkness

The death of soul
Each night by twelve
The self itself a victim
Of darkness

The contrast between my ideals and the reality again came
crashing down. I couldn't accept that I might have chosen
aloneness. The fantasies took off in prolific poetry. By October, I
was writing about death and futility. One poem, though, contains
the resilience and a familiar opening line:

My memory is sharp and clear
About the way it never was
The beauty, innocence of youth
The family, real, a cause

How school was fun and teachers cared
And students formed a group
Together they could learn anew
What it meant to be true

And friendship was forever dear
A need fulfilled by love and trust
Awakened by a sense of one
Unblemished by all selfish thrust

Then I found my love, my soul
And holding hands we galloped free

Of lonely, sad, depressing times
I worshipped him, he cherished me

Life was joy, exuberance
With challenges unceasing
Yet with my family life so rich
The love ne'er stopped increasing

Within a few weeks, the grief changed to anger and renewed strength:

Hark! World, mourn the death of me
I had so much to give, you see
Our rendezvous was ceased by life
All those years of woe and strife

One more thing, cruel world
Resting there with truths unfurled
My life was sapped by bargain
And we will never meet again

The anger was sustaining, enabling an internal consolidation. My sense of humor came back and once again I could laugh at my own intensity:

The respite is sweet
Long-awaited and dear
And I watch the sky
Inspiring and clear

But as I viewed the warming scene
Relaxed, relieved of strife
I fell into a gaping hole
A victim of real life

During that first semester, three of us in the program were invited to a faculty-student gathering, with our spouses. I was the only single person there, and only one of three single people in the whole psychology program. Nervously, I accepted the invitation, knowing it was a command performance. I was never good at small talk, but I hoped the hosts would feel it was their responsibility to keep the conversation going. One of the other guests was the other female in the program, Rosemarie, with whom I was beginning to develop a rapport. We snickered at the dinner fare, sloppy joes on a bun and potato chips. During dinner, I tried to make small talk with the woman next to me, the wife of the social psychologist on the faculty. I was about to admire the pin on her dress, when it started to lurch. My eyes were glued to its movements, as I feigned interest in what she was saying. Finally, I had to ask. She said it was a Mexican spider she had purchased on a recent vacation. It was on a little chain and would wander all over the left side of her dress. I tried to signal Rosemarie from across the table, and worked to maintain composure for the rest of the meal.

After dinner, we were introduced to the entertainment portion of the evening: ping pong in the basement. The room itself was only about six feet bigger than the table, which made for an intimate grandstand. It was quaint, to say the least. The evening was indicative of the provincialism all around.

Political activism had reached even Nebraska by the late 1960s. Though I remained aloof from conventional politics, strong anti-Vietnam feelings ran deep. The feminist movement was catching fire and gaining momentum. More than once, Rosemarie and I marched to the Capitol supporting a woman's right to choose what happens to her body, or decrying U.S. involvement in Southeast Asia. But the study demands of graduate school precluded any real commitment.

A combination of the emotional adversity, the loneliness and isolation eventuated in my re-contacting Leo toward the end of my first semester. The relationship was the lessor of stressors. He had just returned from a disastrous cross-country motoring trip, on which he totaled his car in Pennsylvania. His father sent money for him to return to Los Angeles. We were in mutual need. I missed his support and began writing and calling almost daily.

Though I had hoped the months away had made a difference, I was afraid of being sucked in again. The strong approach-avoidance conflict showed itself in a December 1969 poem:

It is unfair to love him
He cannot be mine
I must let him go
Another I'll find

Inside I know
We will not share
A mutual fantasy
Without tension or flare

But I cannot leave him
Nor let him depart
We're caught in a bind
Doomed from the start

Two months later, I still vacillated between the hopes of reconciliation and the nagging reservations. Leo was in Los Angeles still looking for a job. While I plowed through the Nebraska winter, we corresponded daily and sent tapes weekly. As we approached the second anniversary of our meeting at Valley State, another poem came forth, which I never sent to him:

Contemplating these two years
I was writing festive verse
Telling you of our strong bond
But feeling the reverse

The bond was just restraint of words
Of hopeless lies and plans
The double standard flying high
Structuring your demands

After bitter words and phrases
Intolerance, disdain

The years of broken promises—
I could not stand the pain

And when we spoke from distance far
I could not find your love
With your love so like John Wayne
But softer than a glove

'Twas then I knew it had to end
I sounded very brave
The affect was unusually like
Placing flowers on your grave

Again, I began writing poetry with death themes, feeling hopeless and under continuing pressure in graduate school. In the
anonymity of school, I questioned who really knew me and extended the doubt to Leo. His desire to see me, to put energy into
me was appealing and engaging. When we were on target with
each other, it was magnificent, and totally consuming.

By the spring, I was feeling more positive. Even the poetry was
optimistic for a change:

Don't know what to say
Since my emotions are wordless,
Potent, transcending communication
And all that comes out is "I love you"

The warmth wells up inside
Threatening to burst forth now
A garden of effusive turbulence
Yet all that comes out is "I love you"

I feel your strength, assurance
Engulfing me from miles away
Unspeakable joy in discovered structure
How inadequate to say "I love you"

By the end of that first year, we had decided to risk pursuing the relationship in earnest. The daily communication gave the appearance of depth and substance. His willingness to explore his own issues was the reassurance I needed, the final link in forging the bond.

The wedding was scheduled for August 1970, just before I was to return for my second year. We had gone to dinner in Los Angeles and he had taken me to see a production of *Promises, Promises*, a prophetic title. He formally proposed with his usual romantic flair, on the California beach in the moonlight. When he asked, I carved out "Yes" in the sand with my foot. Then the psychosomatic symptoms began. Though my head and heart had said "Yes," my body was obnoxiously assertive in disagreement.

During the two months between the beach scene and the wedding, I was on Tofranil and Kaopectate. When nausea and diarrhea were under control, I was making decisions about hors d'oeuvres and color schemes. To justify my being in Los Angeles during the summer, I had petitioned the psychology department for twelve credit hours in absentia, establishing another precedent. I was working three days a week at the Sepulveda Veterans Administration Hospital and doing research at the UCLA library.

One evening that summer, we went to see the film *Funny Girl*, the play that had made such an impact on me in New York. I loved the movie and was surprised at Leo's depressed mood as we left the theater. After coaxing, he admitted he was afraid it was a portent for our marriage, that he would be "Mr. Pam Munter." There was little I could do to disabuse him of that premonition, considering how new we were to forging a true equality. From the moment of our meeting, he had been the student, and I the established adult. His sensitivity to that issue led to my decision to take his name, rather than keep my own. He was pleased and it wasn't important enough to me to stage what would have been a nasty confrontation.

At the elaborate Jewish wedding, I was surrounded by my friends and relatives. Two close friends had confided to me that they were worried about me and baffled by my choice of partner.

Pictures taken on that day are filled with nervous smiles and the omnipresent bottle of Kaopectate. The ceremony was beautiful, my three attendants in yellow and orange, a vast display of flowers donated by Leo's uncle. My brother gave me away, which was emotionally evocative because of our renewed closeness. As I stood at the top of the aisle, I heard the final strains of "If Ever I Would Leave You," and laughed hallowly at the prophetic message. I realized then how out of it I had been, to have ignored choosing my own music for this important occasion. There was a rush of anxiety as I flashed on what else I may have overlooked.

Two days later we packed a 22-foot Hertz truck, trailing my Volkswagen, and left for Nebraska. It didn't help that we had to yell at each other over the engine noise, or that my Kaopectate's effectiveness abated halfway there. Leo took it all with his usual aplomb.

The marriage helped my flagging self-esteem, and I was able to finish the Ph.D. in two and a half years, three years ahead of the next psychology student to be granted the degree. It was simply a matter of aversive conditioning: it felt so good when I stopped.

Leo found a position with the Neighborhood Youth Corps, his first real job. I worried about his exposure to all those young girls, as I knew we did not agree on the fidelity issue. He was susceptible to others' admiration, and he was in a position to take advantage. We continued to argue, but with no resolution. I was constantly uncertain, though he was telling me I had no cause.

Surviving graduate school was a result of my motivation and intensity. I had a vivid picture of the lifestyle of professional and personal freedom, in which I did not have to kowtow to anyone. I had had enough of that in my show-biz quest. Success in clinical psychology was totally up to me, and I relished that responsibility. After show biz, I believed psychology was the primary vehicle to a good life. The struggle was so turbulent that the actual receipt of the Ph.D. was anticlimactic. I didn't even attend the ceremony.

After an internship in Wisconsin, I accepted a position at Portland State University in Oregon. We wanted to return to the West Coast and I wasn't prepared for the seduction of Los Angeles.

In 1973, while in Wisconsin, we had decided to get pregnant
with what was to be our only child. I didn't care about the sex of
the child and was pleased when it turned out to be Aaron. He was
one month premature, delivered by Caesarean section. Moist
Lung Syndrome kept him in an incubator for eight days, and I
wasn't in good shape either. In the fourth month of pregnancy, the
physician had diagnosed a uterine tumor which had to be removed
immediately. Thus, the C section was the second major surgery
within five months. A tubal ligation was performed, since another
pregnancy might have been fatal. Fortunately, I had a good friend,
another psychologist, who provided essential emotional support.
More and more I counted on Leo less and less. It was times like
these, though, that strengthened my relationship with myself. I
was the only one I could count on; it was somehow all right.
Within two weeks of Aaron's birth we were all off to Portland to
report for duty.

While the marriage itself was not emotionally satisfying, my life
had settled into a prototypical Superwoman role by 1976. Essentially, I held down two full-time jobs, as an assistant (and then
associate) professor of psychology at Portland State University
and in private practice as a clinical psychologist. I was often
working evenings and weekends, and Leo would bring Aaron to
the office to visit during the day. It was a tough grind.

Upon our arrival in Oregon, Leo had been unsuccessful in his
job search. After a few months, we agreed he would be a house-
husband and raise Aaron while I worked. While we had some
disagreements about what constituted his role, it worked out fairly
well. We would laugh together when he would get caught up in
indecision as to which market he would patronize, or what he
would cook for dinner. When he decided to go for a master's
degree in social work, we adjusted.

In spite of the crowded schedule, I decided I wanted to go
through the process of converting to Judaism. Not one to be
impulsive, I had been studying Jewish thought for more than ten
years. I wanted to formalize my affiliation, to consolidate my own
identity and to present a united front for Aaron. For about six

months, I met weekly with Rabbi Emanuel Rose at Temple Beth Israel. We had a relationship similar to the one I had had with Rabbi Perlman in Boston, but without the emotional intensity. Rabbi Rose was open to my agnosticism and respectful of my existentialism. When I finished the readings, there was a private conversion ceremony in the sanctuary. In an emotional capper to an already moving experience, Rabbi Rose surprised me by giving me the Hebrew name Sarah, that of a strong female role model for the Jewish people.

Though I was still uncomfortable with the ritualism of organized religion, the social activism and cultural values offered a familiar bond. Leo and I attended services on occasion, usually on High Holidays. But the sense of connection with the Jewish community as a whole was the glue for me.

While Leo worked for the degree, he campaigned to join my thriving private practice. I had serious reservations about our working together, for lots of reasons, but I ultimately gave in. We began traveling together, some vacation and some business. It was on one of those business trips that I got the bad news I knew was coming someday.

We were attending a week-long workshop in St. Louis, put on by the Masters and Johnson Foundation. It was full of information and required avid attention. We would go out for a nice dinner afterward and return to our hotel room to talk about the day. Since the content of the workshop had been sex, we began to relate the material to our own sexuality. In the course of the night, he confessed that he no longer found me exciting, not nearly as much as his previous partners. That hurt, but, after all, we were in our sixth year together. It was not a devastating disclosure. Then I summoned the courage to ask what I had never really asked before: Had there been affairs since we were married? After an understandable hesitation, he admitted to several others. I was crushed, though I had long sensed it was coming. He was unable to grasp my pain, as his choices had not violated his values. I was not prepared to deal with the emotional disarray I knew would be caused by a divorce. When I thought about ending it, my body lapsed into psychosomatic symptoms. I couldn't leave the marriage until my body cooperated with my head and gut. Things settled down when we returned to Portland but I knew it was just a matter of time. The disagreements were on core values and apparently non-negotiable.

During the early Portland years, the payoffs in other areas were more sure. I loved being with Aaron and often took him with me to Portland State. He was an active and alert kid, well behaved as only-children often are.

A major fringe benefit of my work at PSU was an occasional opportunity to be interviewed on television. I had done some research on screen actresses as role models, and had presented it to several psychological meetings throughout the country. My thesis was that women over age thirty who admired Marilyn Monroe, Jane Russell and Sophia Loren had different personality configurations than women who admired Bette Davis, Katharine Hepburn or Rosalind Russell. Admirers of Hepburn's group tended toward androgyny, while Monroe's fans were more stereotyped and hysteric. The Portland *Oregonian* picked it up and the subsequent interview made page one of the Day section. In the course of the interview, I mentioned my vicarious relationship with Doris Day.

The following week I was called by the producer of a local talk show, featuring Dick Klinger, Portland's version of Mike Wallace. It was another chance to combine show biz with clinical psychology. As may be imagined, the fantasies were grandiose and pervasive. I hoped that when the network saw the show, I'd be offered at least a spot on Johnny Carson, if not my own talk show.

There was no way to prepare for my television debut. I had always imagined being famous for the real me, and this might be the closest I would come to that. As it turned out, Klinger and I were a good match. Glibness was rampant as we cavorted through extensive material. Klinger, a notoriously close-mouthed guy when it came to personal issues, revealed that he had purchased a white suit after seeing *The Great Gatsby*. After this, other TV appearances followed, mostly on news and talk shows in the 1970s.

Having been disdainful of Joyce Brothers and her willingness to give psychological advice on television, I was careful. I tried to give thoughtful answers, educating the audience. I was in demand as a public speaker, and was one of the keynote speakers at the International Women's Year conference at the Memorial Coliseum. Visibility was increased because I was one of the few outspoken feminists in Portland at that time. My public persona as a psychologist had emerged.

I might have settled for the label of media psychologist had not a serendipitous event occurred in 1976. The family planned to spend Thanksgiving away from home for the first time in our history. Leo and I arranged to attend a hypnosis workshop in Palm Springs, providing a business reason for us to be there. We stayed at a beautiful hotel in Indian Wells where Leo's brother Ed would meet us for our Thanksgiving feast.

NINE

Here We Go Again!

I had met Eddie when Leo and I were going together. Both of them were hippie freaks. I thought Ed, who is younger than Leo, was a bad influence on him. Ed was also then completely into rock music, which I disdained. After we left Los Angeles for Nebraska, Eddie got a job with a commercial jingle house in Hollywood, writing music for commercials. This was ironic, the original anti-establishment hippie peddling capitalist goods. I don't know how he felt about me in those days, but I suspect there was no love lost on either side.

Consequently, I was not looking forward to our Palm Springs meeting. We all went out to dinner. After a few drinks, I was feeling more charitable toward old Ed. When we came back to the hotel, the three of us headed for the giant Jacuzzi and talked for about an hour. Ed was discussing his work, and then it popped out. I told him of my fantasy of recording, of my experiences listening to others record at Columbia, and of my years of singing along with Judy Garland, Eydie Gorme, Ella Fitzgerald and Doris Day. Eddie, also in his cups, asked why I had never recorded anything. This was a little like asking me why I had never starred in an MGM musical. The answer was obvious. He said he could arrange it. Just let him know and he would get us a studio.

The next day in a more sober mood, I questioned him about his offer and he repeated it. Get some music together and the next time we were in Los Angeles, he'd set something up. I knew Ed was no stranger to hyperbole, and I had certainly experienced the disappointments inherent in show biz before. Somehow I believed him. And then I could think of nothing else. I began to prepare, without really knowing when or if that session would take place. But, oh, God, I was back in show biz again. What sweet agony!

One of my mother's favorite stories about me concerns my singing repertoire at the age of three. She claimed that I knew about one hundred songs. Thus, more than thirty years later, it was difficult to select just a few songs to record with Eddie in Los Angeles. I decided to go with a variety, a combination of what I had been singing with on record, what I had heard, and some material that was new to me.

Risking everything on new material was a deliberate decision. It was a bow to the pressure I felt from working with younger people. Though I was only in my early 30s, Eddie was in his 20s and of the rock-and-roll generation. I was embarrassed to sing only big-band tunes, afraid of his reaction to this throwback from another era. I thought a variety of songs might make me more marketable. Of course, it was true that I really didn't know how I would sound doing very much of anything, even the familiar tunes. Leo, Eddie and the arranger were intimidating and their presence pushed me to do what I was afraid to do. I remembered stories of Judy Garland in her last years, unable to learn new material due to her increasing dependence on drugs and alcohol. Those were not my problems, but I wanted to remain flexible and current.

Six months had passed since our Jacuzzi compact. Leo and I made a business trip to L.A., but its real intent was to talk with Ed. To my delight, he met us at his place of business, along with a friend of his, a piano player-arranger. As Gary warmed up on the piano, I felt my stomach turn over and my throat tighten. It was one of those moments that occur only in dreams, when fantasies are dared into reality. So much was on the line for me that afternoon.

We taped a few songs and took them upstairs to hear them on the massive sound system in the boss' office. As I listened, I felt the shiver that I did that first day at Columbia Records. That was me on that tape! I was being captured, almost immortalized, for the first time. Well, at least since my parents used to tape our family gatherings. To my surprise, what I heard was a pleasant voice, a melodic one, a seeming blend of Eydie, Doris and Ella. Truthfully, I had expected Ethel Merman; since my musical comedy days, I had imagined myself a belter. It turned out all that intensity was internal. But it was okay. It sounded fine. I had passed my first test, and was ready for more.

The thought and memory of that sound haunted me for months. It stirred up all the long-ago-diverted performing fantasies. Recording seemed ideal to me. I was afraid of live performances, and I didn't think I was attractive enought to be marketable, anyway. In a recording session, I could exert complete control, as Frank Sinatra did. My musical training would enhance my sensitivity to what was good. I could be in control, at least in this world.

Leo dropped out of the picture at this point. Though he had fantasies of being a rock-and-roll drummer, he had never acted on any of them. This was clearly between his brother and me. Ed and I talked about a "real" session and how that could be arranged. By this time, I was making good money as a psychologist. Leo and I had regular disputes centering on how to spend the money I was making. Since he seemed determined to run through it as quickly as possible, I had my justification for this narcissistic expense. Ed figured it could be done for under $1000. It really wouldn't have mattered if the figure had been ten times that. For that opportunity, I would have hocked everything. My joy was modulated when Dora Hall came to mind. She had also tried to buy her way to fame, and made it to the Jackie Gleason show and assorted other appearances. I wanted to be taken seriously, not merely because I could afford to cut a record. No matter. The opportunity was here. I could hope that talent would win out, the money only greasing the wheels of success.

For the next fourteen months, Ed and I talked frequently on the phone, making arrangements. He and Gary wanted to know what

I would record. We could do two tunes. Perhaps a show tune and one that was more contemporary, though that was harder to find.

Two years earlier, Leo and I had taken a cruise to the Caribbean. It had been a big band/nostalgia cruise, featuring Jimmy Dorsey's band. I had gone to every performance, usually by myself, studying the singers and the band. The singer had done a song I had never heard before, but it had struck me as something suited to my voice. For the next two years, I had tried to track it down in Portland, but without success. On that last trip to L.A., I had happened in a sheet music store on Cahuenga and asked the clerk. He hadn't heard of it either, but would search for it and order it if he could find it. It turned out the song was from a failed Broadway musical with Michele Lee, *Seesaw*, called "Nobody Does It Like Me."

When the sheet music arrived, I picked out the tune on the piano and squealed in delight. This would obviously be one of the songs I could record with Ed. About a month later, I was watching television and Carol Burnett was doing my song! I was incensed! How had she found it? The experience of hearing it on the ship, the two-year search, and the feeling of triumph seemed so personal to me. It was incomprehensible that someone else could have gone through that process. Another lesson from the laws of show biz, I guess: If you don't act immediately, someone else will get there first.

The other tune would be "You've Got a Friend," the beautiful Carole King song. I had played her "Tapestry" album and liked several things from it, but I liked the irony and sensitivity of a clinical psychologist telling someone they could count on me to be there, when they're "down and troubled."

Another business trip to Los Angeles allowed time for me to meet with Gary to set the keys and hear his ideas for orchestration. Both Gary and Ed were part of an L.A. subculture of semi-starving musicians who were just getting by. Neither seemed to be in the musical mainstream, but both were making a living in spite of themselves. Gary was gentle and nonjudgmental, and I liked working with him. He promised to orchestrate the songs soon, so no more time would be lost.

Everything was set up by December 1977. We flew to Los Angeles, this time with the expressed purpose of my recording date. I was being taken seriously as a performer. Ed had rented the Johnny Mercer Studio on Western Avenue for the event. As we went in, he recounted some history. What meant most to him was that the Beatles had done some recording here; what mattered to me was its affiliation with Johnny Mercer. Again, there was an integration of history. I had spoken with Mercer the day after "Moon River" had won an Academy Award, and here I was, working in his studio. Mercer had since died, which made it even more poignant. In the lobby was a bronze of him, a plaque under it in dedication to his extraordinary gifts as a songwriter.

Inside was a studio even more impressive than Columbia Records. Countless boards with an endless series of dials, all behind a glass wall. On the other side, I would do my thing. On this first day, the musicians would come in in small groups to lay down their tracks. First the piano, both electric and acoustic; then the percussion and bass guitar; the horns came in for an hour or so, followed by the reeds, and finally the strings. Each track had an identity and sound all its own. It was like making a cake: Each ingredient was so tasty as to be able to stand on its own, but when it was put together it was a culinary masterpiece.

There wasn't anyone there to talk with about what was going on inside. All those dreams coming together were overpowering. Yet I sat there in silence. Every once in a while, I would wander down the hall, to Mercer's bronze, to listen to the reverberations of the music inside. My turn would come when they were through, probably not until Day Two.

I had remembered the feeling of being transported while listening to the enhanced sound in the Columbia Records studio. Add that sound quality to the emotional power behind the taping and it was a feast for my eyes, ears and soul. The combination produced a sensory synergy I had never experienced before or since. When I let myself feel it all the way down, tears came to my eyes and my heart felt it would burst. There was clearly a need to harness this power; it would be impossible to sing under these conditions.

To resolve the contrast between the task required and the churning inside, I developed a demeanor that appeared cool and in control. Others may have seen me as detached, even cold. It was a constant struggle to keep the enthusiasm within workable boundaries.

Meanwhile, I had to get some rest. Thirty-four years of fantasy would be riding on the performance tomorrow.

The next day I arrived at the shrine that was the Johnny Mercer Studio, ready. We had chosen to stay in a new, fancy Beverly Hills hotel, L'Ermitage, as a token of my new "celebrity." It was a quiet place, filled with Old World dignity, the kind of hotel where a real celebrity would stay to avoid all the autograph hounds.

Day Two was my day, singing alone. I was placed in the big studio, all by myself. Four men sat in silence behind the big glass wall: Leo, Ed, Gary and the sound engineer. I decided I'd better sit on the tall stool, as I wasn't sure I could stand without pacing, which I did at home when I sang. Eddie clapped the earphones on me and signaled for a playback. As the sound of forty musicians hit my ears, my body threatened to go into convulsions of joy. The music was part of my inner being. I could hear it through every pore. I was almost afraid to open my mouth, for fear of destroying the spell. When I did, even that sound was clear and perfect. This was a whole new definition of powerful, of peak experience, of at-one-ness with myself. Again, this was impossible to communicate to anyone. Tears came to my eyes, and I turned away for a moment.

Ed asked that I sing it through once with the playback to get a level, before they tried a take. The initial bars of "You've Got a Friend" began with the sweeping violins, and my heart beat as fast as I can ever remember. My throat felt dry. I sang it through, referring frequently to the lyrics written in front of me on a music stand. I knew this song as well as I knew my own name; I also knew that without looking at the lyrics, I would forget everything.

It's an axiom in hypnosis that attention focused on one object aids relaxation. How much more excited could I get and still sing?

We went over it several times, until some desensitization occurred. This was the first time I had sung this song without Carole King in the background. I began to wish I had had several weeks of rehearsal with a tape. As the time went on, I felt more under control and could interpret the lyrics more personally. The bridge reads, "Now ain't it good to know that you've got a friend, when people can be so cold?" I thought of the treatment I had received at the hands of certain members of the psychology department at the University of Nebraska. They were cold, trying to freeze me out. As I articulated the word, it came out as a sort of curse, giving it bite. By the end of the song, I really had meant every word.

Once we got a take we all found acceptable, someone suggested we go to lunch. Though food was not uppermost on my mind, we agreed on a restaurant on top of an office building, near the corner of Sunset and Vine. We parked the car and walked down Vine Street. History flashed behind my eyes: Jacquie and I standing in line at the old NBC studios, hoping we wouldn't be asked for I.D. That building was now a huge savings and loan. Hanging out at Music City, hoping to hear the latest releases. Bus trips to the Brown Derby to catch a look at a celebrity. All these were within a stone's throw of the restaurant. The voices of the others were an intrusion into my private world. It was all coming together—the past, the present, maybe even the future. As we returned to the car carrying the tape we had produced that morning, I had the feeling I had left something behind. It was a feeling of complete fufillment, not just emotional but of destiny as well.

That day was a confirmation of the merger between a sense of destiny and my own mortality. When I was twelve, my grandmother's death had caused irreparable pain. As with many young people, it was impossible to visualize being old, or even middle-aged. Some time after her death, I became convinced that my own death would come before thirty, probably of a cerebral hemorrhage. That fiction helped me make choices that emphasized the present. With that sense of mortality, there were no minor decisions. While some gratification might be delayed, the emphasis was definitely on the intensity and meaning of the now. This puts into a larger context my urgency at KNXT and the *Christian Science Monitor*.

I walked down that Hollywood street feeling I could expire right there, having fulfilled all my bottom-line fantasies. There was little more I imagined doing. Leaving something tangible behind, such as a product or even a child, had never been important in that way. The sense of destiny and mortality created an urgency to live life at high intensity, but much of that occurred from within. When the first tune was on tape, the enormity of the accomplishment in terms of completed fantasies hit me like a bomb. I was astounded that it mattered so much.

I had more anxiety about doing "Nobody Does It Like Me." Though the lyrics were a perfect fit, I was afraid Gary had pitched the final key too high for me to reach comfortably. The arrangement called for three modulations, each a half-step higher than the previous one, ending on a sustained high note. I returned to what was now the familiar studio, and closed the door behind me. This was a kind of exquisite aloneness, just me and that glorious sound.

Rehearsals reinforced my concern. That last note was a corker and the tempo felt rushed. I was disappointed that there wasn't more of a chance to rehearse. Yet the music transported me into another space. I had to live with the limitations. It took more time to cut this tune because of that last stanza. It was getting late, and we had only an hour to do the mixing and dubbing; we had a plane to catch.

I finished, and returned to my ritualistic tour of the building. As I walked through the empty reception area, I pondered Mercer's head again. I mused that this must be like the graven image people pray to in ancient religions. I listened to the playback sounds of my own voice against the big band sound and felt a smile creep over my face. Thank God no one was around; I felt embarrassed at the enjoyment I was experiencing. A scream threatened at the base of my throat. As usual, I kept it under control.

The atmosphere those last few hours was tense in the control room. We were aware of the plane's imminent departure and we were running out of allocated studio time. Gary sensed he had blown it with the key changes. We were all pushing to finish. I was afraid I was compromising the finished product due to time pressures and the futility of confronting Gary. I understood why recording stars become finicky and controlling as a way of avoiding low-quality material. I wanted very much for the recording to be my best effort, even though the skills were still in flux. It was to be an accurate reading, even if it failed to meet my soaring expectations of perfection. But because of the time, this proved impossible. It couldn't have been helped. Before that rushed weekend, the whole project had been done long-distance. I prepared the only way I could, with Eydie Gorme, Doris Day, Ella Fitzgerald and Judy Garland leading the way. At the time, though, it seemed enough to have produced that peak experience. I told myself I could be satisfied with what I had done.

The final mix was completed and we bolted out of the studio. I quickly hugged Ed and Gary, thanked them, grabbed the tapes and headed for the car. Once we got in, Leo stuffed all the luggage into the back seat and reached for the tapes to put them into the suitcase. No way. I carried them with me on the plane. If the plane went down, those tapes would be found in my lap. At that moment, the product of that recording session seemed like one of the most significant things I had ever done. I had a feeling it was not to be duplicated.

That same year, I began lessons in both tap dancing and jazz piano. It was a chance to pick up old skills and to get close to music again. I had a hard time finding teachers. One of the dancing schools I called was owned by a seasoned former dancer. I shuffled and with some timidity asked about private lessons for adults with two left feet. She shot back, "Oh, don't apologize, dearie. We all want to be Ann Miller."

It wasn't Ann Miller I wanted; it was a more graceful Pam Munter. I joined a class of eight adults, most of them older than I, all of them housewives. We were all a little klutzy, but worked hard. I even signed up for a second year. The lessons were weekly, sandwiched into my already busy Monday mornings; it was the only way recreation was possible. My life was already heavily scheduled. The classes left me panting and sweaty and I barely made it back to the office for my next appointment. Switching gears was part of the challenge.

The teaching of jazz piano was sparse in Portland. Most of the music teachers were of the Hanon variety, emphasizing scales and traditional music. I located Gene Confer, a professional musician who copied his own music for his students. His studio was a one-room affair, in a run-down downtown office building. He introduced me to augmented chords and the sound of jazz piano. While I learned to read his sheet music, I knew that if I didn't practice every day I would forget everything. I could sit down one evening, and play five pieces to perfection. But if I missed a night, I would stumble through each one of the pieces. I didn't know it at the time, but I had a mild seizure disorder, "absences," that prevented the mastery of sequences required to master the piano. It was a frustrating and puzzling experience.

At the lesson on Saturday morning, Confer would politely accuse me of not having practiced, when I would often play for hours each day. However, the slightest bit of distraction would throw me off. I would lose my place and have to take it from the top. The only other area in which I had experienced this kind of frustration had been mathematics. I felt like an idiot, but I kept on. When I was right on, it was fun and I liked the sound. I fantasized about playing in a piano bar somewhere, singing along with my own playing. When the "absences" became more intrusive, I knew that kind of split attention was impossible.

Life in show biz was just fine, but the marriage was slipping. Our feminist/househusband arrangement was not working and I was becoming increasingly dissatisfied and lonely. While I was nowhere near leaving the relationship, I began to wonder about my sense of direction. After attending a workshop with James

Bugental and reading several of his books, I wrote to him, asking for professional time with him.

If the name sounds familiar, it may be because I was once in love with his son, Joe. We had written *Like Wow!* in 1959. I had visited his home in Bel Air many times and had exchanged polite words with both his parents. He had told me his father was a psychologist, but that had no meaning for me then. When I became a psychologist myself and came across Bugental's work, I was pleased at the convergence of thought. Bugental advocated the humanistic/existential approach in an organized and methodical style, the first time I had seen it done so well. I was carrying out my own theory, alone in the clinical wilderness. Finding a "colleague" and perhaps a mentor was exciting. Bugental agreed to two intensive days at his office, now located in his home overlooking the hills of San Francisco.

Though I had read countless psychological authors, I had not been able to identify to the same extent I had with Bugental. Part of me was afraid I would be disappointed with the man; in fact, Bugental had written of this experience himself. Another part was afraid I would fall short in his eyes. The competitive side of me wanted to wow him with my clinical expertise, exchanging observations about clients and the process of therapy with great sagacity. In fact, I wasn't sure if I wanted a consultation about life in general, wise lectures on psychotherapy, or stimulation to clear my own slate.

On the way down to the Bay Area, even the droning of the plane served to elevate my anxiety. Jim had arranged for a room at the local Holiday Inn. A dear friend from graduate school, Peter Tsantilis, picked me up and took me to dinner. We obsessed about the rare opportunity to meet with an honest-to-God psychological guru. I felt honored that Bugental had agreed to my request. It was a no-lose situation, so long as I stayed present and focused.

The next morning, I leaped into my rental car and began the search for the house. As I drove, my mind wandered back to other therapeutic experiences, especially the time with Ricky. My anxiety was nowhere near the magnitude I had felt then. I knew

Bugental valued process and trusted spontaneity; if I listened to what was going on inside my own head, I'd be fine.

I waited for several minutes in the chilly morning air outside the lower level of his house where he saw his clients. When the door finally opened, I held back an urge to hug him. His consulting room was homey, decorated with artifacts from trips abroad. To my disenchantment, he tended to sit at his desk, taking notes as we talked. I worked on withholding my expectations of him personally, since I had chosen the personal avenue instead of the professional and more distancing approach.

I had forgotten about his background in traditional analytic therapy. He let me do most of the talking. At one point he asked me to lie on the couch because he felt I was becoming too involved with his degree of responsiveness. I wanted an interaction, not a monologue. As the hours went on, I gave him my background and the sources of dissatisfaction with my life. We took breaks every few hours and a longer one for lunch. By the end of the first day, we had already met for over six hours. I returned to the motel and made notes.

Pete picked me up again for dinner and we talked about the day. There were several highlights, in terms of insight. One was that I was angry about the marriage, not just sad or distressed. I was not willing to "settle" for the passive-aggressive adversarial relationship, in which my emotional needs were being met outside the relationship. Most of all, I was not willing to live without passion—in this case, emotional involvement. The passion of the recording session was rare and strangely solitary. I had never shared that kind of intensity with Leo; in fact, I was withdrawing from him because of the ongoing discord.

The next day was more relaxed, and I was eager to find out more about myself. Part of me resented that I was doing all the work. Bugental seldom offered insights or observations. I was well acquainted with his therapeutic technique and wanted to see more of the person behind it. However, it was hard to argue with the fact that material was coming out. It certainly conformed to the long-established pattern of doing things myself. My mother was fond of telling others my first words were "Me do it." And who else should take responsibility for my growth?

Day Two revealed the intense feelings about show biz and my puzzling connection to Judy Garland. Until that day I had not seen the unique pattern of show-biz attachment. Many are attracted to the business because they want to be loved or admired; my investment had to do more with my relationship to myself. I came to see show biz as using all of me. Singing, dancing, performing were challenges to the varieties of expression; fantasies of talk-show experiences and writing tapped the person beneath the performance; creating the product and participation in my own management was problem-solving at its best. It was a one-woman show, and I liked it that way.

I began to wonder if I hadn't shut out Leo the same way. There was little I couldn't do and I certainly didn't "need" him in traditional ways. I "wanted" him to be my partner, my accomplice in life. But perhaps he wanted to be needed, to be taken care of in that safe, traditional way. Was this what they meant by irreconcilable differences?

After thirteen hours of therapy in two days, my return home was marked by reflection and more writing. There was no need to make a decision yet. Questions were raised about my settling for my life, whether it was working full time at Portland State, letting the show-biz bug die, or continuing in an unfulfilling relationship.

TEN

The Singing Shrink

Fortuitously, I began to see show-biz people in my private practice. Several local celebrities sought my professional services, mostly for relationship-oriented problems. Of course, we would discuss the rest of their lives as well. I had to wrestle with a potential conflict of interest.

One of the cardinal tenets of psychotherapy is that the therapist's private life remains just that. Disclosure is of emotions, rather than of content. It would have been inappropriate to share my lifelong passion with a client. If I hadn't had that added complication of having a second agenda, there would have been no problem. Instead, I was continually asking myself if any show-biz-oriented question were truly relevant. The only casualty was me. All this double-tracking left me drained on the days I saw those people.

My goal in professional life as in the personal arena is to be as present in a given situation as possible. This requires that my thinking be on a single track, on whatever is occurring in that room. When my mind is on a second or even a third track, my attention is diluted and I am less effective. It often takes considerable energy to exclude those secondary tracks, but the sense of power and focus is phenomenal when I can. When I'm double-tracking, others get the impression I'm not there, that I'm preoccupied with something else. I would be communicating a sense of uninterest, which is seldom the case.

Along with being present, I feel my best when there is no unfinished business. There is nothing additional I need to say, no loose ends. The agenda is clear. I am caught up and ready to tune in to what's going on inside. It is often the time when I experience the most creativity within myself and when the internal messages are most potent. My ongoing intent is to be in this state more of the time.

The divergence between what I experienced within or with friends and what I found at home was increasingly evident. In my naiveté, I had selected an androgynous Jewish male with whom I had imagined an idealized lifestyle. That my own father was a rounder who hurt his family made fidelity a major issue for me. I sought a partner whose loyalty and commitment were at least as strong as my own. I had ignored several obvious violations of my central value system and minimized the irreconcilable attitudes after continual conflict. There were warnings all along, but I wouldn't heed them. When the anger, pain and sense of betrayal turned to emotional inertia, I called a halt.

Since Leo was still trying to make a go of working in my office, he had to get a real job before he could leave. This is what I had hoped he would do all along, but now it was too late. We agreed to a deadline and I respected his request that I help him find a place to live. It was an agonizing time for both of us, but my friends were really there for me. I had prepared myself well for the inevitable break, and of course I still had my work. Things were going well at the office, and the intensity I experienced there was the condition I sought to approximate in my primary relationship. It was the place I felt most alive.

Among the half-dozen show-biz people I was seeing in therapy, there was one client I found irresistible. She was a singer on a part-time basis, but had spent most of her forty years in show biz one way or another. Singing couldn't pay the bills for her and her growing daughter; she had two other jobs. Delilah (not her real name) reeked of the business. Her auburn hair flowed like Rita Hayworth's; her eyes were penetrating and full of pathos; her mouth was sensuous and expressive. She came to me with a series of problems, but what it added up to was exhaustion and an identity crisis. She hated show biz and wanted out. I was disbelieving at first; I couldn't imagine anyone wanting out. She abhorred the late hours and the drunks, the life itself. She was studying at Portland State, with the intention of being a mental health professional. At that point, I would have traded her my degree for a chance to sing one night in a club.

The intrigue wasn't merely from her show-biz connections. Delilah was warm and giving, always interested. I admired her honesty and ingenuousness. I had the feeling she could be trusted completely, that it wouldn't occur to her to be dishonest. Week after week, she complained about her frenetic life. When my secretary left for a better-paying job, I considered offering the job to Delilah. We had finished our therapeutic work, and she was feeling better about herself. It is always a risk, converting a therapeutic relationship into anything else, but I felt confident that we could overcome the obstacles. I offered her the job.

The termination of the therapeutic part of the relationship was propitious. I had planned to separate from Leo and was set to move to new, larger offices and take on the supervision of two students. The timing was not premeditated, but added emotional clout to my relationship with Delilah. Knowing of her eagerness to consolidate her job efforts, I offered her enough salary that she would no longer have to sing for a living. It was quite a while, at least by my impatient standards, before I told her I was also a singer.

I mentioned it after she had been working for me for a few weeks. Her car was being repaired, and I volunteered to drive her to the dealer after work. As we walked to the car, I all-too-casually mentioned that I had recorded some songs and asked if she would be interested in hearing them. Delilah was nothing if not demonstrative. She was excited and vivacious. Of course, I happened to have the cassette tape of my L.A. recording session in the car. Each time I would listen to it, the surging feelings of transcendence would return. I wondered if she would pick up the vibes; more than that, I wondered if she would think I was any good. There had been little feedback, and none that was untainted by relationship. The people who had been in on the recording date made polite remarks, which was to be expected. Leo, Ed and Gary were quietly supportive, but I had been essentially operating in a vacuum.

I was aware that Delilah was working for me, and politics might overcome honesty. But there was that inherent trustworthiness. I felt I knew her well enough to know whether she was hedging. There was also a fantasy that she might help me improve my talents, or at least offer further direction. In Portland, Oregon, show-biz opportunity was not exactly pounding at the door.

As casually as I could, I put on the tape and pulled out of the parking lot. Out of the corner of my eye, I could see her smiling. She grabbed my hand. "You should have told me. You're very good." The praise was welcome and wonderfully effusive. Her reactions that evening set the course for my increasing trust in her, and for my reaching out to her as a friend.

She knew my marital situation and I knew all about her life. One week I suggested we go out to dinner together. After dinner, she asked if I would like to hear some jazz in town. I had never done that in Portland, and had no idea where we would go. Going to listen to music alone still had the connotation of a woman looking to be picked up. Still, it wouldn't be so bad if we went together. Our first stop was the Prima Donna, a well-known hangout for other musicians, featuring soft jazz. I wasn't sure why, but I was nervous. Delilah boldly moved toward the front table.

After a few minutes, three men ambled over to their instruments. Their casualness of dress and lack of professional demeanor was disarming, but their musicianship was exemplary. After the first number, the piano player picked up the mike and introduced the featured singer, an ageless, handsome black man named Gene Diamond. His way with the melody line was fascinating and he knew what to do with his audience. The thrill of being almost on top of the music added to my already escalating adrenaline.

During the break, Gene came over to our table. I had a quick fantasy that Delilah had set me up. Knowing that I had cut the tape, I wondered if she had taken some independent action. This was an obvious extension of the *Confidential* magazine/conspiratorial fantasy that enchanted me. Somehow there would be a happy ending; someone cared. All I had to do was present myself and my talent and it would all fall into place. Isn't this what happened in all those show-biz biographies Hollywood produced in the 1950s?

Gene was a gentle, easy person, hip and sensitive. He didn't pay much attention to me, but that was okay. I was intrigued by his interaction with Delilah. He asked her how her singing career was going; she told him she was trying to get out of it. They commiserated about the late hours and the hard work. I didn't say a word, feeling like an eavesdropper. I was never very good at that kind of conversation anyway, and my bounding emotions further interfered with any sparkling intrusions. Within a few minutes, Gene returned to the bandstand to begin another set. He sang a tune, hypnotizing me again; then he did a startling thing. He called Delilah up to the stand.

Without batting an eye, she got up to the applause of the crowd, kidded with Gene and took the mike. She mumbled a few words to the piano player and began to sing "I Could Write a Book" from *Pal Joey*. When she finished, she launched into another, "It Might As Well Be Spring." These were all new rules, a whole new fantasy. This really happened, a singer doing his own gig would invite another singer to sing? You mean, people can prepare to do this? Hmmm . . .

This scene was to recur each time we would go to dinner. After the first episode, I was hooked. Dinners out and sitting in were to become a weekly ritual. Delilah couldn't afford expenses like this, so I would pick up the tab. When she mildly protested, I told her I enjoyed her company and was learning from her all the time. Both these things were true. There was a nagging conflict, though, that somehow I was encouraging her to do the very thing she had claimed to hate and was trying to stop. We talked about that, but she said it wasn't bad when it was just sitting in; in fact, it was fun.

After several months of hearing her do various songs around town, I tired of just watching. I hadn't shared the fantasy that was obviously clicking in my head. When she would be called up to the stand, it became I who was up there. Realizing the irony, though, my exhilaration was changing to depression. She hated this and wanted out, yet she was the one who was being asked to perform. I thought of little else, particularly during weekends and evenings when I would spend several hours each night singing to records. Yet I was the passive admirer. I had to find a way to tell her.

She took the news well, in her usual supportive way. She offered to set me up with Gene to sit in some night. I was horror-struck. Perform without preparation? No way. I had never sung with a live group, only canned musicians who played in my earphones. Not even my most grandiose fantasies would permit me a risk like that. No, there must be some way for me to prepare so thoroughly as to preclude any chance of blowing the fantasy.

For the past few years, Delilah had worked with a piano player, Arletta O'Hearn, who also backed other singers. Delilah offered to arrange for us to meet and for me to rehearse with Arletta. Nervous to the point of psychogenic symptoms, I wondered if I had perhaps pushed this fantasy too far. The night Arletta was to come to my house to "run a few tunes," dinner was of no interest to me. I asked that Delilah be there to introduce us; actually, her warmth might make this trying experience more comfortable. There was a knock at the door and I stood frozen in my tracks. A moment of truth. Two professionals would soon be standing in my living room, expecting me to sound like a pro. I barely knew what I sounded like without Eydie or Doris or somebody.

When she entered the room, Arletta's soothing presence was apparent. Like Delilah, she was self-effacing and nurturing—in short, just what I needed at the time. We chatted for a few minutes, then she sat down at the piano. I marveled at how easy it is for people to begin performing; no warm-up, no apologies, no cloak. Arletta ran through a couple of scales and asked me what I wanted to sing. I mentioned a few tunes I knew quite well, including my favorite, "It Had to Be You." A consummate musician, she had no trouble at all finding my key or following my style. After an hour or so, I began to settle in. In fact, the evening could have gone on forever, as far as I was concerned. But it was getting late and we all had to get to work early the next morning. Timidly, I asked if Arletta would consider meeting on a regular basis so that I could practice and perhaps build a repertoire. I had begun!

Later I learned that Arletta had called Delilah the next day to ask about me and why I seemed so frightened. She also thought I had a good voice, but was taken aback by my intensity and motivation to work hard. Apparently, both of them decided it must be because I am Jewish—an interesting non sequitur.

We met on a weekly basis for several months. In the subsequent sessions, I recorded Arletta's accompaniment so that I could practice between times. By now I had a nightly ritual, in which I would pick up Aaron after work; we would eat, play for a while, then it would be his bed time. For the next few hours, I would sing with my Arletta tapes. About ten o'clock, the phone would ring and it would be Delilah, asking how I was doing. By then my voice would be getting hoarse, a problem I had long had in singing with records. We would talk for a while, then hang up, do exercises, then go to bed. Weekends, we were still doing our old out-to-dinner, out-to-sit-in routine. I grew more restless, knowing I was preparing to take over. The more practice during the week, the more restless on Friday night.

One October night, Delilah suggested we do a New Year's Eve act at one of the clubs in town. She said they were always looking for entertainment for that night and we could come up with something. I never knew how to deal with her zeal; it confused me. I thought she was no longer interested in performing; she certainly seemed to enjoy her work at the office. Yet she took delight in helping me get ahead with my singing. But, as with her premature plans to have me sit in, I had severe reservations about putting together a big-deal act in two months. It caused me to question her judgment.

In December, Delilah announced she was working for a friend on a Sunday night at the Red Lion, singing with a small group. Arletta would be at the piano. Delilah asked if I wanted to come hear her sing. By this time my enthusiasm was lukewarm at best, but I figured I could always learn more from this old pro. A few nights before the date, she dropped the possibility that I might be able to sit in, since this wasn't a regular gig. I knew I was ready, but was annoyed at the casualness of the scheme. I wanted to be able to prepare, to be sure, to be in control. My long history of irony and close-but-no-cigar experiences had taught me to strike while the iron was hot. I agreed to come to the Red Lion and wait to see if the other musicians would mind if I sat in. I brought my long-time buddy, Pauline Wall, for support. Pauline had been an ally at Portland State. She was an effusive, warm teddy bear. I seemed to be drawn to this kind of person, I mused, as I sat there trying to quell the growing anxiety. A glass of wine helped ease the tension.

At the end of the first set, Delilah came over to the table and said it was all arranged. I could do two songs in the next set. She asked how she might introduce me, something that even my most de- tailed fantasies had not covered. I said I didn't really care, just as long as she did not mention that I was a shrink. I still had not resolved the problems inherent in the blending of the two roles. That would come later. I sat waiting, shaking. As I looked around the room to distract myself from the incipient panic, I noticed it was a large room by club standards, but there were not many people there. Thank God. It would be a fairly anonymous debut. I laughed at myself for wanting that, after all these years. It was a class club and the musicians were good. Besides, Delilah, Pauline and Arletta were there, pulling for me.

Far away, in the deepest part of my consciousness, I vaguely heard her introduction. Something about a singer from L.A. who's here to entertain. A pause, applause, and I watched myself get up and go to the bandstand. It's as though there were two of us, one watching, the other performing. I knew this was an important moment. I leaned over, told Arletta I'd like to do "Just in Time" for openers and reminded her of the key. It was fast, with few lyrical complications, and I have known it for years. I asked her to count off the tempo. As I listened to the four-bar intro, I felt all eyes on me and could see Delilah sitting at our table across the room. The roles were finally reversed and a new era was beginning.

The instant before Delilah called me up to sing I became fully aware of how many levels of functioning were going on simultaneously. First was the fear of making a mistake, including forgetting lyrics, losing the melody, missing coming in on time; second was the fear, more a vague anxiety, that I would not be accepted. While I was convinced the audience would not boo me, there was an undefined feeling about people walking out or expressing their dissatisfaction in some other way. Third was the awareness of the people around me. Delilah, Pauline and Arletta were people to whom I felt some allegiance; I knew they were rooting for me and I did not want to let them down. Fourth, I hoped to impress the other two musicians, since I had some thoughts about forming my own group. Fifth, I was aware of my physical appearance, in terms of what I liked and didn't like. There was also the strong hope that this would be an internally rewarding experience, that it would help to feed the fantasy, the sense of destiny. I needed to meet my own standards, not merely of performance but of fulfilling the dream. That particular pressure was the most emotionally demanding of all.

There was the intensity of the music and the actual singing of the lyrics. I wanted to convince an audience that I believed these words, and to translate my experience into something another person could understand via the music. Here is where the cognitive meets the emotional.

I was also aware of the setting, the lights, the number of people in the audience, their age and sex, where they were sitting and how many were getting up to dance during each tune. I listened to the quality of the sound system. Would I need to sing more directly into the microphone for the lower notes? Pull back for the higher ones?

This was only a part of the mental activity that was going on as I heard those four bars introducing my song. I made a conscious decision to focus on the internal cues and trust my ability to communicate what was happening. I flashed back to all the times I had heard "Just in Time" sung by other singers. Nothing touches me more than someone who is truly involved in what he/she is creating; I tried to be there.

As I sang, I became unified with the music. My awareness of the audience diminished as I felt myself expand from within. I hit the last sustained note and dropped my head to my chest, a gesture that subsequently became characteristic. When the applause began, it was almost an intrusion. Arletta started the intro to my favorite song, "It Had to Be You." Again, there was the complexity of the layers of inner experience. I remembered the first time I had heard it, in a 1944 movie with George Murphy, Joan Davis and Eddie Cantor, called *Show Business*. Channel 9 in L.A. played it for seven consecutive nights when I was a kid, and I saw it every time. The song had a nicely resolving melody line and sentimental lyrics. Later I had heard it numerous times in a Doris Day movie, *I'll See You in my Dreams*, with Danny Thomas.

I was always fond of verses. They are seldom sung today, but they often contain the context the lyricist (in this case, Isham Jones) had in mind when the song was written. I wanted to do it this night as something different. I had taught Arletta the tune for the verse, and as I began to sing it I felt I was educating the audience as well as entertaining them. Again, I felt caught up in my internal reactions. I finished the song, and returned to my seat. Pauline patted me on the shoulder, but the meaning of the evening had not yet hit me. I was relieved that it had gone well, but was looking forward to hearing from others what it was like.

At the end of the evening, Pauline left and Delilah and I went next door to an all-night restaurant to obsess about what happened. Obsessing has always been one of my favorite sports. A major function of friendship is to consider all aspects of a feeling or behavior. I want to be able to share my thought processes and to feel it is reciprocal. If something is on my mind, I want to be able to devote as much time to it as I need to reach closure, even temporarily. In the early years, this was done internally. In reality it doesn't take much time, even with the added interaction. The processing can be done rapidly and efficiently.

Growing up in Los Angeles, I loved to drive all over the city, obsessing about something. It was both relaxing and invigorating. There was a secluded spot near Malibu where a mountain full of daisies came within twenty yards of the surf. The noise of the waves and the smell of the daisies provided a tranquil setting for my thinking. Time to myself has enabled me to resolve and plan anything of importance. It was truly a luxury to have a partner in this pursuit.

Delilah was ecstatic that my debut had been such a success. We sat until almost four o'clock in the morning, going over every detail. Best of all, it seemed I could trust myself on stage, and the hours of training had paid off. After the months of preparation, it was hard to realize that this was my first real live performance.

During these months of working on the singing and the presentation, I was still holding down a full-time job at Portland State. I felt an attachment to the students, especially those who took every class I taught. When they would run out of classes, they took independent study hours with me or just hung around the office. It was flattering, especially when they started calling themselves "Munter Majors." By the time of the Red Lion debut, there were probably a dozen such Munter Majors. A few had become clients as well. Our lives were intersecting in several places. It seemed appropriate that they would also share my greatest passion.

The setting would be a small pre-Christmas gathering, ostensibly a social get-together. Included in the guest list was Arletta, though we had not established a truly personal relationship. As the evening went on, I wandered over to the sound system and flicked it on. Arletta moved to the piano. People stopped talking, of course, and listened. After I sang, their reaction was as positive as I had hoped. Performing in front of people I knew was another way to desensitize myself. What was more important, some of these people had been my clients. I had been concerned about the effect on clients, past, present and future. They were "guinea pigs" in this rather unorthodox experiment.

The unwritten rules of psychotherapy require almost an impersonality between doctor and patient. The doctor knows all about the patient, can ask any question, no matter how intimate. But the rules imply that there be no reversal of that privilege. Thus, most patients know next to nothing about their psychotherapist. In fact, even the medical-model terminology in calling the recipients of therapy "patients" suggests a passive role. Not only did I reject the medical model, I advocated a collegial model, in which the client and I are partners in the psychotherapeutic journey. I was on television with some regularity, and was appearing in a PSU classroom daily. My clients knew I existed outside the therapy room.

The traditional rules are functional in that they allow the client to disregard what they conjecture might be the therapist's personal needs, so that they may more effectively explore their own demons. The doctor is there just for them, to focus exclusively on their life. If too much is known about the shrink personally, it is only natural and indeed polite to ask about the life of the doctor. If my client knows my son has been ill, we may kill the first five minutes of the session talking about my son. This is entirely appropriate if we have a reciprocal social relationship, but it interferes with the limited time we have in a professional situation. For clients who fence and avoid, knowledge of the shrink's life only adds to their evasive choreography.

Being an entertainer lends additional risk. Song lyrics are powerful and personal. To have those emotions evoked by your therapist without mediation could be destructive. It would be easy for the client to associate those words and feelings with the therapist personally and to make disruptive assumptions that could interfere with the therapeutic work. When I sing the doormat lyrics to "My Man," it has nothing to do with my own life, but a client wouldn't know that. Should I take valuable therapeutic time in our session to debrief with them? It's a real bind. Being an entertainer and a psychotherapist adds to the potential for increased transference; that is, a bigger risk that the client will have feelings for the therapist that are not based in reality. While some transference is usually seen as harmless, it is hoped that the therapist will have some control over its evocation. While on stage, I would have no way of knowing what fantasies or emotions might be evoked by my actions. I remembered from my experiences with Ricky how powerful transference could be.

One mitigating factor was my clientele. I had long preferred to work with professionals and intact people. Schizophrenics and borderline personalities were referred to other psychologists. There was good reason to believe that my regular clients would be able to handle my increased visibility. In addition, my therapeutic style included the disclosure of selective parts of my life and certainly of my emotional responses in the session. In the important ways, my clients already knew me. What was missing was knowledge of the passion outside the room. It was a risk I decided to take. When I knew certain clients were in the audience, I would ask them in the next session for their response to the exposure. It would have been the same if I had run into them at the market or the pharmacy. Running into your therapist is a big deal, emotionally speaking. It was important that we talk about it. In the case of the singing, it might even provoke exploration of the client's own issues. One must question why one is not living out reasonable fantasies if one's own shrink is modeling calculated risk.

One of my clients came in with the complaint that she was anxious and depressed because of an unsatisfying marriage. She felt as though she were flailing around in her life. After much discussion, she confessed to a longtime fantasy: She wanted to be able to play the piano and sing for the public. She stated this somewhat apologetically, afraid a moral judgment would come cascading down around her. I supported methodical planning toward getting what she wanted; it would have been inappropriate to share my own strategy. As more sessions were spent on her new career plans, I began to feel as though I were lying by omission. She was entering the borders of my own fantasies and I felt guilty to be withholding such potentially relevant information.

Three years later I was appearing at the Jazz Quarry on my own weekend. My name was in lights on the marquee outside and the publicity was ubiquitous. At the end of the first set, my former client came up to me, all smiles. She said she had abandoned her plans for a show-biz career, deciding instead to return to school. She said she had not known about my singing but was pleased I was doing what she wanted to do. "Now I know why you were so good for me. You really knew, didn't you?"

When I was teaching at Portland State, I became aware of the responsibility and power of being a role model. By acting on the show-biz fantasy, I was in effect telling others to "go for it." Go ahead and dare to dream, but also plan carefully, work hard and execute. You have nothing to lose by trying, and everything to gain.

Shortly after the separation from Leo, I took on two graduate students, and later a business partner, Cheryl Castles. We met weekly so I could supervise the students. It was a supportive group for all of us, the first time I felt a camaraderie with the psychology profession. The students eventually finished their doctorates and moved on, but my relationship with Cheryl deepened and broadened. Soon it was just the two of us in practice, between us seeing more than 75 people a week. But more about this later.

A month after the Red Lion debut, I began a journal in order to reflect on what I thought might be the "Year of the Singer." On January 20, 1979, I wrote, "Singing is a loose end, a high priority item that never stayed filed away. And now it yields a steady stream of fantasy that engulfs me night and day." Calling singing a career felt presumptuous, yet it was "powerful, seductive and addicting."

ELEVEN

Paying My Dues

The question now was, what was the next step? How much energy did I want to apply to this new career? I was already working at two full-time jobs, not to mention raising Aaron. While I waited for inspiration to strike, an article appeared in the *Oregonian* announcing a talent night sponsored by a local radio station. It was to be held at the Jazz Quarry in a few weeks. I was already familiar with the club, since that was Gene Diamond's main place. I had often accompanied Delilah there and watched her sit in. This might not be a bad next move, and there were two weeks in which to prepare with Arletta.

The sessions with Arletta didn't seem to help my anxiety level. As we continued to work, I wasn't as afraid of forgetting lyrics as I was of embarrassing myself. My impression of amateur talent night was that the audience gets entertained at the expense of the entertainers. I had heard the master of ceremonies was egotistical and sexist, which contributed to my feelings of powerlessness. I didn't want to feel tense; I wanted to be supported, and it didn't seem likely that it would come from this emcee, who had a controversial radio show. At the same time, my discovery fantasy was in operation. Maybe if I was good enough, somebody important would hear me. In my heart of hearts, though, I suspected that nobody gets discovered in Portland.

I didn't even have to ask for support from Delilah and the Munter Majors. They were there with fervor. As we drove down to the Jazz Quarry, Delilah kept reassuring me that I could handle it, that my voice was fine, that the myriad concerns that I had were inconsequential. We got out of the car and walked to the door. I had forgotten it was next door to an adult movie theater. I wondered if I had made a mistake in judgment.

The place was crowded, the darkened room making it difficult to see who was there. Within moments, the emcee strutted to the stage and began his remarks to the audience. I was trying to concentrate on calming down and remaining mentally clear. The Sky Trio played a number, then the drummer picked up the microphone. He had recognized Delilah and smiled. Over the mike, he asked her to come up to open the show. Even though I knew she was not counting on this, it bothered me that it would happen again, this time on my night. Within a few minutes she was in and out of "My Funny Valentine," but my concentration was interrupted momentarily.

I had decided to ask Arletta to accompany me, partly out of comfort but also to appear more professional. In an amateur production such as this, no one would bring along a pro accompanist. Arletta was helpful, as always, and it made me feel more at ease. At least I didn't have to worry about the unpredictability of a new piano player. A few people sang, and a couple of musicians did their thing. The emcee announced my name and reached for my hand to pull me up to the stage. I was doubtful about being there, and nervous. As I bantered with him to reduce my anxiety, I noticed that Leo was in the audience with some of his friends. It pleased me that he would bother. My tunes were done uneventfully and received solid applause. There wasn't that same intense concentration I liked to experience, though, because of the distractions of Delilah's impromptu performance and the volubility of the emcee. Afterward, many of us repaired to the nearest all-night restaurant to obsess.

It was certainly a victory to have survived that minefield, but there was no plan formulated to follow it up. Since I had not been approached by anyone but fans, other appearances did not seem to be an option. My only hope was to continue to hang out with Delilah and take turns sitting in around town. While this idea still set my pulse racing, it seemed dead-ended. I wanted to go all the way and be a star, extending beyond Portland's boundaries. Short-term, I would settle for working as a singer.

Within a week, the Jazz Quarry announced that the talent night had been so successful they were going to sponsor an open mike each Thursday night. Anyone who wanted could get up and sing or play with the Sky Trio. I met with Leo and arranged for him to be with Aaron on those nights. This opportunity was an outstanding one to learn stage presence and comfort and to increase my song repertoire. Arletta agreed to work with me one night a week.

My schedule at this point included teaching a full load at Portland State, seeing clients five days a week, talent night on Thursday, Arletta on Monday, sitting in on Friday and/or Saturday night with Delilah, and jazz piano lessons on Saturday mornings. I had stopped my tap lessons. Overkill.

The Sky Trio consisted of three competent musicians, all experienced and patient with us amateurs. Eddie Wied on piano represented many eras of music. He always seemed to be sipping on a glass of something, but he was invariably on target when it counted. Hardly a week went by without some thoughtful remark about my voice or what he liked about my style. Dave Elliot, the drummer, was much younger. Between sets he would come over and talk to us at the table, which made me feel as though I belonged. I appreciated his willingness to chat. The bass player, Vance Lee, was quiet and elusive. He would nod his appreciation of a riff or sweet note, not saying a word. The four of us spent some very emotional moments together, though I'm sure they never suspected it.

After a few months of these weekly showcases, I began to realize that if I stayed later, I might get a second chance to sing. Traditionally, performers were given two slots. If I stayed around, it would get late enough that the others would leave. By 12:30 a.m., there would be ten of us left in the audience, and that sometimes included the owners. By then Delilah would also be gone, as she had to get up early the next morning to work, as I did. It seemed like a B movie—Ida Lupino sitting in some joint pining for her lover early into the morning—except that I was only longing for a show-biz career. Those nights I would seldom get home before 2:30, and my appointments began at nine a.m. It was not an easy schedule.

By December I was troubled by continuing hoarseness after singing two or three hours. This had been a problem for years, but now that I was singing on a regular basis, something had to be done. I contacted a singing coach in Portland and arranged an interview. I figured there must be a problem with the way I was singing, that singing lessons would provide a remedy. I took my L.A. tape, hoping the teacher would settle for that instead of a live audition. As my secretary, Delilah arranged for the meeting and eagerly came along. The teacher was located in the same building as my piano teacher, which settled my nerves a bit. When she heard the tape, she was silent for a minute. Locked in my fear, I heard her say, "I have nothing to teach you." Good news, bad news. Good news that the quality of my performance was good enough that she thought it was beyond her instruction; bad news in that I would continue to hurt. She suggested a speech therapist, as she could think of no way to improve on my already well-developed style.

Speech therapy was the province of the Speech and Hearing Clinic at the University of Oregon Medical School. The therapist and I met in a tiny room one hour a week for six weeks. He gave me exercises for my vocal chords, to be practiced daily. It was hard to hear or feel any difference, but before I knew it, I was singing at the Jazz Quarry without getting hoarse.

Sitting-in experiences became more varied. I was going alone to clubs, hoping for an offer to do a few tunes. As a result of my singing at JQ, other musicians were getting to know my work. When I walked into a club, I was known. That in itself was a strange phenomenon. Pam Munter, singer. Nice ring to it, but still unfamiliar.

Just that Christmas, Delilah's gift to me had been a repertoire book, a bound series of pages in which I would list the songs I knew and the key in which I sang them. It was a beautiful statement of confidence and meant a lot. In short order, it was filled with about 150 tunes that Arletta and I had done together on fourteen volumes of tapes. The book remains a permanent record of my repertoire.

On one particular night, Delilah and I were at the Prima Donna, a classy place I had hoped to perform in some day. Gene Diamond was there, but he never let anyone but Delilah sit in there. We arrived late, but he asked her to sing a few songs anyway. Soon it was approaching two a.m. He began his closing, singing "The Party's Over." About halfway through, he wandered into the audience sitting at small tables around the floor. He stuck the microphone under my nose to sing a line in the song. Problem was, I didn't know the lyrics. I finally had a chance to utter a note in the famous Prima Donna and Gene asked me to sing something I didn't know! It felt like a bad dream, all in slow motion. I tracked down the sheet music the next morning and committed it to memory. Later, when I would occasionally sing that song, I would tell the now-humorous story to the audience.

At this juncture, my idea of being a star was to be able to perform in Las Vegas. This was a change from my days in the recording studio when I wanted total control. Live performing was invigorating, largely due to the degree of risk. The audience was a part of the act, sitting less than three feet away. Las Vegas would bring obvious advantages: money to mount an act with a big band, maybe even backup singers. Most critically, there would be advisers—people who could tell me what to wear and what to sing. It seemed no one in Portland could do that, not even Delilah.

After Vegas, a television special would follow, complete with guest stars. It would have been a delightful irony to have Doris Day as my first guest. I could have polished my piano playing and perhaps have returned to the trumpet to do some tunes with the band. What a narcissistic bang! In the meantime, I was having trouble just sitting in with some predictability.

While I was amplifying my involvement with show biz, Delilah seemed to be getting more frazzled. She was having trouble with her daughter, and her male friend of long standing had still not received his divorce. The complexity of the office work was commensurate with the growth of the practice. And she was sometimes staying out late to keep me company. Though she never faltered in her support, she was getting tired. I continued to offer my time and energy when she wanted to talk. She would not allow herself to be comforted, and seemed to keep much of the stress to herself. I decided a trip to Los Angeles might be just the thing for both of us. We had located an L.A. lawyer who might provide good advice for me in terms of where to go from here. I could also conduct some business there as a psychologist, combining business with pleasure. How could we go wrong?

I wanted to meet with Phil Gillin, the L.A. entertainment lawyer, to solicit advice on how best to advance my singing career. Gillin had represented many celebrities, and had been associated with Sammy Davis Jr. Delilah had written him setting up our appointment. I was delighted when she agreed to accompany me to Los Angeles.

The decision was not an automatic one for her. She spoke of feeling guilty about my continued financial subsidy. Not only was I paying her salary, but I was picking up dinner checks on the weekends. She felt uncomfortable when I offered to pick up the tab in L.A. as well. I was making considerably more money than she was, and it was no big deal for me. Besides, currency can be defined in many ways. Her support was invaluable, the only person who really knew of the passion. There had never been a person in my life who could understand it. Her time and emotional energy were always given freely, though seldom directly requested. L.A. was essentially a business trip; it was only right that her expenses be paid by the business.

We decided to stay at the Holiday Inn in Westwood. Gillin's office was in Century City, very near the hotel. I wanted to show Delilah the city that had fed and fostered my passion. Unless one has experienced L.A., it's impossible to conceive of the influences that permeate the daily lifestyle. We drove to the usual tourist spots and past stars' homes and the studios, at her request.

One night, after we had been to dinner at my favorite restaurant, we entered the hotel to the sound of a bell ringing. As we got into the garage elevator to ascend to our 16th-floor room, the crowd was whispering about a fire. The elevator stopped at the lobby and we got out. People were running around in their nightclothes, looking frightened. In the distance was the sound of sirens. We were directed to a large room off the lobby, to wait for the fire to be extinguished. Apparently it was on the 17th floor.

My first thought was for my Arletta tapes that I had brought to continue my habit of singing daily. There were three "volumes." Though they could be replaced, they were the only possession I would miss having during the trip. With her usual magnanimity, Delilah offered to scale the stairs along with the firemen to retrieve them. I questioned her judgment since everything in that hotel room could have been replaced. The Arletta tapes represented a near-addiction. I would pop a tape into the cassette deck of my car at seven o'clock in the morning, or at midnight at home. When I thought of it later, I realized the tapes were symbolic of my commitment to show biz, of my separateness. Not Eydie or Doris or Ella, but Arletta and Pam.

We were returned to our hotel room by one a.m. The next morning we met with Phil Gillin. I was nervous, but I knew I could count on Delilah to bolster me and to fill in any conversational lapses. He had a cavernous office, with countless cubicles filled with underlings. Dark woods and cork abounded; the atmosphere reeked of wealth and power. I could feel myself being engulfed.

Phil himself turned out to be a genuinely nice guy, seemingly unspoiled by his juxtaposition to fame. He listened to my tape on a superb sound system in his office, and asked what I wanted to do. In a burst of risk, I told him of wanting to record. He said I obviously had talent (Did he say that to everyone who braved the intimidating environment?) but noted that jazz singers were not commercial anymore. He said Doris Day, Eydie Gorme and even Ella Fitzgerald don't sell records. He advised me to get as much experience as possible, and to gain confidence as a performer.

While he didn't say anything earth-shattering, talking to a real record producer and entertainment lawyer made me feel more professional. When we left, I felt triumphant.

Several months later, I received a phone call from Gillin, asking how I was doing with my career. The call was an absolute surprise, and went on for more than an hour. I felt very fortunate to have found such a powerful and interested mentor. Though nothing ever came of our association, he was helpful in ways he never knew.

Augmenting the high of our L.A. meeting, Delilah had told me of an old friend who had accompanied her when she was on the road. He was in Southern California somewhere, and she began scouting the telephone books trying to locate him. She found his name at last, and put in the call. Amazingly, though she had not seen or talked with him in six years, the close connection was immediately resumed. He was playing in a private club in Riverside and asked that we join him the next evening. Delilah said this was a good opportunity for me to sit in again, this time in a unique setting.

Rancho California was a *nouveau riche* country club with a lounge/restaurant. Bill Hathaway had a console consisting of electronic rhythm, piano and organ. We met him at his house, twenty minutes away from the club. A few feet inside the door, it was apparent that music was his whole life. The living room was dominated by a console identical to the one he used at the club, along with several tape recorders, various musical instruments and large piles of sheet music. When he entered the room and hugged Delilah, he reminded me of a sideman from the old Duke Ellington band. His weathered face was deeply marked by smile lines, and his eyes widened with interest as Delilah began her pumping-up-Pam spiel. He asked me to sing for him there, and gave me a file of sheet music from which to select. I was only a little nervous by now, and the notes came more easily than I had expected.

One concern was that I had been working on a cold for about a week. The voice would come and go, which was one of the reasons

I had brought Gillin a tape, rather than risk singing for him on the spot. While I sounded okay for Bill in his living room, I wondered what increased anxiety, fatigue and a microphone would do to my consistency. We hadn't had a chance to eat all day, and I knew that would add to the uncertainty.

It had been only a year since the "absences" had been diagnosed, those very brief moments in time when my memory went completely blank. The absences were more inconvenient than alarming. I had had headaches for ten years and assumed them to be vascular and psychosomatic. Several physicians had dismissed them over the years, and I tended to do so as well. Finally, though, they became intrusive and I was noticing that I was forgetting what I was saying in mid-sentence. When teaching large classes at the university, the lapse would be momentary and I would vamp until I remembered what I had been talking about. All those myths about "absent-minded professors" came to mind, and it was easy to write it off as that. Finally a neurologist noted abnormal spiking in my electroencephalogram that correlated with the concentration gaps. It was a very mild seizure disorder and was treated with medication. There was a question concerning the bout with encephalitis in 1969. Had it been a cause or an effect? And were these absences related to the encephalitis?

I had noticed problems remembering my piano music, but that was a private embarrassment. When I started singing and forgetting lyrics, that was a whole new situation. Lyrics are more difficult to cover, even in jazz singing. It happened with some frequency at home, so I knew it wasn't a stress reaction. I had much fear about trying out these lapses in public. After all the preparation and hard work, I knew it would be easy to write off the lapses as lack of commitment or nerves. Thus it was really the concern about singing which ultimately sent me to the neurologist.

It certainly clarified other long-standing mysteries. Why could I never do well in math, when I would get such good grades in most everything else? Why did I have trouble sequencing, remembering such things as tunes on the piano or dance steps? After all the years of coping with these glitches, I assumed it was idiosyncratic. There was embarrassment when it would happen, thinking it was stupidity. I was almost relieved to have it confirmed to be organic. The medication worked like a charm, so long as I got plenty of rest and plugged in the protein every few hours. Obviously, I had good cause to worry about the Riverside performance.

As usual, Delilah sang first and sounded great. After a while, she handed me the mike. I handed the repertoire book to Bill. He picked the songs and continued to play, one song after another. For the first twenty minutes, all went well. The transition from song to song was smooth and effortless. Then the voice started to crack. Because the cold had settled in my ear, I couldn't trust when I was on key. It was terribly unsettling. Not only might I forget lyrics, but I wasn't even certain I was in tune. I could feel myself in an internal race, coming close to losing a lyric, finding the next word just in time. On one tune, though,—"You Are the Sunshine of My Life"—I blanked out at the beginning of the second chorus. I reached down to Delilah and thrust the mike in front of her. She sang a few lines, then the lapse was gone. I signaled to Bill that I was through for the night, accepted the crowd's applause and headed out the door in tears. Delilah was right behind me.

She couldn't understand why I felt so awful. She knew I was missing some notes, but her tolerance was greater than mine. I felt like crying. To make it worse, we had taped it for later study. All those mistakes would be remembered forever. It was especially disappointing to fail so badly in Los Angeles. Earlier that day, I had stared out of our 16th-floor window swearing to make L.A. sit up and take notice of me. This wasn't what I had in mind.

My journal recorded the sense of despair: "When Bill played the tape back, I ran . . . I might have to admit that perhaps I shouldn't be doing this . . . I was so scared it was all over . . . There was no return from this kind of travesty . . . What if I cannot duplicate the success that occurs in my living room?"

In spite of the Riverside fiasco, the trip had been productive. We had stopped at a large music store in Hollywood and picked up new sheet music to master. And there had been that excellent meeting with Gillin. Delilah and I had had a good time personally as well. I hoped it would relieve her tension when we returned to Portland. But it was several months before I could hear "You Are the Sunshine of My Life" without wincing.

After Los Angeles, watching Delilah sit in became more difficult. There would be the initial joy at hearing her sing, then the anxiety that she might call me up there. This was followed by anger that it was so easy for her, and disappointment when the moment was over and my chance had passed.

As important as singing was, the process of waiting to sit in was demoralizing. There were no guarantees that I would be able to perform, but I had to come prepared and geared up. If I was not invited to sing, there was a tremendous letdown. It wasn't as bad when I was alone, as I could kibitz with the musicians during the break, or with the owners while the set was going on. If there were friends along, waiting was tense. Though they knew the precariousness of the situation, I felt embarrassed if the musicians did not make the overture. It was not often that I was ignored, but the threat was always there. I looked forward to the day when that uncertainty would not be there and I would have more control.

As time went on, others began to comment on Delilah's erratic emotional behavior. One friend observed that Delilah seduced people into being emotionally dependent, then abruptly and unexpectedly pulled away. One day she would give total unconditional positive regard with high energy output; the next day, she might be totally within herself, moody and short-tempered.

Meanwhile, I was maintaining my vigil in the local jazz clubs. A journal entry on February 11 documented the first time I admitted to another that I was a singer, without apologies or explanations. The label itself was magical to me, like a title of honor, to be earned. The journal continues, "How quickly I could get sucked into that lifestyle, sitting in around clubs whenever I can. It's certainly not enough in the long run, but its strong appeal is amazing to me."

The obsessing about singing dominated the journal. Every page describes the intensity and absorption. There was an awareness of falling short: "I haven't given all I can when I perform. I feel inhibited and wonder if it's general or specific to the people I know are watching... Can I get support without judgment? Or without fear of judgment?"

Later that month, the perspective becomes more realistic: "It's a funny, precarious lifestyle—clients/friends/Munter Majors/employees all tied together. Had a quick fantasy today of them sitting together in a problem-solving session about difficulties in relating to me. And then rejecting me and going off by themselves. It's exciting and scary to be the center of all this attention. I know it's short-lived and conditional but so neat and warm."

It was one of the few times I felt part of a group, but I was well aware that it would all stop if I didn't produce. It was a clear quid pro quo, but it beat no support at all. I was used to pouring out support to others, both clients and students. This was a rare reversal, and I drank it in insatiably.

Late February of 1979 was the first time Gene Diamond asked me to sit in. He stood in the back of the room at Antoine's, listening carefully. I had waited for this opportunity for a long time and my nervousness was apparent. I sang "The Lady is a Tramp," then launched into a better "Cry Me a River." After the set, Gene came over to the table, all smiles. "Great timing. Boy, you were sure cool up there. Where did you learn to phrase like that?" His comments sent me on a heroin high. I asked for constructive criticism, but he refused to offer any. Evoking suggestions was a problem through the singing years.

Dissonance characterized the return to work at Portland State the next day. It felt good to be good, as a singer. So what was I doing here? Again, the journal: "It was all there in that second song—body, intonation, successful risking, intensity. The audience seemed to pick it up and even the musicians got into it... Can't believe the degree of positiveness... I even missed the ramp to the freeway on the way home; was in another world. Superlatives fail me."

The next week was another triumph at Antoine's. Gene called me up to the stand soon after I ordered my glass of white wine.

When I finished, he said, "You sang your ass off." I told myself, though, I wasn't a real pro until I would be able to sing all evening and be paid for it. The journal crowed, "I sound good, look good. Wonder what's next?"

Delilah's moodiness began to contaminate the office. Even clients asked what was wrong with her and she made several major financial errors. She had moved in with her still-married male friend two weeks earlier and was lavishing all her energies on him. There was little left for her office duties and none for me. My grief response was almost physical. How could anyone be so destructive with so little malevolence?

As Delilah withdrew, my efforts to sit in escalated, often resulting in less than five hours of sleep a night. I was almost afraid to be alone with myself too long, though I knew I had to face the war that was being waged within. Here was the person most responsible for my fantasy being fulfilled, screwing up badly at work and abandoning me personally. My gratitude would allow me to withstand the personal loss. But my psychological career was at risk if she made any more major errors. Action would need to be taken, and soon.

I didn't realize how soon. A week later, we were working when her daughter called to say she had just wrecked her car but was unhurt. The event seemed to upset Delilah disproportionately to the situation. As the days went by, she became more agitated, making mistakes at work that would have been unthinkable earlier. She stopped calling me at night and spent more time sleeping. I felt powerless. When I would ask what was going on and how I could help, she was unresponsive, retreating into herself. To compound her already complex life, she had agreed to house-sit for three months, requiring an immediate move. Though I insisted on helping her, the tension was palpable. Her deterioration was beyond my control. She wasn't letting anyone in.

Within twenty-four hours of the Riverside trip, I had decided it was time to do something more drastic about my throat. Tonsillitis had been a problem all my life, but now that I was going to be using my throat to earn a living, it was even more important to stay healthy. I met with an otolaryngologist and scheduled a tonsillectomy. I had expected Delilah to be my mainstay, but her agitation and distance were clear messages that I should look elsewhere. I knew I could count on the Munter Majors and particularly on Pauline Wall, my old friend. The surgery was short, requiring a week at home and at least a month without performing. It was bound to be a restless time.

To my surprise, another person emerged to coordinate my friends' efforts to keep me sane. Cheryl Castles had been my professional peer first, then my client, and finally my business partner. We had terminated therapeutic work together and she had gravitated toward the group that hung around my office. I liked her intensity, her earnestness and her honesty. She scheduled friends' visits, arranged for my meals and kept me company when no one else was available. I did not yet know if I could trust her with my show-biz passion, but her continual presence told me it was worth a risk. As soon as I could talk with ease, we began talking. I had found an equal.

The Sunday night before my scheduled return to work, the phone rang. It was Delilah, sounding very shaky. She was giving me her two weeks' notice. It was not unexpected, but I had hoped she would do it with more class, like a personal conversation explaining what was going on. I happened to be alone that night, so there was intense internal processing. Given her feelings and her unpredictable ways lately, it seemed better for her not to return to work at all. Hanging on for the two weeks would have been unbearable for me and probably for her, too. I called her back and told her I would pay her for the two weeks, but I wanted her not to wait out the two weeks on the job. As I hung up, I shook all over. Her obvious anger frightened me. Would she seek retribution? But what had I done? I couldn't understand, and that bothered me as much as anything. Since I was still bedded after the surgery, I called Leo in desperation and asked him to retrieve the financial books from the office, along with any cash that might be lying around. At that point, I didn't trust her. It was an awful ending to a relationship that had had so much meaning.

As time passed, I realized the early clues had been there. She had little life of her own, with no real friends. She had no hobbies or interests, moved with unusual frequency and had a disturbed relationship with her daughter. Within a month of coming to work as my secretary, she had become completely immersed in my life. Much of this was without my request, though I welcomed it. She seemed to enjoy taking care of me. Given her lack of longevity in jobs and in relationships, I probably could have been less entrenched emotionally. But she held the key to a lifelong fantasy and the risks were worth it.

In the end, she cut me off as my father had done, by denying me access to her internal process. In contrast to the complete disclosure that had previously characterized our relationship, she stopped telling me anything. She also stopped asking what was going on with me. I made the decision to give her the room to deal with things on her own. Somewhere, we had reversed roles: she had become my musical therapist, showing me the path into show biz. Her resignation was the only way she could get out from under what must have been oppressive for her. The end was much harder for me than my divorce, for which I had been well prepared. And it took me longer to rid myself of the sense of loss. In her own way, Delilah had been more nurturing than Leo and an active partner in that boiling cauldron that was my show-biz fantasy.

My journal continued to be an outlet, especially since Delilah was no longer accessible. While I began to fear being forever trapped within my own passion for singing, I thought about Delilah:

"Interesting pieces fall into place. The first song I ever sang for her was 'Someone to Watch Over Me,' and that was exactly what I hoped she would be, though I didn't realize it. A mother, a professional mentor, a caring person. The last thing she gave me was the lyrics to 'Second Hand Rose,' the way she conceptualized herself and what largely contributed to her downfall. I recall all the times she told me she could only express her feelings when singing.

Ironic, our relationship could be chronicled in a song. And I still can't believe she's gone."

It had been an extraordinarily powerful relationship. Though there had been no overt sexuality, I realize the relationship had reeked of subtle sensuality.

Within a week, we had hired another secretary and were picking up the pieces. No one else understood Delilah's behavior, but no one was surprised that she had resigned. A friend heard that she had subsequently admitted herself into a local hospital. I guess she needed to leave all of us behind to be able to do that. She never could say no.

Everyone else was coming through. As soon as the physician gave his approval, I began the excruciating sitting-in process again, confident that few obstacles would now stand in my path. My voice sounded better than ever, the surgery having increased its range. Certainly I was comfortable more of the time and could take bigger vocal risks. With the support of my friends and the inroads I was making in the jazz community, I could hardly wait to see what developed next.

TWELVE

Moving Toward Congruence: "Me Do It"

Shortly after the tonsillectomy, arrangements were made for a trip to the consummate peel-me-a-grape resort, La Costa. I had made the trip other times, but never alone. It was intended to be a recovery period and a general time out. The week would be filled with five exercise classes daily, along with facials, massages, manicures and pedicures. My breakfast would be delivered promptly at 8 a.m. to my room, together with the *Los Angeles Times*. I wouldn't be far away from Hollywood.

It was a propitious time for reflection. The physical exhaustion from the day precluded much evening activity, but the calm promoted introspection. I began to feel whole again and realized singing was a way to express that. I experienced a need to be deeply understood. My attraction to Leo had been based to some extent on his enchanting efforts to get to know me, but he turned out to be too insubstantial. Delilah, of course, had understood the passion. I had erroneously assumed she was capable of understanding the rest of me.

The annual Academy Awards night happened when I was there. La Costa was an appropriate place to be, a frequent retreat for celebrities. I had seen Barbara Walters, Don Adams, Bette Davis, Milton Berle and John Belushi there. Being there this time of year put me in the thick of things.

I wrote in my journal, "Oscar night! The place is buzzing . . . THIS is what L.A. is all about . . . I get caught up in all that excitement . . . On TV now, they are doing an historical overview of Warner Bros. God, it sends my juices flowing. Wonder what's behind that? More than a lifelong interest. After all, the excitement of hearing 'Hooray for Hollywood' is past, no? Why do I identify with all that? . . . How to be surfeited? Perhaps it's only my ability to empathize . . . Just can't seem to get enough."

Among the books I read was one on the psychotherapeutic experiences of celebrities. It caused me to write about my own. "Certainly one who had an impact was Ricky. Those nine months were very heavy and anxious. Wonder how she would describe it? I can recall wanting to go so much, but undergoing so many psychogenic reactions I could hardly function. There is so much that she did of which I'm critical, but I have trouble remembering the process. Don't recall any developmental discussion. Topics come to mind—can remember feeling distinctly one-down, being afraid of her teasing manner which seemed judgmental. Yet she encouraged my career plans and was probably flattered by my identification with her. Too much so—she never really dealt with my transference . . . What did she do for me? Bought me time for decisions, encouraged my feeling and plans, gave me a temporary role model, and some general personal validation. But the negative was strong, too. She eventually became just another person I cared about who let me down."

After La Costa, I felt refreshed, refocused and ready to begin anew my attack on show biz. My next solo trip to Antoine's was characterized by confidence and patience. As I sat there, listening to the boys play a set, the fantasy was emerging with increased clarity. Opening night, media people, television interviews, big crowds. Only a matter of time before it went national. Absolutely no doubt in my mind that I would pack 'em in. Give me a chance and stand back.

And yet, there was another part of me, the part that knew the change in lifestyle that would be required. Though there was a sense of commitment now, with the nightly hours of singing, learning new songs, meeting with Arletta, I knew there would have to be more. Wardrobe, more promotion and ever-increasing intensity would have to be forthcoming. I longed for someone to come in and take over, as a personal manager. I needed a person to coordinate the clothes, tell me what sounded good and what was awful—an objective critic with my best interests at heart.

I could feel the manic spiral engulf me so that little sleep was required. Apart from time with Aaron and clients, most of the energy was spent in conferring with friends about my career. There was enough sleep to produce a dream. In it, I visited Judy Garland's mother in the house in which Judy was raised. There seemed to be lots of friends in the house who wanted access to it, apparently to search for memorabilia, which were not in evidence. As I walked through the house, it was strangely familiar. There was a sense of comfort and peace, as I knew I could return to it at any time. Her mother and I began to talk. I became tearful and she handed me a Kleenex. I told her of the ironies in this house and that I sensed Judy everywhere in my career. Yet if she were alive, she would have little to do with me because I am a shrink. I told her mother that I liked to sing Judy's repertoire and it seemed to please her. She was planning to give me something of Judy's when I left, which was highly unusual for her to do. As I walked out the door, the intensity of the feeling struck me, a sense of being haunted.

Through April and May of 1979, there was a full thrust forward on all fronts. I had an expectation of success and was intolerant of any interference, especially on my own part. If I had a cold or a headache, it was unacceptable. Any pain seemed superfluous and almost silly. It was generally disregarded, unless it concerned my throat. Professional progress was measurable. It was now possible for me to sit in at two clubs almost whenever I wanted. That was the good news. The bad news was that I still had to cater and defer to the musicians and the singer in order to do it. In spite of my best of efforts, it was beginning to sink in that I was going to be Portland small potatoes. I felt like some supercilious dilettante, at the mercy of less adequate people.

It was this realization that produced another revealing, even graphic dream. I was at a friend's house, surrounded by lots of supportive people. It was an informal gathering and people were getting up to sing, some with records. Others had brought their own piano player. When I decided to participate, I called to Eddie Wied (the piano player from the Sky Trio), but suddenly there was a rush to the stage and it became a competition. I waited for my turn because I didn't want to engage in the physical pushing to get up there. I mumbled something about it being too cutthroat and started to leave. Then I realized I didn't have my car and there was no way back. I was hoping Eddie would pave the way for me to sing but this didn't happen. Before long, I found myself out walking in a strange area, trying to find my way home. When I had almost reached home, it occurred to me that I might have had a chance to sing if I had merely outwaited everyone. My stamina, which was sufficient to have gotten me home over a long and unfamiliar distance, would have won the day. I kicked myself for having walked out, but there was no way to return.

The dream told me I still had confidence in my talent but my patience for the external impediments was growing short. There was an internal voice, though, that told me if you stop now, even in the face of frustration, you will regret it later. Having long ago learned to trust my inner self, I continued to persevere.

One of the regular weekend nights at Antoine's was especially well attended by friends. The singer was being petulant and controlling, putting off my sitting in until after midnight. A good friend, who knew of my political battles at Portland State, asked why I was willing to put up with the politics of show biz but not at Portland State. I was stunned. It hadn't occurred to me that there was any connection at all. But she was right. Practically since the first day I arrived at PSU, I had waged a battle for my autonomy. First there had been the war to be able to maintain my private practice; then, the battle over working hours. I didn't see any need to hang around the department when I wasn't holding office hours, participating in meetings, or in class. I had been clear there, and eventually triumphant. It was harder to be either of these with show biz. Being clear and assertive was counterproductive. Was I going against myself to continue the war in this zone? The possibility of this personal violation and the juxtaposition mentioned by my friend was devastating. I started to cry. Before anyone noticed it, I quickly paid the tab and left the restaurant, my friends forgotten in my frustration.

Later that week I had another of those dreams that seemed to be telling me something. I walked into a smoky jazz club. Singers were waiting to sit in, even though the mike system was crummy. It wasn't until I finally took my turn that I realized the piano player knew only a few tunes. I began to sing and felt good rapport with the audience. The owner of the club walked up on the stage, interrupted me and took me aside. He said he would never pay me to sing, and why should he? He pointed to all the aspiring singers and confidently noted they were always willing to provide the entertainment free. I returned to the stage, finished my song, and tracked down the owner again. So why wouldn't he pay me? Was the real reason that I was no good? No, he said, that wasn't it. Then why? I was too aggressive, he declared. He was confused as to why I cared so much. As he walked away, I realized I had my answer. I became depressed by the reality that I was being destroyed by my own passion for performing. I knew that I could continue to pressure him and that I might be successful. I also knew that I would have to apply that pressure continuously to be successful.

Toward the end of May, the stress reactions began that were so typical for me: isolate and insulate. I let some opportunities go by to visit the Jazz Quarry and Antoine's. I didn't want to continue to set myself up, but there was some confusion about whether I was accepting failure or merely not persevering toward success. Was my criterion for success changing? It still seemed like a waste to let it go. That was atypically passive for me and unacceptable. I wasn't ready to make a proactive decision of that magnitude, but the decision had been made to make a decision.

With ironic timing, another biography was released on Judy Garland. Though Doris Day had been my idol during my early teen-age years, it was Judy Garland who reached me on a gut level. I never "admired" her in that sense, but was fascinated with her, as were so many who knew her. She was talented, misunderstood, dedicated, alone in important ways. I could identify with that. It caused me to reflect on what existentially-oriented psychotherapy might have contributed to her life: a complete reconstruction of her inner life, replacing the hysteria and externality. With her lifestyle, the only way therapy would have been effective would have been for her shrink to travel with her, which would have put Judy firmly in control again. The therapeutic relationship would have been a critical vehicle for the success of the therapy. It seemed that most of her therapists were medical model men she either conned or set up as L.B. Mayer surrogates. No wonder she scoffed at therapy. When I spoke to Jim Bugental about her dying on the toilet, I cried. "She never had a chance," I said. "She never met me."

The day I finished reading the biography of Judy, I had another dream. I was visiting a set on the MGM lot when Judy was just a child. I was trying to warn her. "I know what your life will be like," I said, "listen to me." But she paid no attention. I woke up and immediately wrote in my journal, "While I'm really feeling the sadness now, the rational part is critical. It derides me for being a savior, for having such delusions of power, for letting fantasies get out of hand. I never met her, never even came close. I wasn't even in graduate school when she died. Now she'd be in her late fifties and even more resistant and demanding. Would I drop everything to see her in therapy with my present way of life? Wonder what those ten years would have done to/for her. And I still wonder why she haunts me so."

As I reread my entry, the words came into focus: "Such delusions of power . . . letting fantasies get out of hand." It sounded like my singing career. Now I really was confused. So many conflicting messages, all from within.

By the next month, Cheryl had ended a binding relationship and began spending more time with me. She didn't seem to mind going with me to odd places and keeping the strange hours that were required of a musical supplicant. I certainly felt better not going to those places alone. Though my demeanor clearly said, "Stay away," there was always the threat of being picked up by some creep. As I got to know her better, I began to share some of the passion with her. Much to my amazement, she seemed to understand, though the whole idea was completely foreign to her. A native of Portland, she knew nothing about Hollywood-style show biz. But I liked the fact she was comfortable dwelling on a deeper plane, whether it was sharing the show-biz passion or discussing the emotional impact of events. She was capable of functioning on more than a few levels and intriguingly complex. As we frequented clubs, we were sometimes asked if we were sisters; the resemblance was external as well as internal. As we got closer, I asked her to take a trip to L.A. with me.

There were several reasons for the trip. The ostensible one was a family therapy workshop at the Beverly Hilton. The two real reasons were to pick up more sheet music at the huge shop on Cahuenga, and to take another shot at Riverside.

I didn't know how Bill would feel about my sitting in again, only six months later. And I had no idea of his tie with Delilah. Had she called him to complain about me? I decided to take the risk. He was most gracious, and we arranged to meet at his house again.

This time I was more comfortable. Not only did I have another six months of repertoire-building and performing behind me, but I felt I had a strong, no-strings-attached ally in Cheryl. This time, everything went well. I forgot the lyrics to "Just the Way You Are," but it was no big deal. Besides, I covered it well, unlike the last time when I thrust the mike in Delilah's face to bail me out of "You Are the Sunshine of My Life." I was feeling more and more the pro.

The camaraderie with Bill reinforced the musician network I was building. And I hadn't needed Delilah this time to make it work for me. We stayed until the last song was sung, at two a.m. As Cheryl and I drove down the Riverside Freeway back to the Beverly Hilton, I felt that old exhilaration. I had never experienced that feeling before I began performing in public, and thought of the irony of that. With all my worship of Doris Day, I had visualized myself as a canned performer, most comfortable in film and records. There, mistakes could be redone; live performing was scary, and I had done it only in plays and while playing a musical instrument. I truly liked the immediacy and electricity of the nonverbal interaction between me and the audience. I still felt within myself as I sang, however. It was seemingly impossible to communicate myself at all the levels with which I directly experienced the music.

As a longtime teacher, I was good at transmitting ideas and thoughts. I was a good classroom entertainer, able to make a dry idea interesting. As a psychologist, I could communicate the intensity of a feeling using words. As a singer, it was more of a challenge to bring it all together. There was the message of the lyricist, the mechanical techniques of singing, staying on pitch, adding creative embellishments, blending with the band, relating to the audience. And all the while there were the private images, integrating all the levels of internal history, that elevated the experienced intensity. It was a limitation I never felt was overcome.

The kinetic energy made me want to record again. It had been two years since the Los Angeles gig in the Johnny Mercer Studio. With the tonsillectomy and the additional experience, I had come a long way. I called Arletta and asked her to set up some musicians for the session at a local recording studio. We had a single rehearsal and did the taping two days later. I chose seven tunes, all of which we taped in three hours. To my surprise, I could have gone much longer, even with the tension of the session. As I listen to that tape today, I still hear all the flaws, but there is a distinct improvement from the earlier recording session. I still had not learned, however, to trust my own judgment.

In this session, we recorded simultaneously, which divided me between the taping and the pressures of live performing. It had none of the insularity of the L.A. session. Though it was more natural, I felt the burden of settling for a take after two or three, even though I could have done it better. I understand why Streisand and Sinatra have the reputation for being perfectionists. While I had the inclination, I didn't have the courage. Unfortunately, it was to be my last recording session.

Enter the era of sitting in out of town. In addition to Riverside, I sang at the Maui Surf in Maui and the York in Monterey, California. It felt quite cosmopolitan to know I could fit in with any musical group. I was portable; all I needed was knowledge of my keys and a song title. By this time my repertoire was extensive and I was ready for just about anything. It was during this time that I finally had an opportunity to sing at the famed Prima Donna. Gene Diamond was performing there one night and wasn't feeling well. He asked if I would do a few tunes to give his voice a break. I had sounded better myself, but I sang two of my "safe" songs just to be sure: "Love Is Here to Stay" and "I Could Write a Book." Another milestone. Still, the boss was not in that night, so my fantasy of actually working for pay was not yet an option.

The summer continued to be busy and stressful. By mid-June, I received an official notice from the chairman of the psychology department that my contract would not be renewed. This could be done, even without cause, because I did not have tenure. According to the rules of the American Association of University Professors, PSU had to give me a year's notice. In effect, I had a year of grace. Unless I chose to fight.

Delilah's unemployment hearing was scheduled for a few weeks later. Though she had quit, she realized she would not get her benefits unless she had been formally fired. She contended that my letting her waive the two weeks' notice was the equivalent of terminating her. There was so much unfinished business between us that I dreaded facing her with others around. Pauline was kind enough to volunteer to represent me at the hearing, and I was relieved. In the hearing, Delilah had the opportunity to clear up her unfinished business, getting out all her anger. While she accused me of dominating her time, she admitted she never set limits and became enmeshed voluntarily. She claimed that I had taken advantage of her. There was a lot of truth in her allegations, but I was angry that she couldn't or wouldn't deal with me directly. I had never heard any of that anger. I understood her avoidance, though. I was having ambivalent feelings myself. I was glad it was over.

The studio taping had been in July. By September I was dreading returning to school. I had been living with the reality of having been canned and now had to face the music for a year. The more I thought about it, the angrier I became. I was a good teacher, always receiving top ratings from the students. I had served on countless committees, including the politically difficult Affirmative Action Committee. I had been an effective mentor for both graduate and undergraduate students, having set up a training setting for them at Portland Habilitation Center. The more I thought about it, the more I became convinced that it was a little group of four that wanted me out. The group consisted of three experimental psychologists who lived in their rat lab on the fifth floor, and the chairman. I thought the chairman was personally threatened by me and resented the money I was making in private practice. I had also recently confronted one of the four on an ethics violation. He had been sleeping with a member of the encounter group he was leading, which is an ethical no-no. I had informed him that I knew about it, and would report it to the American Psychological Association if he did not desist, as is required by the APA bylaws. While he never denied the violation, I knew he resented my interference in his sex life. I was teaching psychology of women, among other courses, and was known as the resident feminist. It was not a popular position with the four macho males, who had numerous sexual conquests among the students. We were natural enemies in that regard. I decided to fight the firing.

The October promotion and tenure hearings would be the setting. This was the first year I was eligible for tenure and I decided to pursue it actively. Though I had technically been fired, I was still able to present my case for tenure, a loophole in the system. I asked a friend in the department to act as my spokesman for the closed meeting and advocate for me. I was counting on the department as a whole to override the minority of four.

Before the meeting, I had officially appealed the firing on the divisional level of the university. The Social Science Division was led by another "good old boy" who was a friend of the chairman. I figured I wouldn't get a fair hearing. Seated around the rectangular table were representatives from the other departments in the division. Also there were two of the four enemies. They accused me of never being at my office and of not producing a sufficient amount of scholarly research. I defended myself from their allegations, which were thinly-veiled references to my private practice. My position involved documenting my presence in my office, and equating community service with scholarship. I had been a prolific maker of speeches to local groups and was serving on the board of directors of the Northwest Film Study Center. The committee adjourned to consider its next move.

In the meantime, the psychology department met to decide the tenure issue. Everyone knew the decision would be evaluated by many outside the narrow politics of the department. As usual, I was hoping facts would prevail over emotion. I had covered all possible bases, but was well aware that politics was not my forte, in psychology or in show biz.

Anxiety kept me awake the night before the meeting, though I knew there was nothing more I could do. It was up to the persuasive powers of my friend and the integrity of the department itself. I went to my office the next morning and waited. Within an hour of their convening, my friend emerged with a smile on his face. I had won! It was unprecedented, not only overruling the chairman and the other three powerhouses, but also unusual to be awarded tenure the first eligible year. I felt vindicated, but I knew the enemies would reorganize more effectively next time. They had underestimated me and they wouldn't make that mistake again. But victory was mine and I savored it for months.

Soon I heard from the Social Science Review Committee that I had won there as well. The firing was overturned and my record was cleared. That "good old boy" had come through, much to my surprise, and had considered the case on its own merits. My community service and teacher ratings were praised in an official letter from the dean. Toward the end of that semester, I was even invited to a special tea in honor of the top teachers in the university. As good as all that felt, I knew it was only a temporary victory. But it bought me time to return to other issues.

As if all this political garbage weren't draining enough, December of that year (1979) was noteworthy in that a courtroom appearance was required to finish off the divorce. As with many divorcing people, I thought the terms unfair. Leo had hired an attorney not-so-affectionately termed "Slime" by my friends, a killer who went for the jugular. In my humanistic naiveté, I hired a nice guy, who couldn't compete with the aggressive tactics. It was another case of sticking by my principles. I wouldn't have done anything differently, but it hurt at the time.

The one area in which we agreed was custody. We still shared the value of good parenting, though our ideologies were vastly different. It was important that Aaron come to know both of us, so joint custody was established. After nine years of marriage, the last eighteen months apart, it was finally over.

By this time, Cheryl was spending lots of time with Aaron and me, so much so that we became like a family. To underscore our *esprit*, we called ourselves "The PAC"—Pam, Aaron and Cheryl.

That Christmas we threw a party, an activity I had long avoided. We had enough bucks to hire a caterer and musicians, and I would handle the entertainment, along with Arletta and a bass player I had worked with at the Jazz Quarry. In spite of the more than 75 people at the party, I was at ease because I was singing most of the time. The fact of my singing was still a surprise among the professional community, so it was another stage of the coming-out process. I wanted to know what my psychological colleagues thought of this rather untraditional hobby.

Almost everyone seemed pleased, even my allies from the psychology department at PSU. My former mentor sat on the couch glaring at me. He had been one of the psychologists at PSU who had hired me and had been extremely helpful in setting up my first office. We had been strong allies at the university since we were the only full-time clinicians for a time. Some time during the divorce, though, the dinner invitations started going to Leo and I was cut out. There was an obvious tension between us, though nothing had been said. While I was confused, I had no hard feelings. I suspect he felt the distance that came from my pulling out from under his influence. The show-biz stuff didn't help.

As the others crowded around me at the party, it seemed the torch was being passed. I was now the star, so to speak. From that time on, he had little to say to me.

Though I was scrupulous in avoiding any mention of being a shrink when I sang, the word began to get around. Clients began to come in to the office who had seen me sing, and even some of the musicians who had backed me. Again, the transference issues came up. If I spent several sessions exploring the life of a piano player, could he treat me as just another singer when we worked together? It turned out it was comfortable to everyone but me. As I would wait to sit in, the musicians would sit with me during their break. My client would come over and just continue his session in the lounge. It was distracting. My role as a psychologist was a different kind of intensity than what I felt as a singer. It came from a different place, and I wanted to keep them separate. I was relieved when he terminated because of limited funds.

In January 1980, I was asked to be the first female guest host of a local television talk show, *Town Hall*. The topic was "Kids and Drugs." A Munter Major had suggested to the producer that I might want to do a one-shot in that capacity. Of course! Open the refrigerator door and I'll do twenty minutes! While it didn't involve singing, it was a public performance in which I would get to play myself.

The night of the taping was also the night of one of Portland's famous ice storms. The entire city was frozen in. I was disappointed, thinking I had lost my chance to be a moderator of a talk show. However, Channel 2 had experience with Portland weather and commandeered a taxi to pick me up and return me home after the show. The audience consisted of the show's participants, all of whom had some personal acquaintance with the subject. Many were former drug addicts who were there to speak of their experiences with the system. It was an unusual challenge to think on my feet, but I had prepared for the task by reading everything I could find about treatment programs and the psychological problems of the addicted personality.

This was new for me in that I did the promos as well and the whole show was spontaneous. There was no script to work from, no teleprompter or cue cards. I cued the commercials and kept the show running without a rehearsal. It was fun and stimulating, and I knew the show-biz disease had been given a booster shot. Station executives were on the spot and were laudatory. No offers were forthcoming, and another fantasy of discovery had bitten the dust. I decided to do something drastic.

THIRTEEN

Going Pro
and Withdrawal
from Addiction

For the past several years, I had been on the board of directors of a new school, the Oregon Graduate School of Professional Psychology. At various times I had chaired the curriculum committee and was director of admissions. It required major amounts of time and commitment, but it was a worthy project. As is typical of new ventures, the school was having financial problems. While the board consisted of talented and intelligent psychologists, none of them had experience raising money, or knew much about public relations. It was a strange feeling of having power to run the whole show if I wanted to. It led me to an interesting idea. Why not offer to produce a fund-raiser for them, with me as the performer? We could rent the Jazz Quarry for a night, pay the musicians scale, split the drink receipts with the management. I would handle the publicity, make all the arrangements, provide the entertainment and donate the funds to the school. OGSPP only had to show up. Such a deal!

The idea had come at a good time. Despite the fact things were going well, my inner voices of doubt and depression came back. With tenure behind me and the benefit ahead of me, I wrote in my journal:

"Am feeling the pain turn into anger. It's almost a routine now. We go out for a nice dinner, visit a club or two and see what no-talent bozos are making it. I'm not. It seems clear. My contemporaries are working. I'm not . . . What the hell is going on? I was just another voice before I identified myself as a doctor. Now all the comments are directed at the Doctor. What can I do? What am I doing wrong? Is there anything I can do? Powerless, fatalistic.

"I have to buy the house to sing for a whole evening. Will that do it? What is it going to take? I sound better than I ever have. Power, range, repertoire. Goddamn it. The one thing that has really mattered . . . Am I setting myself up for this? Does it only count because I can't have it? So many things are going well for me now, but this. This controls me. It interferes with my good feelings about myself. April 2 (the OGSPP benefit) will be my last chance—my debut and my swan song.

"My head hurts. My gut hurts. Psychosomatic, obviously. I want to tell them all to go to hell. Vindication fantasies. I've won everything else. I feel . . . almost suicidal. Seems silly, really. People kill themselves over lost love, terminal illness, a hopeless life. Not because they can't sing.

"Over a year now at JQ. The writing is on the wall. I can see I'm going to have to beg. And then it will be over because there's nowhere to go after you beg. I'll have to go back to psychology as though none of this mattered. And come up with some snappy lines about making choices. Wonder if anyone else can know what I'm feeling. Even I'm afraid to experience that feeling as deeply as it goes. Why can't anyone hear the pain? Why can't anyone do anything? Why can't I do anything?

"It's so raw. I can smooth it over, rationalize it, and I'm sure I will. I'll have to. But I wanted to record the raw emotion somewhere, to remind myself how much it hurts to suppress a passion, a significant part of self. I don't want to forget this. Ever."

Those moments of hand-to-hand combat with my emotions were episodic and seemed out of synch with the external achievements. The singing was getting better and I was developing a real following. The April benefit was a logical extension of my attempts to integrate the psychology with the show biz.

The Munter Majors were mobilized for the OGSPP benefit. We drew posters, had photos taken, appeared on local TV shows to plug the benefit, everything necessary to complete preparations. The Sky Trio offered to cut their salary as a donation to the school.

I paid for rehearsal time, just for the reassurance it would provide. I covered all expenses and donated that to the school as well. After all, it was my show. To have total control, I would also need to be in charge of the budget. I could do anything I wanted. A local television personality, Rick Meyers, offered to be the master of ceremonies. It would be fun working with Rick; we had known each other for several years. He was a professional, competent and well-prepared. His wife, Sara, would tape the performance, and was one of my boosters. The show would be the first on my own, an opportunity to sing all evening. I was the featured performer, not just someone who was sitting in for someone else. People would be coming to hear me. A red-letter occasion, to be sure.

Arletta and I rehearsed extra hours for several weeks before the benefit, mostly to desensitize me to singing long hours under the pressure of performance conditions. The show would run from nine p.m. to two a.m. I was in the habit of singing several hours a night at home, of course, but I really didn't know the impact of having an audience there. In Riverside, it was very low key and nobody knew who I was. For this performance, many would be coming out of curiosity. Some probably expected a psychology lecture.

Cheryl and I drove to the Jazz Quarry that night. I was aware of feeling tingly and nervous, but felt well prepared to deal with everything that was under my control. My worst fear was that the upscale tickets would not sell and I would be singing to the board of directors and an otherwise empty house. As we walked in, I saw my fears were unfounded. The place was packed and more were waiting at the door. The capacity of the house was 130 but there must have been 150 or more squeezed in there. I went into the small office adjacent to the bandstand by myself, and waited for Dave Elliot to introduce Rick, who would introduce me. My hands were clammy; I was quite alone in every way for those few endless minutes of waiting. I wondered if my chutzpah had gotten me in too deeply this time.

Historical feelings intruded into the moment, as Doris, Eydie, Ella and Dinah were all in that room with me. Was this what it was like for them? Not quite dysfunctional; there was an electricity within that defied description. I wanted to be alone; the feelings produced an isolation anyway. I thought about who might be out there, how they might react to this new Pam Munter, a side few of them had known. I wondered if I might be jeopardizing my professional standing in the psychology community. Then it struck me that I didn't care. If acting on one's most passionate fantasies meant being a disreputable psychologist, then we were advocating different kinds of standards of professionalism. That worry passed quickly. I hoped the dress would be okay and I wouldn't trip over the uncomfortably high heels. I reminded myself to maintain my entertainer's demeanor, to keep working to translate the internal to the external and not lose myself within myself. And I reviewed how to vamp in case I forgot the lyrics. I had psyched myself up and I was ready.

Soon Rick introduced me and I stepped up to the bandstand.

During the brief rehearsal, I had given the trio a list of each tune in the set along with my keys. Some of it was specially prepared material that I was trying for the first time. Included were gimmicky songs like "Let's Do It" and "Second Hand Rose." I figured five or six sets, with seven or eight songs in each set. I knew this was a musical feat. Four or five tunes is more typical, with long breaks in between. But when a singer does this, I get impatient. If I come to hear someone sing, I want to hear them sing, not watch them take a break. It was dogging it, in my opinion. I decided to really give the audience a performance.

To my surprise, I felt comfortable enough to make witty comments before and sometimes after each song. It was like an act I was doing for friends; the words just came rolling out. If I was about to sing "My Man," I would make a comment about this being a song for hysteroid neurotics who needed to be seeing someone. This was a crowd supporting a psychology graduate school, after all. It was fun and almost seemed naughty. I was spoofing psychology, having my cake and eating it too. I was a hero to the school, a singer to the audience and an integrated person to myself. It was a feeling similar to the one I had had after recording the first song in Los Angeles. I could have died then and my life would have felt complete.

The school raised more than two thousand dollars, which was more than it had ever seen. I felt I had done my share to work toward the school's success. Shortly after the benefit, I resigned from the board. Many board members had not worked to sell tickets, and did not even choose to attend their own benefit. I was burned out from the extent of my efforts over the past few years for the school. Now it was someone else's turn.

Of course, the perennial phoenix of the discovery fantasy was there again. I just knew that once the owners of the Jazz Quarry saw what I could do they would hire me immediately. If I could pull all those people in for an expensive show and make money for the bar, they surely would be convinced I could attract people when admission was free. A week after the benefit, I sauntered into the club, hoping the boys would approach me. As usual, Dave asked me to sit in. That was the extent of the action, and I started to get irritated. In the past, I had felt the motivating anger that comes from being an underdog, the person who is dependent on another for a break. I had proved myself. I had come through for everybody. I decided to confront Brad, the younger of the two owners. I asked him what it would take to get a job singing there. He was remarkably open and tentatively set a date over the Labor Day weekend. It was low risk for him, as most people are enjoying the final weekend of the summer out of town. He informed me he paid a new singer $50 a night. I reminded him that they had been looking me over for two years and I had demonstrated my drawing power the previous weekend. He capitulated to $70 a night for a two-night gig.

It was strange to be ecstatic over making $70 a night when I was making that much in a forty-five-minute session in the daytime. Obviously, money was not the motivator here. Negotiating with Brad was for the principle of it, not the cash. I wanted to earn a little more than the average new singer, but the actual amount wouldn't have made any difference. I had reached a major goal in my life. I was being paid to sing, at last!

I was beside myself. Was this what it took? Was it the directness? Was it the two-year apprenticeship? Was it the success of the benefit? Did he have trouble filling the time slot? At that point, I didn't care. This was make-it-or-break-it time, now-or-never, and all those other black-and-white cliches. Two years was a long time to maintain the intensity. It wasn't as though I expected the world to open up, but I was tired of being at other people's mercy. If this weekend didn't propel me into professionalism, it just wasn't going to happen. Before admitting defeat, I would give it everything I had.

I had waited for this opportunity all my life. It was a benchmark, a goal in itself. Unless significant progress was evident, it would be time to call it quits. The weekend took on a disproportionate importance. It was disenchanting to discover it to be a myth that if you work hard, sing well and please the audience success will inevitably follow. I was learning that you're a success only if management says you are.

After the benefit, some realities had come into focus. The intense commitment I had made to singing was in contrast to my teaching experiences at Portland State. I was putting in considerable effort at PSU and remained at risk of ongoing personal attack by the rat men. Singing was at least emotionally rewarding, while lacking the perennial threat.

Portland State teaching had been a consuming but exhilarating experience for seven years. I had battled and won promotion to associate professor and tenure in a relatively short time and was teaching about 250 students in three classes a quarter. The opportunity was there to learn while I earned as I taught courses in abnormal psychology, personality, psychology of adjustment, psychology of women, community psychology, family therapy, counseling, mental deficiency and my favorite, psychology and the media. It was in this course that I opened with a two-week discussion on the life of Judy Garland. I had written an article on psychobiography, the art of using psychological information to look at a person's life. Using records, photographs, videotapes and various biographies, I pieced together her psychological life and her interaction with the times. It was fascinating for all of us and one of those experiences that had kept me at the university.

But it was a sexist environment as well as fundamentally anti-clinical. There were regular purges of the clinicians, as the experimentalists opposed the notion of private practice. We maintained that in order to teach, we had to keep up in our field by working in it. They claimed it detracted from our responsibilities at the university. It was a no-win situation for me, as I was not about to give up my practice. The pressure caused me to feel a deep sense of dread each night before having to go to PSU. The mornings became a test of stamina in pulling myself out of bed. In the seven years of battles and attempts at intimidation, the balance had swung from the positive to the negative. It was time to leave. Life was too short to spend that much time in such nonproductive activity. I had won all the battles, but lost the psychological war of nerves.

My solo singing appearance in September was preceded by a media blitz. I plowed about $500 into newspaper ads, radio ads and a public relations adviser to produce them. We used the last recording session tape as a backdrop for the voice-overs in the radio ads. I wrote a feature article on my show-biz background and sent it to the jazz writer on the *Oregonian*. He printed it as his lead story the week before the Labor Day weekend. The word was out. I had announcements printed on blue paper that resembled engraved wedding invitations, and blitzed the community with them. If nobody showed up for this, it wouldn't be because nobody knew about it.

I followed the same plan of careful preparation as I had for the benefit, including a week at La Costa. It helped me feel special and toned up my body and my breathing, a fitting prelude to the weekend. I spent more time than usual planning the wardrobe, since I would have to wear two different ensembles. When I sat in, I could wear pants and a sweater, or a pantsuit, something comfortable. Dresses bound me in more and sometimes made breathing more difficult. To look my best in those slinky dresses, I stuffed myself into my first "Rawhide" bra—you know, round 'em up, push 'em out—and spiky "bitch" shoes. I became aware of having to move differently, especially with the heels. It was a minor annoyance, when I wanted to be spending all my energy on singing. The costuming was in sharp contrast to my rampant feminism, but I wrote it off to the "pretending" inherent in show biz. As it was, I felt like a one-person show. Sometimes it was overwhelming. There was still no place to get informed feedback, and I was making all these important decisions using only my own judgment.

The first night arrived and boy, was I ready. All that media hype. I knew I had to come through, but I also felt confident. There was a new strength there, in contrast to the first time at the Red Lion when I tentatively made my way to the bandstand. Once again, Cheryl and I entered the Jazz Quarry not knowing what we would find. As we walked in, a hush came over the room, then scattered applause. I looked around and saw a sea of familiar faces—friends, clients, Munter Majors. Even my mother (who was now living in Oregon) was there, and she never went out at night. The evening was a peak experience, never to be replicated.

It was reminiscent of a dream I had several years before. It was "Pam Osborne Day" at Paul Revere Junior High School. All my classmates were to pay tribute in glorious statements of vindication and retribution. Banners were everywhere. I entered the auditorium, which was crowded and humming. As my former drama teacher, Vicki Nagel, introduced me, I walked to the podium and saw that the audience was composed of today's kids, not the kids who went to school with me in the late 1950s. This was the wrong audience. I didn't know what to say to them.

This night at the Jazz Quarry contained the right audience. It showed my clients that fantasies are important to fulfill, and that they can be executed with determination and preparation. It showed my friends that I had gone to a good deal of trouble to entertain them, and that I was letting them in on my passion. It was another culmination of a lifetime of dreams. It was "Pam Munter Night," no doubt about it.

Once again I crammed the sets with songs. This time I grouped some tunes together. There was a Judy Garland medley, a Frank Sinatra medley, and one that seemed especially appropriate, a retribution medley. This opened with "Who's Sorry Now?" continued with "After You've Gone" and ended with "Goody Goody." The medley was a kick to sing and pleased the audience. Almost everyone can identify with the "screw you" lyrics. I added the psychological rap with it that explained the context in humorous pop psych terms. The evening was a triumph. The only way I could let it go was hoping it would be repeated the next night.

And it was! Many people came back, and others joined them, via word of mouth. Another SRO crowd. Brad told me later the JQ set new records in bar receipts, a sure sign of financial success for them. The audience was friendly, familiar and supportive, leading me to try new riffs, new sounds. I was looking forward to the career I sensed was beginning that night. I had seldom experienced such a feeling of internal success coupled with external validation. The unanimity at the JQ produced a new high.

You would think I'd know by now. Life is full of ups and downs, as the cliché goes. My life in show biz was full of both extremes, and my tolerance was growing short. I had hit my peak, the ultimate up. I suspected the truth after the Saturday night performance was over. How could I follow that?

I waited around a few days, expecting a call from Brad offering me more weekends. I had played by all the rules: watching, waiting, providing free services, auditioning over and over, playing a benefit, contributing money to the owner by bringing in big business. When the call never came, my worst fears were confirmed.

The journal contained fewer entries these days. The emotions were almost too intense to chronicle, the internal messages too numerous to sort out and too painful to record. As is typical, I was far more eloquent in my failures than in my successes. After the two-night stand, I captured some of what was happening. After describing the positive feelings, the other half came crashing through.

"Since those eventful weeks of preparation and especially since JQ, I have been out of it. Not much energy, a little down, hard to concentrate. Trouble getting excited about anything. I fear the best is over. There's nothing ahead. I've shot my wad. I suppose there's still the old fantasy that once I 'came out,' the world would stand back, awed and cheering . . . I'm feeling humbled. Like I staged a big party and no one came. Feel foolish. Now it's over, like a weekend on 'Fantasy Island.' Now I have to go back to the grind as though nothing had happened . . . What do I do now? Do I pursue it? What can I do? What do I want to do? I'm afraid to want anything now. Getting bits of it seems to lead to an empty place."

All this didn't fit with the major triumph just a few days before. It was an ending. Like I had gone to the top and it just wasn't enough. I wanted more.

The following weekend Cheryl and I visited the Jazz Quarry again, hoping to force another encounter with Brad. I saw both the owners sitting at a table. Dave, the drummer, waved to me and I knew he would ask me to sing. After the benefit and the SRO performance weekend, sitting in just wouldn't make it anymore. I had outgrown that kind of subservience. There was no other part of my life where I had tolerated that role very long. I was in an enormously successful private practice, helping to shape people's lives. And here I was delegating a significant part of mine to people whose perspective was on a whole different level.

Brad smiled at me from across the room and went on with his conversation. As the status-quo message was transmitted, I became angry, too enraged for a productive meeting with him. The dawning came, as I realized the futility of my position. I would always have to grovel in uncertainty, and that was clearly unacceptable. We got up and walked out the door. It would be three months before I returned.

This was the beginning of an extremely sensitive period. For the past several years, most of my leisure time had been spent singing or preparing to sing. There were always tapes or records playing, and I would even practice in the car as I was driving. Now I found music to be intolerable. The news station assumed permanent status on the car radio and the record player grew dusty from lack of use. We stopped going out on weekends to hear music.

I continued to run experiments periodically, more out of curiosity than anything else. What I was experiencing remained puzzling. One Wednesday evening in October, I put on a Frank Sinatra tape. For the first time in a long time, I let the tears flow. In a single moment, the intensity came rushing back and focused the melancholy I was avoiding. Though my own peak experience had happened only a month earlier, it all seemed years ago. In that time, I had shut down the intensity, flattened out the emotions. After the tape clicked off, I reached for the journal.

"It's hard to face the possibility that I may not have the charisma I thought I did. Other people said so, and I believed it. I felt it. That powerful sense of destiny. The actuality that would . . . pull me into a larger-than-life life. But it's not happening. Now it dawns on me that it never will. What do I do with that?"

Two months later, I was still preoccupied. The feelings would be triggered when I would inadvertently hear music or run one of my emotional experiments. One night I dreamed I was watching an amateur production of a musical play. When it was over, the singers all passed by me and I avoided congratulating them on their performance. There were two important lessons there. One, it was the first dream in many years in which I had not wanted to perform. Second, it seemed that the anger had returned along with the hurt and sadness.

Just before Christmas, I came home from an evening with my mother, put on an Arletta tape and sang. My voice sounded good. The vocal endurance had gone, after only four months. I guess I wanted to see if I could "do it" when I wanted to, some reassurance that "it" had not disappeared forever. Then I put the Sinatra tape on again. I was still amazed at how little it took to get to me through music. It seemed to reach into the deepest part of me. The chord progressions, where and how the melody goes, the instrumentation, his phrasing. I could hear each instrument section together and by itself. I could appreciate the sheer power of the arrangement. I believed in myself, that I had an ability to "do that." The feelings began to change, away from a deep sadness to a feeling that I was missing something powerful inside.

A few weeks later, I became impatient with what I perceived to be an overreaction to the whole situation. I had let my fantasies get away from me again, taking singing too seriously. I was out of step, expecting too much. After all, I was pushing forty and I wasn't sleeping with anyone who could do me any good. What could I expect? My cynicism led me to experiment with visiting jazz clubs again, selecting places where I wasn't known. I didn't want to sit in.

Poor Cheryl did not know what was going on a lot of the time, and probably questioned the duration and extremity of the response. We would go to a club after a pleasant and stimulating dinner and sit down. We would order a drink and the music would begin. Within a few minutes, tears would be cascading down my face; the pain was obvious. I felt as though I would implode. Listening to music touched me so deeply, hearing someone else singing, knowing my time was over—all of this caused involuntary shuddering. The pain was self-inflicted, which made it worse. I could have continued to sing, under the identical conditions I had performed under for over two years, always waiting for opportunity. My self-respect could not survive that emotional ringer.

After a number of evenings of hastily scribbled notes to each other in the darkness of a jazz club, we agreed to avoid them for a while longer. It was nothing we said, though by now she knew clearly of my ongoing pain. We would continue to go out to dinner with some frequency; we would make it an early evening. Instead of rolling in at two or three o'clock, it would be more like ten. I felt as if I were in mourning. Life seemed slowed down. Over the next year, there would be some sitting in, usually at the request of a friend. It would be in strange places where I wasn't known. I didn't return to the half-dozen or so clubs I had frequented. What is interesting is how a person can suddenly disappear like that and no one investigates. I had been in the Jazz Quarry on a regular basis, had that successful engagement, then was gone. It was as if I hadn't mattered. That made it worse.

By July, there was more emotional distance. I had gotten tired of myself and the preoccupation with avoidance. I had isolated myself from my friends and had thrown myself into my work, which could be emotionally consuming. When I thought of singing, it was as though all that had happened to someone else. The journal reads, "Still have that melodramatic image of being on my deathbed, getting ready for the famous last words—and still sense they would relate more to my disappointments than my successes. It will soon be a year since the weekend at the Jazz Quarry. And I wonder even now—how could I have been so at ease, so comfortable, so good—and not have been more successful? . . . I am now totally out of the limelight, known only to my clients and a few others. I hadn't intended it this way, but I'm going to have to learn to live with it."

Thus for most of 1981, there was little show biz in my life. I was still trying to bury the corpse, but it wouldn't stay in the ground. Every time I would put music on the stereo, or hear a tune in the background in a restaurant or an elevator, the sense of loss would come rushing back. My show-biz dreams even stopped, to be replaced by dreams of death and grieving. Sleep would come easily enough, but I could not stay asleep longer than a few hours. Memories of performances would come back and the sadness would grip me, preventing slumber.

To escalate the desensitization, Cheryl, Aaron and I decided to take tap-dancing lessons. Aaron also signed up for a jazz dance class. It was challenging for the part of my brain that had trouble with motor sequencing, and I felt I was using the wrong part of my body. I should be singing. At this point, though, dancing was all I could tolerate; and it was sometimes touch and go at that.

One of the most provocative events of my life occurred during that year as well. Some time during the summer I was contacted by an executive from ABC Television's *20/20*, who asked if I knew anything about a phenomenon known as Lifespring. As it happened, I had worked on several wrongful death lawsuits involving it. Many of my clients and PSU students had been involved with this organization, and I had a whole collection of anecdotes.

We filmed with Geraldo Rivera in my office in August and the show was televised nationally in October, in two parts. Though the interview had taken about a half-hour, my part on the show consisted of about thirty seconds. It was disappointing, but exciting to find myself on network television, under any circumstances. Local TV was becoming a matter-of-fact experience by now; this was something really special.

As with my other imagined triumphs, there was little reaction immediately after the show. Within a month, though, mail came in from all over the country and the phone rang asking for interviews for radio shows from coast to coast. That was pleasing, but not enough for the kid from Hollywood who was still waiting to be discovered.

Still, the show kept me on a high for a while. One January morning, however, I arrived at work to find I was being served with a subpoena. Lifespring was suing everyone involved with the program, including one Pamela Osborne Munter, for over one hundred million dollars. Did I say I wanted fame?

FOURTEEN

The One Hundred Million Dollar Lawsuit

I had been teaching psychology at Portland State for only a few years when I began to hear of Lifespring. My classes were typically held in an amphitheater, a lions-and-Christians setting, in which the students were elevated in tiers above me. At the appointed time, I would walk into the room and open the class, asking for questions. This was my favorite time of the class, when I could demonstrate my knowledge and versatility. One of the students commented that I handled the class like Carol Burnett's famous show opening. It was very show-bizzy; I could be funny and glib, yet informative at the same time.

Students would sometimes ask if I knew anything about Lifespring, a new organization that had moved into Oregon. People shared their perceptions and experiences during class. I didn't like what I was hearing. Early reports were of a five-day basic training, in which a large group of people would meet continuously (except for sleep) to work out problems in their lives. It sounded like encounter group theory but with an authoritarian base. Bathroom breaks and eating periods were strictly regulated; glasses, watches and medicine were confiscated. If people left the sessions without permission, they were followed, confronted and entreated to return. It sounded frightening in its degree of control and the potential consequences for the human spirit.

Some time during this period a graduate student asked to interview me about these new quasi-therapies. I was far more familiar with EST and more conventional marathons and encounter groups, but was becoming more interested in Lifespring since it seemed to be concentrating its efforts locally. During the interview, I expressed reservations about these types of "therapy," commenting on the transience of positive result and potential danger.

The student's material apparently was published for I began to hear from radio stations around the country, asking for comments on these groups. Among the callers were casualties of Lifespring. Parents of children who had sought out Lifespring called the office at Portland State, and began to show up as clients in my private practice as well. Lifespring seemed to be hazardous under some circumstances, but I didn't know what to do about it.

I spoke with several colleagues at professional meetings. Many were similarly distressed, but lacked even my rudimentary knowledge. Apparently there was no psychologist involved with the Lifespring group in Oregon. Under the ethical precepts of the American Psychological Association, if I see a possible ethical violation, I must inform the APA, which I was intending to do. Without a professional in charge, the APA had no jurisdiction. I was not an injured party, only a concerned one. I continued to read what I could find and to talk with anyone who would tell me anything about the group.

One day in my PSU office, I received a phone call from Bill Newgent. He sounded frantic, his voice tremulous. In a rushed manner, he told me of the recent death of his daughter, Gail Renick. An asthmatic, she apparently left a Lifespring training session to retrieve her medication. She collapsed a short distance from the meeting place and died later in a Seattle hospital. Newgent blamed Lifespring for her death. I wasn't sure why he was telling me all this. When he asked if I would be interested in any written material, I jumped at the chance. While I had heard of emotional distress during and after the trainings, this was the first death, as far as I knew.

Within a week, Newgent had sent a large packet of material. He had reproduced an article from the Seattle *Post-Intelligencer* detailing her death, and had written some trenchant questions in the margins, implying Lifespring had murdered Gail Renick. At the time, he sounded like an hysterical, bereaved father, looking for a logical reason for his daughter's death, perhaps trying to locate a scapegoat so he could begin to work through his feelings. I continued to read his articles and remarks for several months. After a while, though, reading the voluminous material became too time-consuming and I began to place it in a file.

In the meantime, some of the interviews I had been giving about Lifespring had hit the media. The only way I knew was a phone call one afternoon in my Beaverton office. It was John Hanley, founder and president of Lifespring, from San Rafael, California. He said he had heard of my concerns about his group and wondered if I would take a few minutes to share them with him. I told him about the lack of screening of trainees, which I believed to be a serious flaw. They had little idea whether their trainees were unstable, psychotic or even retarded. I could find no evidence of training the trainers either. Who were these people who entered into the intimate lives of the trainees? Did they know what they were doing? I didn't like the relentless tracking down of the trainees at their homes or place of business if they made a decision not to return to the sessions. And I had heard no evidence of systematic follow-up.

Hanley smoothed over my grievances. I had the feeling he had attended a Dale Carnegie course. He asked if I had spoken with his psychological consultant, Dr. Everett Shostrom. I had not known Shostrom was involved, and was surprised. Shostrom was known to me as the narrator of a psychotherapy film classic that is used in undergraduate courses in counseling. His narration is well done and always stimulates good class discussion. It was hard to believe that he would be involved in Lifespring. What could he be doing?

My answer came quickly. Within minutes of hanging up with Hanley, the phone rang again. It was Shostrom. With the same smooth manner, he repeated the identical questions asked by Hanley. I wondered if they had spoken, and if they had even been in the same room together. I gave Shostrom identical answers. He said he had not been aware there was no screening, which was confusing. What, then, was he doing there? It seemed irresponsible not to screen in an endeavor as sensitive and potentially volatile as an encounter situation. Impressed by his previous credentials, I gave him the benefit of the doubt. Maybe he had just come on board and honestly wanted the information. I didn't want to believe that a psychologist would knowingly turn his head the other way.

I didn't give the calls much more thought, other than to wonder why they found me so threatening. I was just a college professor, after all. There must have been others with more clout who were vocal. It is still surprising to discover that was not the case. To this day, few of my colleagues have spoken out against such groups as Lifespring.

In July of 1979, I wrote to Newgent thanking him for the latest batch of materials and detailed some of my reservations. By this time, I felt some support for him. He didn't seem to be getting over his daughter's death, and I felt some therapeutic concern. By this time, his letters raised some questions in my mind about Lifespring's role. In my letter, I shared my feeling that Lifespring might victimize the consumer in the maintenance of total secrecy. The group would hold an open meeting in the evening, throw around some pop psych cliches and ask people to sign up, without adequate warnings or hard information about what they were going to experience. I had no idea that he was planning to sue Lifespring in a wrongful death action, or that it would lead me into a more public role in criticizing the group.

Then I received the letter. An attorney in Seattle wanted to consult with me on the Renick case. I had never heard of Richard Stanislaw, but then northwest lawyers lack the glamorous notoriety of big-city attorneys. He asked that we meet to discuss the possibility of my being retained as an expert witness in the case of Newgent v. Lifespring.

I was surprised that there was a lawsuit at all, and initially saw it as a therapeutic move for Bill Newgent. It was flattering to be considered an expert witness. While I had searched both the literature and the experiences of those around me, I had not directly experienced Lifespring. I was usually willing to speak out publicly on controversial issues, but involvement in a legal action? Well, that was more serious.

I had served as an expert before, in pornography cases for Multnomah County, in divorce and custody cases and even in murder trials. This case had more ins and outs, greater complexity. There was also the possibility of establishing precedent for similar "sudden growth" groups.

My first meeting with Dick was pleasant enough. He struck me as a real character, craggy, with icy eyes, clear and insightful. As we talked, he confessed a weakness for Haagen-Dazs ice cream, and mentioned that his sister was a reporter for a Seattle television station. We had some things in common. Dick seemed knowledgeable about Lifespring, and believed it had contributed to Gail Renick's death. As was usual for me, I was put off by his strongly maintained viewpoint. I knew a little about the organization, but I found it hard to believe that it would knowingly contribute to the death of one of its trainees. For one thing, I couldn't believe that any group would be that ignorant of the basic safeguards. I felt somewhat like a devil's advocate.

When he offered me records and depositions to read, I leaped at the chance. When he offered to send me the actual training manuals, I could hardly contain myself. I had tried to obtain as much information as possible, and here was the opportunity to get the original documents. At last I could read for myself, without the intermediaries of attorneys or frustrated students or even successful Lifespring trainees. I could hardly wait for the stuff to arrive via Federal Express.

When it came, I secreted myself, very much like a sequestered jury, to take the time for study. It was important to decide for myself, away from the hysteria of the victim, away from someone else's experience.

To use the parlance of the day, I was blown away. It was as though someone had read a book one day and framed an organization the next. The naiveté and potential destructiveness abounded in almost every exercise. The founders had attempted to codify the trainer's job by producing a training manual that would be used in every training offered anywhere. But the exercises were set up without any of the usual safeguards I had learned were so important.

Even the most elementary therapeutic course in college emphasized the importance of screening the applicants. If someone was in crisis, the groups would probably be of little help. The success of the group depended on the perpetuation of the feelings of groupness, a collective loyalty that would transcend but enhance the individual. The only way that worked would be for all the members to be relatively healthy. Lifespring had no real way of screening out crazies. There was one item on the questionnaire that asked if the person was in therapy. If so, the consent of the therapist was sought. That was so naive as to be laughable. Often the most unstable people were those who had not sought out therapy. There was no real testing of emotional status, or any query about a person's defense system. I was appalled.

The exercises themselves seemed calculated to induce emotion without any guarantee that it would be handled by Lifespring trainers. The emphasis was on catharsis: feel deeply, go ahead and lose control. Humiliate and humble yourself—it is the true path to mental health. If you can survive this training, you are stable and healthy and can survive anything, it seemed to imply.

Numerous powerful techniques were employed toward this end. From my own experience, I knew the power of music to evoke feeling. For those less stable, it could produce long-buried memories, with little structure or support to put them in a constructive context. Frequently the exercises were conducted with music in the background while the trainee sat with eyes closed. The trainer would drone out instructions intended to evoke feelings. It was reminiscent of a mass hypnotic induction, encouraging the abandonment of the usual defenses. While a healthy person might be able to withstand this kind of emotional assault, many could not.

Gail Renick was in the fifth day of her basic training, the last of the intense workshop. The days had stretched long into the night, the only interruption being her going home to sleep. All meals were taken with the other trainees, with breaks dictated by the trainers. And for her spare time at home, she had been given homework of an emotional nature which she had apparently completed. In the middle of a particularly evocative exercise on Sunday, she had an asthmatic attack. Since she had surrendered her asthma medicine on entering the training, she had little recourse. Either she would accept the trainer's judgment that the attack was a "cop-out," or she would have to leave to go home to pick up her stronger medicine. After a period in which she had trouble breathing, the trainers apparently became concerned and asked that she go downstairs to the basement to sit quietly and work it out on her own. Within a short time it became apparent to her that she needed the medicine. After abortive telephone attempts to retrieve the drug, she left to pick it up herself. By the time Lifespring gave her permission to go, the situation had become desperate. Within 200 yards of the training site, Gail Renick collapsed in the arms of an employee of a nearby restaurant, cyanotic and dying.

I could understand why Bill Newgent suspected foul play. The irresponsibility of Lifespring was almost implicit in its training manuals. After reading the basic training manual and the facts of the Renick case, I was surprised that no other deaths had occurred. Other interesting facts soon came to light. Gail's car keys were later discovered some distance from her person; a Lifespring employee had them. Her car was also located a distance from the restaurant. What would account for this? Wouldn't she be in possession of her own car keys, since she was going for medicine? If a Lifespring person had been helping her by driving her to her apartment, where was he or she? Did he/she panic when Gail became cyanotic? The mystery was intriguing, but just the facts in the training manual convinced me of the dangers of Lifespring. I agreed to work with Dick Stanislaw on his case. And I began to understand Bill Newgent's anger and suspicion about his daughter's death.

Somewhere during our conferences in Portland, Dick introduced me to his associate, Dan Jacobson. Dan was younger than Dick and very quick-witted. Between the two of them, the conversation was supercharged with acute observations and acerbic remarks. I looked forward to meeting with them; we formed a mutual admiration society. It was refreshing—and something of a relief—that there was never a suggestion of sexual innuendo between us. I had seldom experienced that freedom in working with men in an intense professional relationship. It also felt good to know that they valued me as a professional, without my having to "pay dues." It made our relationship comfortable and stimulating.

Then the team of Stanislaw and Jacobson offered me another challenge. A young man in Portland had drowned in the Willamette River while enrolled in a Lifespring training. His family claimed Lifespring had unduly influenced this man to try to swim the heavy current; in fact, Artie Barnett could not swim and was known to be afraid of the water. Why would he want to swim across a swift flowing river? The facts of the Barnett case were even more intriguing, primarily because more was known about who he was.

Artie had gone through Lifespring's basic and intermediate training levels already. He was training to be a trainer in the advanced session when he had been asked by the trainer to swim the Willamette as part of his "grail." The culmination of this particular training was to conquer one's biggest fear, and Artie had said his was of water. It was only natural to Lifespring trainers that his grail would involve some triumph over water. As the facts unraveled, I became even more convinced that Lifespring could be hazardous.

Artie Barnett could have been a well-drawn character in a novel. He was from a blue-collar home and worked for a local sawmill. Depending on whom one believed, he was either a stable, warm family man or a loner-type daredevil. He was known to have taken risks on occasion. Following a near-drowning incident in childhood, he developed a fear of the water. During the period in which he was involved with Lifespring, he was required to fulfill a grail. It was a gimmick to indebt one to the program, and to preclude making excuses for not bringing other trainees into the basic training. The latter was the main thrust of the advanced training program in which Artie had enrolled. All were required to attend weekly "sales meetings," where a trainee's progress in enrolling other trainees would be strictly monitored. The grail was usually assigned during the second of three weekends. People were to work in pairs in order to document the accomplishment of the feat via eyewitness report.

Artie and his buddy arranged to meet after his swim across the Willamette. He drowned before he was able to meet her in downtown Portland. Lifespring lawyers maintained that he was reckless and had violated the rules of Lifespring, and they therefore were not responsible. Stanislaw and Jacobson alleged Artie was a walking time bomb and should have been screened out at the start. Lifespring pushed him beyond his limits in a reckless manner, without regard for proper safeguards. The capper was that his buddy did not know how to swim well enough to rescue him, even if she had been there that frosty Sunday morning.

Both the Renick and Barnett cases required depositions, so that the Lifespring lawyers could assess my position as expert witness. They tried to prove bias, that I might have some personal grudge against the organization. It was relatively easy to elaborate on my views and to provide clinical testimony of the dangers of Lifespring's methods. During one of the Barnett depositions, the two opposing attorneys got into an oral brawl. Stanislaw objected to the Lifespring lawyer standing over me at my desk while he asked his questions. I thought this technique theatrical and rather pathetic. Though I felt in control, I was pleased that Dick would defend me. My experience in other depositions has sometimes been that attorneys let me twist in the wind; Stanislaw obviously would be aggressive in seeing that my rights and my comfort were protected. It only increased my confidence in him.

Some time between the first and second Barnett deposition I received the long-distance call from *20/20* producer Dan Goldfarb asking me what I knew about Lifespring. We chatted for a few minutes and I followed up with a letter outlining my concerns. We made arrangements that Geraldo Rivera would interview me in my office some weeks later.

My schedule at the office was rather hectic. Goldfarb and I made explicit plans for the taping so that my clients would not be disturbed and no one would have to be canceled. However, on the day of the taping, Rivera and his crew showed up several hours early and asked if we could do it right then. I was in the middle of an assessment of competence for a local attorney and would not interrupt it. Rivera and company cooled their heels for about an hour.

I had not met Rivera before, but I had seen him on television. I knew I had to be careful, since I was not able to reveal any information obtained as a direct result of my expert witness role. I was aware of wanting to be fair, and not participate in a witch hunt, if that is what it turned out to be. We talked on camera for about five minutes, then he asked them to stop for a minute. He leaned closer to me and asked me to reread my letter to Goldfarb, which he had brought with him. Apparently I wasn't being direct enough. I reread it, but resolved not to toughen my stance. We spoke for another ten minutes or so on camera, and they left. I had no clear sense of how well I had communicated, but I was confident I had been conservative.

The program was aired several months later. I appeared for only a short time, and I was disappointed. Others on the show had been more acutely negative.

The following January, Cheryl and I attended a conference in San Francisco on the role of the expert witness. One night we enjoyed a particularly lavish meal in the Carnelian Room overlooking the lights of the city. We talked of many things. I remember musing, "I wonder what John Hanley is doing tonight." His headquarters were only a short drive away.

Within a few weeks of our return to Portland, I found out. He was suing me, along with another mental health professional, Geraldo Rivera, Roone Arledge (the head of ABC News), the producers and others connected with the show for the largest amount in legal history. They claimed that Lifespring had been seriously damaged by the broadcast, that revenues were down dramatically. People were staying away in droves. I knew that the Oregon branch had gone broke, and there were more telephone calls with requests for information and/or help since the program was aired.

The notice that I was being sued was delivered to my office and ran only a few pages. I had never been sued before, though I knew it was a common practice. The fact of the suit surprised me, in that the broadcast seemed very accurate. I did not understand why Hanley would want all that aired again, this time in detail in open court with all the media watching. My limited expertise in reading about such suits told me that it might be intended to scare ABC and silence me. I had become a danger to them and the suit was an intimidating move to prevent me from testifying further in lawsuits against Lifespring.

My feelings were mixed. While I never felt any vendetta against the organization, its harassment troubled me. I felt more determined than ever to educate the public about the group. Lawsuits were a way to force Lifespring out of business, or at least to pressure them to modify their practices. Of course, I was frightened. It wasn't the legal process that bothered me, but the possibility of Lifespring actually collecting even a fraction of the more than one hundred million dollars they were asking. It was beyond comprehension. Later I was asked if one of my fears was of being professionally discredited if Lifespring should win. I had no such worry, as I felt schooled in my opinions and sure of my facts. I was pleased with my conservative statements, considering what I might have said in less guarded moments. Mostly, I just felt overwhelmed. What should I do now?

I knew by now that nothing angers me as fast as feeling out of control of my own life. The lack of control and its subsequent frustration was one of the reasons I had abandoned singing, not to mention the marriage. Harassment at PSU had underscored the helplessness, and here it was again. I had thought I was doing a good job in a tough situation; there had been no malevolence. The rest of my life was going well, and I sought to contain the pain, to compartmentalize the discomfort.

I called Dick Stanislaw and asked for advice. In a way, he had gotten me into this, by soliciting my work as an expert witness. I hoped he would not object to my calling him. He seemed undaunted, and also conjectured about Lifespring's intent to silence my opinions. He said the ABC attorneys would probably be contacting me soon and not to worry. Right.

Several days went by with no word. When it went into a week, my anxiety started growing exponentially. Finally I saw a note in my box from Jeanne, our office manager, saying someone named Warren Wilson from a San Francisco law firm wanted me to return his call. I hoped it wasn't the Lifespring lawyer. It turned out to be the office of Lillick, McHose & Charles, who had been retained by ABC to represent them in the suit. As I heard a voice on the other end of the phone, I was relieved they had contacted me. At the same time, I was angry that I had to wait, and that ABC had not called me with reassurance this would be handled somehow and not to worry.

Wilson sounded careful and evasive. He wanted to know if I knew of the suit and what I planned to do about it. That's what I wanted him to tell me. He casually mentioned the possibility that his firm might represent me, but that it would have to be approved by ABC. Such approval had not yet occurred. Great. First they put me on national television, then stand by and watch me be lynched. I never expected gratitude, but I did expect loyalty. Wilson's elusiveness offended me. He offered nothing, but asked if I would cooperate with them in the defense of the suit. Of course, I agreed. But after speaking with him, I called Dick again. He was an ally I could trust.

We discussed the possibility of his defending me, but the costs would have been altitudinous. He suggested I check into my malpractice insurance policy and my homeowner's policy. Sometimes homeowner's policies provide protection against statements made if I had made them as a private citizen. I began to explore these possibilities, writing lengthy letters to each company, explaining my plight. All this time, I was getting more frightened and increasingly angry at this monumental interruption in my life. Even with two sources of coverage, I never heard of insurance that would cover a person for a hundred million dollars.

After getting reassurance from my local insurance agents that they would support me in any way they could, Wilson called again. He said ABC had agreed that Lillick, McHose & Charles could represent me and that ABC would pick up the legal fees. Again, there was relief tinged with anger. Why did they make me writhe in worry? And there was still the issue of indemnification. Who would pay the hundred million, if Lifespring somehow won the case?

Stanislaw said ABC should indemnify me, which echoed my own sentiments. On Wilson's next call, I told him of this view and he became defensive and hostile. He could not understand why I would expect ABC to assume this risk. After a few minutes of discussion, I began to lose my cool. I told him if he expected any cooperation from me, he had better consider covering me. And if he did not, I might sue ABC and Lifespring for whatever costs or judgments might result from the suit. I was angry and profane. The phrase, I believe, was that I would "sue the shit out of all of you." It made a dent, anyway. He said he would speak to ABC and get back to me.

It seemed like an eternity. The two-part broadcast had taken place in October and November 1980, followed by the filing of the lawsuit in January 1981. It wasn't until March that Warren Wilson called to say that ABC had approved the indemnification. They agreed to cover any losses I might sustain in the event of a judgment against me. But Wilson and I had had several acrimonious conversations by the time the good news came through. On the day he told me about ABC's decision, I wasn't sure who the enemy really was.

My angry outburst on the phone seemed to quell Wilson's defensiveness. In a curious turn of events, he became more solicitous and even obsequious. Each time he called it was usually bad news. Since I was new to the world of the sued, I did not know the red tape involved in defending oneself. I had to prove what I had said not only on the actual broadcast, but also on all the outtakes that never appeared on TV. When I referred to having had many clients who reported negative experiences with Lifespring, the attorneys asked me to document every conversation, including the name of each client. Lifespring subpoenaed my appointment records, setting the scene for the major battle as I saw it.

Indeed, I had been talking with people for years about Lifespring. Revealing any information that might identify a client is not only unethical, but illegal, under the privilege law in the state of Oregon. Many states have such laws, and psychologists have been relentless in getting them passed. Confidentiality is the very basis for the therapeutic relationship. We are unable to talk to anyone about who said what to us, without the client's consent. Without this legal and ethical guarantee, clients would be reluctant to reveal their innermost selves. I was prepared to do what was necessary to protect this important precept.

In sending my appointment book, I included only those pages in which ABC was involved in some way. I took special care to white out every name but those belonging to Dan Goldfarb and Geraldo Rivera. Of course, the Lifespring lawyers wanted all my client records, in order to have a list of people they could question as to whether or not they had been in Lifespring. For trainees to even discuss their Lifespring experiences is a major crime within the organization. Trainees were isolated in the training, to increase the impact of the intense five-day basic training. This violated my personal ethics.

Though I had been expected in graduate school to keep careful, detailed records of my clients (usually for purposes of supervision), I figured out quite early as a result of my legal reading that written records could be easily subject to subpoena. Since my practice of psychotherapy was largely of an existential nature, I did not require extensive historical documentation and felt no conflict about not keeping notes. Over the years, it has been surprising to me that I could remember many details about a person just by being completely "present" in the conversation. I tended to remember what was important, and the knowledge stuck in my head for years. When a client would return after five or six years, I was able to recall the original issues, down to remembering names of significant family members. It was a matter of the practical and the philosophical coming together.

It took almost a year of legal haggling for Lifespring attorneys to run dry on the fictitious issues. Both of them came up again during the formal *20/20* deposition, but that wasn't until much later. In the meantime, they pressed me for details on how I knew about Lifespring, what I knew and when I knew it. It was obvious to me that these were the real issues for them. How formidable an opponent would I be in future trials in which I might appear as an expert witness?

One of their intended ploys worked. Wilson advised me to stay away from the media on the question of Lifespring until the case was resolved. I had to turn down several television programs, much to my regret. I continued my work with Dick Stanislaw, but after the Barnett case was settled out of court, even he backed off. Dick felt I was under enough pressure as it was. I wanted to continue working. Dick's withdrawal made me feel even more isolated in my defense. Certainly there was not much support from Wilson.

Most of 1981 was spent fending off requests for materials and/ or providing the ones with which I felt comfortable. The first wave of interrogatories was produced in early 1982, and a second wave came later that year. By 1982 the anxiety had turned to annoyance and low-level tension. The pressure for documents tapered off and it was easy to avoid thinking too much about the suit until Wilson would call. By this time, he had seen the dangers of Lifespring himself. He had the fervor of a born-again muckraker.

We met personally twice, both times over dinner at Trader Vic's in Portland. Wilson's appearance belied his earlier aggressive posture with me. He looked like a Chamber of Commerce executive, cool and sanitized. Any residual fear I may have had about dealing with him left with our first meeting. It seemed to make a difference for him, too. Though it never occurred to him to be supportive of me as a person, his emotions came out against Lifespring, which was almost as good. At least the detached lawyer was gone. I still had heard no direct word from ABC or from anyone connected with the network.

Among the co-defendants, only Dr. John Clark had the courtesy to call me. Clark was a Harvard psychiatrist who had been openly critical on the program. On the phone, he sounded friendly and encouraging and convinced of the evils of Lifespring. He was a renowned expert on cults and had more experience than I had. I was flattered by his calls but did not know whether to encourage the contact. Wilson never mentioned the other defendants and only occasionally gave me information about what was going on. As a consequence, I became almost paranoid about conversing with anyone about Lifespring. I didn't know if I could trust Jack Clark. Subsequent events and an eventual meeting with him in Boston led to my feeling foolish for questioning my trust. But in the days of 1981 and 1982, I was still in the dark.

By mid-1982, with the suit in its second year, Wilson and I developed an understanding. He was still my only ABC contact, yet I began to feel more at ease with him. Then, as suddenly as he had appeared, he was gone. I received a copy of a letter announcing a shift, not only of attorneys but of law firms too. I regretted losing my contact person; talking with another lawyer was like starting over. It was consistent that I never did hear this directly from Wilson or ABC. It was merely a copy of a memo. Nonetheless, I felt sorry for Wilson, who had put in prodigious amounts of time. With his new-found convictions, he was immersed in a personal way. I wrote him a brief note, telling him I was sorry he had been replaced and wishing him well. Ever consistent, he never responded.

It was to be another month before I heard from the new law firm. Three new characters emerged, two of them women. James Forrester was the partner responsible for defending the ABC gang, including me, but it was Linda Shostak and Christina Hart who worked most directly with me. Chris was a genuine person and it was a relief to talk with her. She was guarded sometimes, which was disappointing, but I knew the pressures she must have been under. It took the new firm several months just to read all the materials Wilson and his firm had collected.

Chris was present at my deposition in the ABC case. She had some of the toughness of a Stanislaw, but was still less knowledgeable about Lifespring than Wilson had been. I spent time helping to educate her. I had lost count of the number of unpaid hours I had spent defending myself in this case. All of it was unreimbursable, of course. I decided then that if there were any judgment against me, I would sue Lifespring for harassment.

The deposition would be a culmination of the case against me. The attorneys could ask just about anything and it would all be on the record. It might be their only direct opportunity to find out what I knew. While no one wins in a deposition, it is possible to lose. By saying something unclear, or misleading, or by exaggerating, I could be attacked later in court. It was to be a time of carefully weighing each word. I took half a day off before the deposition, to confer with Chris and to rest.

As with most previous depositions, this one was held in my office. I was on comfortable grounds, feeling in control. I felt confident of both my position and my attorney. It turned out the Lifespring attorney was a woman, which was a surprise. I knew it was not beyond Lifespring to throw a woman lawyer at me to relax my guard, appealing to my well-known feminism. I assumed she was out to get me, which kept me on my toes. It was anticlimactic. She had no teeth at all. Her questions seemed procedural, repetitive and downright boring. At the very least, I expected to answer difficult questions brilliantly, with all the subtlety of which an experienced clinician is capable. The deposition lasted all day, but left me feeling empty. Chris seemed pleased at my demeanor. I knew there had to be still another deposition. Surely Lifespring would not go into court without more specific responses. Had it accepted my refusal to provide confidential information? I wondered what it was doing with the information contained in the depositions from the Barnett and Renick cases. I knew my work there was at least partly responsible for the group's having to settle with the plaintiffs. They were letting me off the hook. I wasn't sure if I should feel relieved, or begin preparing for the other shoe to drop.

Within a few months, settlement was discussed. Chris called to sound me out. I would be pleased to settle, but I didn't want to give Lifespring any money, even if it wasn't mine. That might be construed as a defeat, an admission I had done something wrong. And I did not want any more silencing. I wanted the freedom to continue to tell the story of Lifespring.

It is an interesting postscript that during the suit, Lifespring did change some of its procedures. While the screening did not improve, some of the more dangerous exercises were omitted, including several that seemed intended to humiliate the trainee. That was reassuring, but there were other aspects to which I continued to object. Since the group had moved out of Oregon, I seldom received direct information about what it was doing. It seemed the whole process was coming to a halt.

The work on the final settlement escalated in the summer of 1983, two and a half years after the suit was filed. It had come to represent the major unfinished business of my life. I guessed Lifespring would eventually settle. It was not in its best interests to proceed to a public trial, where the information might be so damaging as to eliminate whatever hold it might still have. While Chris did not keep me apprised even as episodically as had Wilson, I had the feeling her firm was on top of things. When word of the settlement came through, I approved it. It required only that I not initiate any press coverage of the settlement. No money would be exchanged, and each side would reimburse its own attorneys. It had cost Lifespring a pretty penny for over two years of harassment. I wondered if it had been worth it to them.

FIFTEEN

Staying Present

I was still angry. My life had been disrupted and upset. The ongoing tension had been exhausting, and I had done little else but defend myself emotionally against the pressure I felt. The singing career had unraveled and I felt estranged from my show-biz fantasies. The whole lawsuit had left me feeling that little had been gained. While I had felt competent and strong working with Stanislaw and Jacobson, ABC had given me little sustenance. There was no acknowledgment, no gratitude, not even a mutual rejoicing when it was finally over. It seemed like business as usual for ABC. In a funny way, I received another show-biz education in what it's like to deal with a major television network. In the Lifespring case, I was essential to ABC. I felt abused all the way around. It caused me to look again at the fantasy of being a television personality, to have to do business with a network.

There were some haunted moments during the lawsuit. Among other things, it brought back in spades my long-dormant *Confidential* magazine complex. In childhood, it represented fantasies of being important enough to be watched, as I hoped my life would prove interesting enough that others would be fascinated by my every move. When the Lifespring case hit, I was concerned that I would be monitored, both at home and at work. Recent cult cases had involved such spying operations and invasion of privacy, and I didn't know the limits to which Lifespring would go.

I wondered if the office was bugged. When clients would ask about Lifespring, or would talk of their own experiences with the group, I became immediately split between the person there and the person who might be listening. I began to monitor my own conversations for bias and/or potentially incriminating comments.

Several months earlier, a man from Synanon had been indicted and convicted of putting a poisonous snake in the mailbox of a dissident. The victim was bitten, but recovered. It made me aware of the possible dangers of speaking against powerful groups. One afternoon as I was cleaning the house, I heard a helicopter hovering over the house and got chills when the paranoid fantasies came to life. A few nights later, I was lying in bed ready for sleep. I looked up to the window above the drawn curtains and saw a silhouette in the trees that was unfamiliar. I imagined it to be a camera, obtaining pictures with which to blackmail me into silence. I knew, of course, all of these things might be in my own head, but it made me more alert than usual when I walked to my car in the deserted parking lot in the dark after work.

When I began work on a national committee of psychologists studying about cults, I found my fantasies were not so fantastic. Colleagues related experiences such as cult members sifting through their garbage, bugged telephones and anonymous calls to employers with fictitious defamations. While I never had any such experiences with Lifespring, I'm glad those committee meetings happened after the lawsuit was dropped.

Lifespring did do me a perverse favor, though. So much of my attention became focused on defending myself from the suit that my preoccupation with the disappointments of the singing career abated. It was a moratorium, in a way, buying me time to reflect on what happened. As a child, the fame fantasies were a guarantee of acceptance, admiration and safety. As an adult, show biz came to symbolize a peak experience. Rather than a need for admiration, it became a need for transcendance, a total integration of self. The need was filled early merely by singing in my own living room. Later, entertaining others added to the risk and heightened the effect. Like an ice skater training for the Olympics, it was thrilling just to be out there. It was only by appearing in public that I could fully participate in the fantasy—that singular combination of live music and stage lighting. After that, I couldn't get the same charge out of singing by myself. Now I knew what was possible.

Still, I never know when the show-biz blitz will intrude once again. In January 1984 I received a call from the local ABC affiliate, asking me to discuss a made-for-television movie, *Something About Amelia*. The film depicted a family riddled with incest and was done in excellent taste. I came in a few days before the interview to preview the program. The Monday it was to be broadcast, I appeared in a half-hour segment on a local morning show. We received lots of phone calls because the show seemed to speak to many people. I no sooner got back to the office than our phone was ringing off the hook. One of the calls was from a radio station. Its reporter wanted to interview me later that day in my office. A few minutes later, a television news team made arrangements to do a live remote from my office for the evening news. It was a true media blitz, sandwiched between my clients and my normal work load.

It was an isolated day. There have been other television appearances since then, on various topics. There have been several productive therapy sessions as a result, and that makes it worthwhile in itself. It still feels as though I'm in training. I wonder if that will ever go away.

When I feel down, I still ruminate about what went awry in the singing career. There were so many elements out of my control. I was approaching forty, which is probably too old for club owners to feel confident of my ability to attract a consistent crowd. I have never been a sex symbol. Though much money was spent on clothes, there were no experts to consult to determine the best look. I ran on the seat of my pants.

A side issue was the nature of the audience. When my appearances were publicized, a significant portion of the audience was gay. It could be that my androgyny was attractive; I don't know. I am not in the least judgmental, and am certainly empathic with a closet struggle. While Cheryl would accompany me when I went to clubs, the other singers would be surrounded by men.

There were undoubtedly assumptions being made about my sexual orientation. I couldn't help that. I still don't know why the club owners failed to pursue; I know that their decision was not based on my drawing ability. Each time I performed, they made nothing but money. It makes me wonder what my impact might have been in a larger city where alternate lifestyles are more acceptable. The mystery of my singing failure has not been solved to my satisfaction. I still think about it, but it is without the abject grief that surrounded that topic for so long.

While the show-biz passion burns on, the fantasies of singing professionally have extinguished themselves. The unhealthy relationships, the phoniness, the late hours—all contributed to their decline. Singing demanded "not-me" behavior and an abdication of control over my own existence. Ending the singing might have been less labored had there been one apocalyptic event, such as a "Pam Munter Night" at the Jazz Quarry when no one came, or a club owner telling me I had no talent. As it was, I created the beginning and I was the one who decided to end it. The only way to exert control was to pull out. It came together for me when I realized my sense of destiny required an external locus of control, a delegating of personal power to others. I think of singing now with residual pain, but also—finally—resignation.

These days, my life is enriching. Aaron is a joy. His dance lessons are his own idea, and I work very hard at not being a stage mother. I am supportive of his performing several times a year, as is his wont. He regularly participates in school programs as well. In the spring of 1984, he was spectacular in the lead of *Fiddler on the Roof*. We had it videotaped, for his later viewing. I get tearful and excited when he's up on the stage, but it's very different for him than it has been for me. He enjoys it, takes pride in a good performance, but does not have the same set of driving fantasies. His emotional life is currently invested in computers. One day he told me he would not be a professional performer because success in that field is uncertain and transient. Smart kid. I hope he grows up to feel the intensity I have felt and to develop a broadly based lifestyle, as I have tried to do. He could do without the pain.

Raising Aaron has forced consolidation of years of reflection and experience. In contrast to my own childhood, authenticity and disclosure are valued. Though I take full responsibility for being his parent, Aaron seldom feels one down; we have an actively egalitarian household where all views are respected and solicited. Dinners are my favorite time of day, when we catch up with each other and often get involved in deeper conversation. There is also much laughter and genuine wit exchanged.

When Aaron was a toddler, he would come to me when he was hurting, physically or emotionally. We designated a black leather rocking chair as our "snuggle spot." Now, our meeting place is halfway up the stairs, where mother-son dialogs often take place.

PAC talks are held when one of us has an issue or stimulating topic to share. Probing questions sometimes open the conversation, such as "What's your ideal day?" or "What are three qualities you like and three you would like to see modified in each of us?" Often coincidental with eating out in restaurants, PAC talks can assume an intellectual tone, such as discussions of current events or politics. They are invariably fascinating and tend to solidify the respect and affection we have for each other.

I have participated in Aaron's show biz life, to some extent. I volunteered to sing as well as dance in the annual recital for Deborah's School of Dance and Gymnastics. There were some concerns, as expressed in the journal. "I will be singing in June for the dance recital, almost a 'walk on' I never thought I'd do. But it's part of the unraveling of the passion . . . If I sing under trivial enough circumstances, maybe I won't get that supercharged feeling and the phenomenal let-down afterwards."

Arletta and her son, Robert, backed me in two performances. The four tunes were all different, and gave me opportunities to play with singing. Each involved a costume change. We had searched through a Goodwill store to find clothing so I could be authentic with "Second Hand Rose," which was mercilessly campy. "Ten Cents a Dance" called for a slinky gown and a come-hither approach, while "Cabaret" was upbeat and Minnelli-like. In a lapse toward the sentimental, I opened with "Nobody Does It

Like Me," my first "find." The sound system was inspiring, the audience responsive. The resulting feelings were different. There was no let-down. After singing at the Jazz Quarry, I had often felt an increased longing for fame, a sadness of the dream falling short. I ran the risk of those feelings returning with a vengeance. There were good but not triumphant feelings, perhaps because it was so shared and had very little pressure. Much of my attention was on Aaron, who appeared in two dances. At the end of the show, he was recognized as the "Most Improved Junior Tap Dancer," which pleased me every bit as much as singing had.

By late 1982 I had come to terms with the reality that show biz was no longer a focal point for my life. In the journal is written, "My life has shifted toward more internal activity. Few people. Most of the intensity occurs on the job. Peace of mind has come largely through simplification. Given that model, the challenge is to push for the optimal amount of complexity within that framework. Keeping alive, turned on, vibrant."

The irony is that with the simplification, life has become rich and full. Aaron is in an especially interesting period of his life as he prepares for adolescence. After a few years of study, I am involved in managing the financial portfolios of the corporation, as well as our personal stocks and bonds. It is another kind of validation. Having read *Daily Variety* for over twenty-five years, I am conversant with the business side of entertainment. Among the stock gains have been "killings" in the stocks of MGM/UA, Orion Pictures, UA Communications and General Cinema. At least all that study has moved on to still another manifestation of the passion.

Another fantasy was completed when I played two seasons on a women's softball team. I had been the coach/manager for Aaron's Little League team, but I had not had the chance to really play organized ball. I was able to play first base on a recreational league team, a dream going back thirty years. To my surprise, I was a dependable singles hitter, batting over .600 each season. Winning the league championship was almost superfluous, though I proudly displayed the trophy in my office. I was pleased to find that my body did what I wanted it to do, as I threw it around the diamond, sliding into bases and leaping for errant throws. It was the latter, though, that did me in. Consistently high throws caused me to jump and stretch, resulting in a rotator cuff injury. After five months of physical therapy, I decided to hang up the spikes.

Living out the baseball fantasy led me to think about what else was unfinished. Though I had gone through the conversion to Judaism and joined Temple Beth Israel, there was still more to be learned. After a year of study with a small group of compatible adults, we participated in a B'nai Mitzvah ceremony, a group Bar and Bat Mitzvah. I labored with the Hebrew and faltered a bit reading from the Torah, but my part in leading the service brought back those feelings of public mastery. We have a Jewish household and are involved in living out the cultural values as best we can.

Clarity and simplicity seem to go together these days. There is no unfinished business. Each transaction, each day, is complete within itself. Long-term goals are in place, but maintaining an openness to experience is mandatory. I can see that each era in my life has its own dimension and identity and this one is characterized by peacefulness and enthusiasm.

Life seems more centered, simple but elegant. As I listened to an early Judy Garland record, I wrote in the continuing chronicle of my life that is my journal: "Wonder what it was like to spend all day grooming oneself—acting, singing, dancing—to please an eccentric mogul. A kind of satisfying narcissism, I think. But frustrating because other people's standards assumed prominence over one's own.

"That's the ideal part of my life. Not having to meet other people's standards. 'My Way,' as Sinatra sings. I do miss what I judgmentally call the narcissism . . . mostly the performing itself . . . I look for hard work. That was among the best memories I had of singing . . . the long hours of rehearsal, the times I was scared and took big risks, the resultant exhilaration.

"I'm deeply touched by people who give their all, especially if they triumph. I wonder when I've given my all. Singing, sure.

What else? Relationships? Yes, I think so. In therapy, yes. I'm all there most of the time. It's a rewarding life."

Now in my fifth decade, I have learned that the show-biz fantasies are so much a part of me that they will never completely disappear. Perhaps they will remain dormant for a few years, reincarnating in still another form.

I am always on a threshold. I can hardly wait.

ACKNOWLEDGMENTS

This book stands as an acknowledgment of people who have helped me along the way. In addition, I thank those who participated in putting the actual volume together and who provided the support throughout these last two years.

Technical assistance was invaluable, coming from the articulate Kiki Canniff and Susan Applegate, a talented and hard-working book designer. Jim Estes did the editing in a sensitive and professional manner, while Mark Beach labored unstintingly on a marketing strategy. Additional photographs were by the Photo-Graphic and by Barbara Gundle, both of whom took the time to get it right.

I was touched by the generosity of my readers, who volunteered to wade through my early drafts. Richard Stanislaw proofed the Lifespring material so I wouldn't get sued again and Susan Reese read the rest of the book toward the same end. Susan was also helpful with her substantive comments and provocative questions. Dr. Alan Morgenstern graciously took the time to make extensive suggestions along existential lines, prodding me into more disclosure.

All kinds of logistical and emotional support were tendered by Dr. Cheryl Castles and Aaron Munter, who were available night and day. The project would never have been completed without them.

INDEX